THE
ULTIMATE
BARBRA

THE ULTIMATE BARBRA

ERNEST W. CUNNINGHAM

RENAISSANCE BOOKS
Los Angeles

Library of Congress Cataloging-in-Publication Data
Cunningham, Ernest W.
        The ultimate Barbra / Ernest W. Cunningham.
            p. cm.
        Includes bibliographical references (p.), filmography (p.), discography (p.), and index.
        ISBN 1-58063-041-3 (alk. paper)
        1. Streisand, Barbra—Miscellanea. I. Title.
ML420.S915C86 1998
782.42164'092—dc21
[B]   98-39329
                                                         CIP
                                                         MN

10 9 8 7 6 5 4 3 2 1

Design by Robert Aulicino

Manufactured in the United States of America
Distributed by St. Martin's Press
First Edition

Contents

PART III: HER WORLD

Acknowledgments

Academy of Motion Picture Arts and Sciences: Margaret Herrick Library, Archive Photos (Michael Shulman), Israel Bick and Lorraine Pollock, Rick Carl, Lloyd Curry, J. C. Archives (John Cocchi), Ken Joachim, Jani Klain, George Marcelle, Museum of Television and Radio (Jonathan Schwartz — Research Department), Photofest (Ron Mandelbaum), James Tamulis.

And a deep bow to James Robert Parish and Allan Taylor, and to Bill Hartley for his continued encouragement.

I especially want to thank these women:

Pauline Kael, for her passion for film.
Arleen Schwartz, for her passion for Barbra.
Diane Fain, for her pursuit of beauty.
Sharon DeRosa, for her friendship.

Preface

Barbra Streisand once asked how *A Star Is Born* (Warner Bros.,1976) could be declared a disaster by the movie critics but then make a fortune at the box office.

The answer is . . . well, that's show business!

And then she asks how it is that some people call her ugly and ask where she parked her broom, while others praise her beauty and compare her to an Egyptian princess. And how can she be on "worst-dressed" lists and "best-dressed" lists at the same time?

The answer is, each to his own taste. Or, different strokes for different folks. Or, that's show business!

More seriously, Barbra asks how she can be called an egomaniacal monster . . . while she donates millions of dollars for cardiovascular research, pediatric AIDS, abused and disabled children, and for breast cancer research.

The response this time borrows from nineteenth-century poet Walt Whitman's poem "Song of Myself" in his collection *Leaves of Grass* (1855):

> Do I contradict myself?
> Very well then I contradict myself.
> I am large, I contain multitudes.

To their credit, the writers of the major Streisand biographies acknowledge their subject's duality, expressing shock at her monstrousness while lauding her very great talents. Because it's all part of the package deal. This book strives to achieve the same balance.

I like to cite another poet, Oscar Wilde, who wrote, "It is the feet of clay that makes the gold of the idols precious."

PART ①
THE
WOMAN

CHAPTER 1

Things Said

The Ten Best Nice Things Said About Barbra

1. Robert Ruark, syndicated columnist, February 26, 1963:

"Her nose is more evocative of moose than muse, and her eyes at best could be called Nilotic [Egyptian] only by way of mascara, but about 2 A.M., when she sings 'Any Place I Hang My Hat Is Home,' she's beautiful, even if home is only Brooklyn. Her name is Barbra Streisand. She is 20 years old, she has a three-octave promiscuity of range, she packs more personal dynamic power than anybody I can recall since Libby Holman or Helen Morgan. She can sing as loud as Ethel Merman and as persuasively as Lena [Horne] or Ella [Fitzgerald]. She is the hottest thing to hit the entertainment field since Lena Horne erupted, and she will be around 50 years from now if good songs are still written to be sung by good singers."

2. Tony Parsons, (London) *Daily Telegraph*, April 21, 1994:

"Streisand has an ability to talk directly to an audience's heart that is surpassed only by [Frank] Sinatra. When [she] takes flight, she makes music that is full of memories and a sense of loss. She is unquestionably the last of the great romantics."

3. Cecil Beaton, designer, *On a Clear Day You Can See Forever* (Paramount, 1970):

"She is a self-willed creation."

4. Rosie O'Donnell, TV talk show host, November 21, 1997:

"You were a constant source of light in an often dark childhood and you inspired me and gave me the courage to dream of a life better than the one I knew."

5. *Time*, April 10, 1964:

"This nose is a shrine. It starts at the summit of her hive-piled hair and ends where a trombone hits the D below middle C. The face it divides is long and sad, and the look in repose is the essence of hound. She is about as pretty, in short, as Fanny Brice; but as she sings number after number and grows in the mind, she touches the heart with her awkwardness, her lunging humor, and a bravery that is all the more winning because she seems so vulnerable. People start to nudge one another and say, 'This girl is beautiful'."

6. Jule Styne, songwriter of *Funny Girl*, in *Time*, April 10, 1964:

"The real force of her talent comes from an individual spirit that is unique, a kind of life force that makes her even more of a personality than a performer. She carries her own spotlight."

7. Stanley Kauffmann, *The New Republic*, November 9, 1968, reviewing *Funny Girl* (Columbia, 1968):

"It's always irritating when a conceited person is as good as she thinks."

8. Pauline Kael, *The New Yorker*, November 10, 1980 (reviewing the new Bette Midler film *Divine Madness*, Warner Bros., 1980):

"When Streisand sings, her command of the audience is in her regal stillness; she distills her own emotions. You feel that she doesn't need the audience—that she could close her eyes and sing with the same magnetic power."

9. Richard Rodgers, songwriter, testimonial on the back of the *Simply Streisand* album (1967):

"Nobody is talented enough to get laughs, to bring tears, to sing with the depth of a fine cello or the lift of a climbing bird. Nobody, that is, except Barbra. She makes our musical world a much happier place than it was before. Sincerely, Richard Rodgers."

10. William Wyler, director of the film *Funny Girl*:

"She fusses over things, she's terribly concerned about how she looks, with the photography, the camera, the makeup, the wardrobe, the way she moves, reads a line. She'd tell the cameraman that one of the lights was out—way up on the scaffold. If the light that was supposed to be on her was out, she saw it. She's not easy, but she's difficult in the best sense of the word—the same way I'm difficult" (Axel Madsen, *William Wyler, the Authorized Biography*. New York: Crowell, 1973).

The Ten Best Mean Things Said About Barbra

1. John Simon, *The New Leader*, July 6, 1970, reviewing *On a Clear Day You Can See Forever* (Paramount, 1970):

"More than by the heroine's ability to make flowers grow miraculously, I was struck by the sprouting of Barbra's ego, which starts as a single giant cactus and ends as a one-woman rain forest." Simon also says: "Directing Streisand must be like trying to get a rogue elephant to cross a street on the green light."—*The New Leader*, June 22, 1979.

2. Stanley Kauffmann, *The New Republic*, July 18, 1970, reviewing *On a Clear Day You Can See Forever*:

"Miss Streisand is possibly the only fishwife ever to become a star. She has broad abrasive theatricality, and she sings well, though without much individuality. But since *Funny Girl* [Columbia, 1968], her performances grow repellent. In that first film she played Fanny Brice, who was Jewish. In the first half of *Hello, Dolly!* [Twentieth Century-Fox, 1969] (which is all I saw of it) and in most of *Clear Day*, she keeps trying to fight her way back to the Jewish vein of *Funny Girl*, which seems to be the only vein in which she is comfortable. What we are getting from her is the return of the nineteenth-century stage Jew.

This is about as timely and ingratiating as the return of Stepin Fetchit would be."

3. Jack Kroll, *Newsweek* film critic, commenting on Streisand not being Oscar-nominated for directing *The Prince of Tides* (Columbia, 1991)—although the film was nominated for Best Picture:

"Many in Hollywood consider her self-absorbed, difficult and controlling. . . . [The snub may have been] less sexism than Barbrism."

4. Walter Scharf, veteran film composer-arranger who worked with Streisand on *Funny Girl*. He declined to participate in two subsequent Streisand films:

"Once was enough" (Walter Scharf/Michael Freedland, *Composed and Conducted by Walter Scharf*. London: Vallentine, Mitchell & Co., 1988).

5. Omar Sharif, actor, costar of *Funny Girl* and *Funny Lady* (Columbia, 1975). In a Rex Reed interview quoted in James Spada, *Streisand: Her Life* (New York: Crown, 1995):

"I think her biggest problem is that she wants to be a woman and she wants to be beautiful, and she is neither."

6. Walter Matthau, Barbra's battling costar of *Hello, Dolly!*:

"The trouble with Barbra is she became a star long before she became an actress. Which is a pity, because if she learned her trade properly she might become a competent actress instead of a freak attraction—like a boa constrictor. The thing about working with her was that you never knew what she was going to do next and you were afraid that she'd do it" (quoted in Shaun Considine, *Barbra Streisand: The Woman, the Myth, the Music*. New York: Delacorte, 1985).

Also from Matthau, the much quoted, "You haven't got the talent of a butterfly's fart!"

7. Vincent Canby, *New York Times*, June 22, 1979, reviewing *The Main Event* (Warner Bros., 1979):

"The pushy cosmetics executive . . . seems to be an extension of the role played in real-life by Miss Streisand, who co-produced the movie, stars in it and seems to have ordered every close-up and line-reading.

Miss Streisand has become a contradiction: she's too much without being enough."

8. *Time*, January 3, 1977, reviewing *A Star Is Born* (Warner Bros., 1976):

"Hearing her light into a rock song is like listening to Al Jolson sing Leadbelly. A concert sequence, where the debuting Barbra brings a hostile audience to their feet with the wonder of her funkiness, is a milestone of piquant absurdity, equivalent perhaps to having Kate Smith conquer Woodstock."

9. Lewis Segal, *Show*, July 23, 1970, reviewing *On A Clear Day You Can See Forever*:

"In *On a Clear Day You Can See Forever* clouds appear . . . to assist in what must be called The Ascension (if not The Assumption) of Barbra Streisand, who, accompanied by the swelling strains of the title tune, disappears On High to presumably join a recast Trinity consisting of Father, Son, and (at the lady's present weight) Holy Cow."

10. Paul Williams, songwriter, musical supervisor for *A Star Is Born*:

Williams came to think of working with Streisand and Jon Peters as "having a picnic at the end of an airport runway."

Williams also said, "Barbra is working on a tree—you know, only God and Barbra Streisand can make a tree."

The Silliest Things Ever Said About Barbra

1. John Barbour of KNBC-TV, praising *Funny Lady*:
"Barbra Streisand's incredible artistry as an actress and singer deserves more than an Oscar; it deserves a Nobel Prize."

2. United Press International reviewer, on *My Name Is Barbra*, (CBS, 1965) her first TV special. It is a one-woman show with full orchestra, but *no* guest stars:
"She is so great it is shocking."

3. Bruce McCabe, (Boston) *Herald-American*, reporting on Barbra's concert at Festival Field, Newport, Rhode Island, July 30, 1966:

7

"Listening to Barbra . . . is something like having your soul massaged. Like being infused with an electric charge . . . that's Barbra. Barbra of the thunder and lightning, wind and rain, spring and fall, darkness and light. One is captured, enslaved by her."

The Best Things Barbra Ever Said About Herself

1. A reporter asks Barbra why she is so successful:

"The only way I can account for it is that whatever ability other performers have, I must have it plus. Onstage I am a cross between a washwoman and a princess. I am a bit coarse, a bit low, a bit vulgar, and a bit ignorant. But I am also part princess—sophisticated, elegant, and controlled. I can appeal to everybody. When I am not performing, however, I don't think I have that definite a personality. I think

She sings of the simple life while trying on the extravagant goodies of Bergdorf Goodman. This is a pose from CBS's *My Name Is Barbra* (1965), her first TV special, her first Emmy Award.
PHOTO COURTESY OF PHOTOFEST

maybe I have nothing" (quoted in Anne Edwards, *Streisand: A Biography*. Boston: Little, Brown, 1977).

2. As producer of *Nuts* (Warner Bros., 1987), Barbra worries about the budget, the director, her own role:

"I want so much to be liked and understood. But I have to be in control, because so much of the world is so stupid!" (quoted in Spada, *Streisand: Her Life*).

3. A reporter asks, "Do you think your personality has been captured by the press?"

Barbra: "Captured? (she laughs) Slaughtered, barbecued, pickled!" (quoted in Derek Winnert, *Barbra Streisand: Quote Unquote*. Avenel, N.J.: Crescent/Random House, 1996).

4. Sophia Loren says, "I would give anything if I could sing like you."

Barbra: "If I could look like you I wouldn't even wanna talk!" (Winnert, *Barbra Streisand: Quote Unquote*).

5. On the difference between theater and movies:

"Making movies is easier because you can't hear the coughing of audiences, but harder because you can't hear the applause" (*Los Angeles Times*, November 27, 1967).

CHAPTER 2

Forget the Nose–
Look at These Fingernails!

Legend has it that at the time Barbra Streisand was portraying a secretary in the hit Broadway musical *I Can Get It for You Wholesale* (1962), her "obtuse" mother didn't believe her daughter had a future in show business, and urged her to learn the skills necessary to be a real secretary

By that time, however, Streisand was positive she was going to be a Star, that she would never be a secretary. One of the endearing stories about Barbra is that, back in high school, she had carefully grown her fingernails extra long so that she would be unable to take typing lessons.

That's about it for endearing stories about Streisand's fingernails. From her first public appearances in 1960, her lengthy talons have provoked a steady stream of ridicule and criticism from audiences and critics, culminating in a 1992 feature story in the *Los Angeles Times*.

*   *   *

The reviews for the London stage production of *Funny Girl* (1966) contained this observation: "Miss Streisand has a neat, pocket-size humor, expressing itself in small, mocking gestures, and alarming fingernails that would interest a vampire" (Harold Hobson, [London] *Sunday Times*, April 14, 1966).

*   *   *

Biographer Anne Edwards describes a confrontation with director William Wyler when production began on *Funny Girl* (Columbia, 1968), which was Streisand's screen debut:

"Wyler insisted that a Henry Street waif (Fanny Brice) in 1910 would not have two-inch Mandarin fingernails. 'Why? Why not!?' she kept screaming. 'The Chinese have worn them for centuries!' Wyler gave in, which was a mistake because her feline claws present a jarring image on screen with the period costumes" (*Streisand: A Biography*. Boston: Little, Brown, 1997).

*   *   *

Reviewing *The Prince of Tides* (Columbia, 1991) film critic Georgia Brown wrote: "I'm sorry but I have to talk about the fingernails. Here's this $150-an-hour psychiatrist between Park and Madison, inhabiting an office that looks like it's part of the Morgan Library, and she has these grotesque little finger-extensions like Freddy Kruger or Ming the Merciless. It must be all her patients dream about. The fetish is Barbra Streisand's, but when she plays a role like Dr. Susan Lowenstein, the ravishing Jewish psychiatrist . . . she brings her talons with her. It's an amazing solipsistic directorial act. (As director, she also gets lots of shots of the nails, like walking up the back of a man's dark suit.) The nails are like the movie—perverse, tacky, anachronistic. Silly, but you can't take your eyes off them" (*The Village Voice*, December 24, 1991).

Several other commentators also poked fun at the scene in *The Prince of Tides* when the psychiatrist's son feigns throwing a football for his mother to catch and she exclaims, "Oh, no, my nails!"

*   *   *

"Barbra! Scratch the Nails," by Paddy Calistro, was a feature article in the *Los Angeles Times*, January 17, 1992. (It's reprinted in Ethlie Ann Vare, *Diva: Barbra Streisand and the Making of a Superstar*. New York: Berkley/Boulevard Books, 1996.)

Paddy Calistro interviewed amateur and professional psychologists on Barbra's fingernails in *The Prince of Tides*—Barbra's talons were seen as a gaffe at a time when short, tailored nails were the trend.

Beverly Hills manicurist Rando Celli said, "She wants us to understand her power and control. Those long, strong nails say, 'Keep your distance.' "

Psychotherapist Christine Maginn of Glendale, California, reasoned, "Women who aren't comfortable with their appearance often fixate on one feature that they like and take special care to call attention to it."

Brentwood, California, psychologist Fanya Carter interpreted, "Streisand's hands are her one special feature; if she calls attention to them, she distracts audiences from her nose."

*   *   *

More recently, the March 1998 *Vanity Fair* featured a "speculative draft" of a prenuptial agreement between Barbra and James Brolin: It has the First Party being in no way liable for potential injury to the body of the Second Party resulting from contact with the fingernails of the First Party.

A tale of two noses: one trouper welcomes another in *Color Me Barbra* (1966), her second CBS-TV special and another one-woman tour de force.
PHOTO COURTESY OF PHOTOFEST

13

CHAPTER 3

The Men in the Life of Barbra Streisand

*"It's not the men in my life that count
but the life in my men."*—Mae West
—*The Wit and Wisdom of Mae West*
(New York: Putnam, 1967)

Barbra Streisand says she looks up to Marlon Brando, movie critic
Pauline Kael, and whatever man happens to be in her life at the time.

There usually is a man in her life.

Despite her unconventional looks—or maybe because of her unconventional *beauty*—many different men have been attracted to her.

Some spent a number of years with her—Elliott Gould, Jon Peters,
Richard Baskin. Other reported romances, like Peter Jennings, may
have had more substance in gossip columns and tabloid headlines than
in real life. Other "dates" were probably that and little else.

In her middle years, she caused comment over the younger men she
was attracted to—tennis star André Agassi, actors Don Johnson and
Peter Weller, composer James Newton Howard, tycoon Edgar
Bronfman Jr.

Actor James Brolin, who is just one year older than Barbra, entered the picture in 1996. They were married two years later and Barbra put her flaming youth behind her.

But, oh, didn't she ramble!

* * *

In the spring of 1992, twenty-three-year-old tennis star **André Agassi** was the sport's latest pinup boy when he called Barbra to say how much he liked *The Prince of Tides* (Columbia, 1991). That September, Barbra was in the stands watching André play. A commentator said she looked at him like he was an ice cream cone with a cherry on top. It was said she jumped up and down, screaming his name . . . but then left early, saying she didn't want to distract him.

She went to England, June 1993, to cheer him on at the Wimbledon tennis championships. The press ridiculed the twenty-eight-year age difference and reported that Agassi had never had sex with his long-time girlfriend Wendi Stewart because of strong Christian religious convictions, and wondered if his relationship with Streisand had gotten past the platonic.

Agassi was also seen as homophobic. He was widely quoted as saying, "I'm as happy as a faggot in a submarine!"

Then Agassi married tall person Brooke Shields, age thirty-two, in 1997.

* * *

When Baskin-Robbins ice cream heir **Richard Baskin** (born 1950) introduced himself to Barbra at a 1984 Beverly Hills Christmas party, he told her how much he loved *Yentl* (MGM/United Artists, 1983). She told him how much she loved his coffee ice cream.

Baskin was probably tempted to groan out loud over that cornball remark, as he had worked hard to establish his own identity as a composer. He was musical director for such films as Robert Altman's *Nashville* (Paramount, 1975) and *Buffalo Bill and the Indians* (United Artists, 1976). Baskin appears briefly in *Nashville* as the musician called Frog.

Barbra hired him to produce several tracks for her then-upcoming *Broadway Album* (1985). He soon moved into her Carolwood Drive house in Holmby Hills and stayed for three-and-a-half years, moving out in the fall of 1987. When Barbra's 1988 relationship with actor

Don Johnson plotzed, she started dating Baskin again. Little is known of the Streisand-Baskin relationship . . . which might be some indication of its seriousness. Biographer James Spada insists Baskin is one of her great loves, along with Elliott Gould and Jon Peters.

*   *   *

When actor-teacher Allan Miller and his wife spent the summer of 1958 acting in stock at Harmon's Clinton Playhouse (Clinton, Connecticut), they took Barbra Streisand along as babysitter. Barbra played Ellie May, groveling in the dust for turnips, in Erskine Caldwell's *Tobacco Road*. Handsome newcomer **Warren Beatty** had major roles in most of the theatre's productions.

Ten years later, even though he then was involved with British Oscar-winning actress Julie Christie, Warren Beatty invites Barbra up to his penthouse suite at the Beverly Wilshire Hotel, thus adding her to his lengthy list of sexual conquests.

The liaison with Beatty proved disappointing. "She demanded more than good sex from a man. She expected commitment" (Anne Edwards, *Streisand: A Biography*. Boston: Little, Brown, 1997). Warren was just one of her flings (and, certainly, vice versa).

Shaun Considine wrote of their "brief passionate affair of 'mutual use' " (*Barbra Streisand: The Woman, The Myth, The Music*. New York: Delacorte, 1985).

*   *   *

In 1971 Barbra began filming *What's Up, Doc?* (Warner Bros., 1972), costarring Ryan O'Neal and directed by **Peter Bogdanovich** (born 1939). She was enamored of thirty-year-old O'Neal at the time (who was married to, but separated from, actress Leigh Taylor-Young), but his ever-roving eye soon doomed their relationship. In retaliation, she dated Czech-born director Milos Forman, actor Steve McQueen, and—maybe—had a brief affair with Bogdanovich himself.

*   *   *

The *Star* tabloid for April 16, 1994, featured the headline "GOTCHA! Streisand goes ballistic as she's caught in steamy clinch with **Jeff Bridges**." The story goes on to claim that she "flirted outrageously" with married actor Bridges (born 1949, making him forty-five to Barbra's fifty-two) during the filming of *The Mirror Has Two Faces* (TriStar, 1996), that they were caught kissing passionately, "oblivious to everything." But the photo evidence shows Bridges smiling at the photographer; Streisand has her arm on Bridges' shoulder: They could be dancing, or he could be helping a lady across the street.

In 1998, another tabloid tried it again: The mighty *Globe* (March 31) revealed "the secret [veteran actor] Lloyd Bridges took to the grave": that the Bridges clan was nearly torn apart by Barbra Streisand's fatal-attraction crush on Jeff. The family assembled to convince the actor that he would destroy his family by abandoning them for Barbra. A spokesperson for Barbra denied the alleged romance.

*   *   *

A supermarket paper called **Edgar Bronfman, Jr.** (born 1955) Streisand's "Mr. Right." A handsome Canadian tycoon thirteen years her junior, Bronfman is the wealthy, dashing heir to the Seagrams spirits fortune. He skipped college in favor of a career as a Hollywood producer, and was named head of the House of Seagram in 1984. He's a divorced father of three. Barbra told a friend, "I suppose I've always wanted a real strong man who won't be in awe of my status." (*Star*, September 8, 1992)

When Seagrams bought into MCA/Universal Studios, Edgar Bronfman, Jr., became the seventh most powerful man in Hollywood (according to *Entertainment Weekly's* "Power Issue" of January 8, 1998). Just think: If their relationship had gone differently, Barbra Streisand might today be the power behind the power of a major movie studio!

*   *   *

In the spring of 1982, British superstar **Richard Burton** (1925–1984), at age fifty-seven, gave several interviews in which he intimated that he and forty-year-old Streisand had been romantically involved. The supposed affair took place after Burton's breakup with his actress wife Elizabeth Taylor in 1973 . . . which is when Barbra met Jon Peters. (*Barbra* magazine, no. 8, 1982)

*   *   *

Barbra met and dated **John Calley** (born 1930), Warner Bros. production chief, at the time she was making *What's Up, Doc?* for that studio.

*   *   *

Sydney Chaplin (born 1926), Barbra's costar in the Broadway *Funny Girl* (1964), is the son of legendary screen comedian Charlie Chaplin and his second wife Lita Grey.

At the time Sydney was contracted for *Funny Girl*, he was best known for the Broadway musicals *Bells Are Ringing* (1956) and *Subways Are For Sleeping* (1961). In this period, he was wed to dancer Noelle Adams.

At the beginning, Streisand and Chaplin hated one another. By the second week of tryouts in Boston, Chaplin became friendlier—and Barbra encouraged him, realizing that her scenes would play better. By the time the show reached Philadelphia, the two were having an affair—and there were rumors that she was pregnant.

However, during the pre-Broadway out-of-town stopovers in Boston and Philadelphia, as Barbra's stage part was being beefed up, Chaplin's role was being trimmed back and his songs eliminated. Finally his one remaining solo, "You Are Woman, I Am Man," was gradually changed from his romantic seduction scene to Barbra's comic seduction scene.

When their affair ended, Chaplin turned ugly, and would even curse her under his breath during performances. She brought him up on charges before Actors Equity, but no action was taken. Producer Ray Stark finally agreed to buy him out. Chaplin left the show in June 1965 and was replaced by singer Johnny Desmond.

*   *   *

Barbra Streisand had a brief public encounter with **Charles, Prince of Wales** (born 1948) when he visited the Burbank Studios in 1974 while she was recording the soundtrack for *Funny Lady* (Columbia, 1975). Members of the sound stage orchestra remembered the intense eye contact between the two. "Sparks flew," one musician observed.

Twenty years later, in London for her world tour, Barbra recalled that she had been distracted by her work and was ungracious to the prince that day. She joked to the audience, "Who knows? If I had been nicer to him, I might have been the first *real* Jewish princess!" (In a 1997 interview, she said she might have been "the Blintzes Princess.")

Barbra and Prince Charles met again at a champagne reception before the concert, and she warmly clasped his hand in hers twice during their five minutes of conversation, neither seeming inhibited by the others present.

The Prince of Wales (sometimes rudely referred to as "Jug Head") admitted that over the years, Streisand had been "My only pinup . . . she is devastatingly attractive and with a great deal of sex appeal" (James Spada, *Streisand: Her Life*. New York: Crown, 1995). Barbra and the Prince of Wales? Are they star-crossed lovers . . . or just being silly?

*　　*　　*

On September 16, 1992, Barbra met Presidential candidate **Bill Clinton** (born 1946) and his wife Hillary when Streisand headlined a fundraiser held on the Beverly Hills estate of film producer Ted Fields. At the affair she sang "On a Clear Day (You Can See Forever)" and "Happy Days Are Here Again."

Four months and three days later, Barbra performed at the inaugural gala for now-President Clinton. In March of 1993, Streisand quietly spent several nights in The White House.

A political miniscandal (one of many) erupted in 1997, when it was disclosed that President Clinton enticed potential campaign donors with offers of a night in the White House, letting them sleep in the historic Lincoln Bedroom. (Steven Spielberg was said to have contributed $446,023; Chevy Chase, $55,000; Ted Danson, $10,000; and Barbra Streisand, $85,000.) In Barbra's case, there are rumors that she didn't sleep alone.

"Wild White House Nights" screamed the cover of the *National Enquirer* (February 17, 1998). TV's *Night Court* star Markie Post is the new blonde babe revelation—but Sharon Stone and Streisand are also included in the gossip.

Barbra gets a third of a page and three photos in the *Enquirer* tale, one showing her and the President hugging. "No one makes Hillary Clinton more jealous than Barbra Streisand," says the story. The two were said to have become cozy when Hillary was away. Says Streisand: "For Hillary to fear that Bill and I could be romantically involved is silly."

*　　*　　*

Barry Dennen (born 1938) is an actor-writer credited with suggesting that Barbra approach songs as mini-dramas or as acting exercises.

He's also usually identified as her first lover.

They met as struggling young actors in a 1960 off-Broadway production of Karel and Josef Capek's parable play *The Insect Comedy* (1921) and became friends. Dennen tells her of the amateur contests at The Lion, a neighborhood gay bar in Greenwich Village.

He has her listen to his extensive record collection of the great song stylists—Edith Piaf, Gertrude Lawrence, Lee Wiley, Libby Holman, Billie Holiday. He helps her choose songs and styles. Streisand then wins at The Lion, is booked at classier night spots like The Bon Soir, and The Blue Angel, cuts records, stars on Broadway, and becomes famous and rich. However, over the years she has never acknowledged or credited Dennen with having any part in the making of her career.

In his book (*My Life With Barbra, A Love Story*. New York: Prometheus, 1997) Dennen tells of their relationship, when she moved in with him and they became lovers . . . although Barry was gay. He says that she said the word marriage. Dennen seems to say that the relationship didn't work because the sexual angle didn't work.

Biographer Anne Edwards says Barry Dennen's greatest contribution was to help Barbra feel beautiful, desired, and confident.

*   *   *

After the breakup of her relationship with Jon Peters in the 1980s, Barbra was seen with a number of eligible males, including the Arab playboy and would-be movie producer **Dodi Fayed** (born 1955), who would later woo Princess Diana and die with her in Paris on August 31, 1997, in a car crash.

*   *   *

In 1971 Barbra dated Czech-born movie director **Milos Forman** (born 1932) on the rebound from her relationship with actor Ryan O'Neal, he of the rampant libido. Since then, Forman has won two Academy Awards for Best Director: for *One Flew Over the Cuckoo's Nest* (United Artists, 1975) and *Amadeus* (Orion, 1984).

*   *   *

Elliott Gould (born Elliot Goldstein in August, 1938) is Barbra's first husband and the father of her only child, Jason.

Elliott was the teddy-bearish leading man of Broadway's *I Can Get It For You Wholesale* (1962) and Barbra was the show-stopping Miss Marmelstein.

He may have lost his virginity to Barbra at the Bellevue Stratford Hotel in Philadelphia during the show's pre-Broadway tryout. He moved into Barbra's barren Third Avenue apartment that smelled of fish . . . and then into her Central Park West penthouse when she hit it big.

Gould had an early success on stage, then a decline, and then hit it big again with such movies as *Bob & Carol & Ted & Alice* (Columbia, 1969), *M*A*S*H* (Twentieth Century-Fox, 1970), and *The Long Goodbye* (United Artists, 1973). Then mostly darkness descended upon his career. It must have been miserable being called Mr. Streisand after *Time* magazine, in 1970, had labeled him a "star for an uptight age," and predicted that he would have a bigger and longer-lasting career than Barbra's!

Barbra and Elliott Gould were married on September 13, 1963, in Carson City, Nevada (when she was appearing in Las Vegas). Jason Emanuel Gould was born on December 29, 1967, and the couple divorced on June 30, 1971.

Over the decades, Elliott Gould has spoken at length about Barbra, defending her, explaining her, sometimes attacking her. In one interview, he seems to blame the homosexuality of their son, Jason, on Barbra for not having time to love him (Edwards, p. 18).

The *London Evening Standard* (January 9, 1997) quoted Elliott as saying, "I think the poor baby [Barbra] is miserable. She must be the most miserable person I've ever known. She keeps herself occupied with so many things because she's so afraid to fail, so afraid of the truth."

*   *   *

Anne Edwards describes Barbra's **Secret Lover** as an Arizona businessman and entrepreneur. They met in London: He was there on business, she was taping her TV special *Barbra Streisand . . . and Other Musical Instruments* (CBS, 1973). Edwards described him as "vital, Jewish, fifteen years older than Barbra." She was so in love "she glowed with it." He "wound Barbra around his finger." Barbra said, "I actually enjoy being subjugated to him." Through the years she renewed this affair but nothing changed—he remained married.

In James Spada's *Streisand: Her Life*, the Arizona businessman is identified as Sam Grossman.

And their secret love's no secret anymore.

22

*   *   *

Barbra and composer-musician **James Newton Howard** (born 1950) had known each other for years. A former keyboard player for Elton John, Howard had worked on her *Songbird* (1978) and *Emotion* (1984) albums. He's tall, good-looking, and the ex-husband of actress Rosanna Arquette. He had success scoring the films *Pretty Woman* (Buena Vista, 1990) and *Flatliners* (Columbia, 1990).

In September, 1990, Barbra hired the thirty-nine-year-old composer to write the music for her film *The Prince of Tides*. Soon he and Barbra were romantically involved. When the work was done, so was the affair—apparently with no resentments on either side. "Relationships with Streisand don't seem to end so much as evolve into friendships" (Kein Sessums, *Vanity Fair*, September 1991).

*   *   *

President Clinton's first state dinner at the White House, June 13, 1994, was the first public appearance of Barbra with ABC news anchorman **Peter Jennings** (born 1938). The pair received much media attention and rumors of romance.

Jennings is a distinguished-looking news reporter with great popular appeal. At that time, he had just separated from his wife. Speculation had it that Streisand saw in him the intelligence and political savvy that earlier drew her to Pierre Trudeau.

*   *   *

Few of Barbra's romances attracted as much attention, and ridicule, as the affair with **Don Johnson** (born 1949).

They met in February, 1987, at the Grammy Awards at the Shrine Auditorium in Los Angeles. Barbra was formally introduced to the blond actor, star of the popular TV cop show *Miami Vice* (1984–89).

At Christmas they met again in Aspen, Colorado, and by January 1988 they were "Hollywood's newest odd couple." A *Bloom County* comic strip dubbed Johnson "Streisand's Toy Boy Goy." At the time she was forty-five and he was thirty-eight.

The lovers recorded the duet "Till I Loved You" from the unproduced pop opera *Goya . . . A Life*. (It's on Barbra's 1988 album of the same name and also on Don Johnson's *Let It Roll* album.) Scoffers insisted that Johnson was using her to further his recording career. Nevertheless, she did a walk-on in a *Miami Vice* episode.

By winter it looked like the romance was over. Barbra was said to be "disturbed by Don's suggestion that they embark on a non-monogamous open marriage" (Spada, *Streisand: Her Life*). A tabloid reported that Don was disturbed that Barbra wanted him to be circumcised.

Then Barbra was shocked when Johnson and his actress ex-wife Melanie Griffith announced that they would remarry—Barbra says she didn't see it coming. The media was not kind to her.

(Don Johnson and Melanie Griffith became sexually involved in 1971 when she was fourteen and he was twenty-two. They posed nude for *Playboy* in 1976. They married, divorced, remained friends . . . and remarried in spring of 1989. Melanie ran off with Spanish actor Antonio Banderas in the mid-1990s, which led to her and Johnson divorcing yet again.)

In 1985 Barbra went to a party at the home of Pamela Des Barres, a former lover of Don Johnson. In her book *I'm with the Band* (New York: Jove, 1985), Pamela describes Johnson as an enormously endowed sex god.

Later, talking of the women in his life, Don Johnson says, "We all consider each other family. Patti [D'Arbanville, an ex-wife] is part of the family. Miss Pamela is part of the family. Barbra [Streisand] is part of the family" (Riese, *Her Name Is Barbra*. New York: Birch Lane, 1993).

*   *   *

Barbra and singer-actor **Kris Kristofferson** (born 1936) had enjoyed a brief affair in 1970 before he met his future wife, singer Rita Coolidge, and while Barbra was separated from Elliott Gould. The word is that Kristofferson dropped *her*—that she was too demanding. Kristofferson told a reporter that during their affair "she was being a superstar and I was being a country shit-kicker, both playing games" (Spada, *Streisand: Her Life*).

When it came time to cast *A Star Is Born* (Warner Bros., 1976), Barbra felt that the old chemistry between her and Kristofferson would likely be special. It was special: According to published accounts, filming was characterized by everyone shouting at everyone else, fighting for control. Kristofferson's threat to Jon Peters, her boyfriend and producer of the film—"When I want shit out of you I'll

24

One of the earliest publicity photos for the movie version of
Funny Girl (1968). The airbrushed simplicity and
sweetness of this shot wouldn't be seen again.

PHOTO COURTESY OF ARCHIVE PHOTOS

squeeze your head!"—has gone into the vernacular.

At the moment of the filming of the movie's bathtub scene, Kris slid into the tub and waited for Barbra—completely naked. When Jon Peters saw this situation he went ballistic.

25

*   *   *

While filming *On a Clear Day You Can See Forever* (Paramount, 1970) in England in 1969, Barbra was attracted to **George Lazenby** (born 1939), the Australian actor who is the James Bond no one remembers (*On Her Majesty's Secret Service*, United Artists, 1969). The affair was apparently unconsummated because Barbra didn't want a casual affair, she wanted Lazenby to be her one and only.

*   *   *

In the spring of 1965, Barbra hired French composer **Michel Legrand** (born 1931) as musical director for her album *Je M'Appelle Barbra* (1966), on which she sings in French. Legrand's score for the musical film *The Umbrellas of Cherbourg* (French, 1964) had just been nominated for an Academy Award.

The two worked together into the early hours of each morning in the deserted Broadway theatre after *Funny Girl* performances. *Barbra* magazine (no. 8, 1982) reprints a French interview with the married composer, who admits that their relationship became "almost intimate," but other rumormongers say it went all the way.

Legrand also speaks of her temper: "It's unbelievable—Barbra in anger. An angry Barbra is all of a sudden a usually courteous and delicate woman seized with fury and capable of the most foul vocabulary."

The composer worked with Barbra again on *Yentl*, writing the music for the songs by Alan and Marilyn Bergman.

*   *   *

Another date in the early 1970s, which proved to be yet another attempt by Barbra to get back at faithless lover Ryan O'Neal, was with **Steve McQueen** (1930–1980). This heroic antihero action star of the 1960s and 1970s is best known for *The Great Escape* (United Artists, 1963) and *Bullitt* (Warner Bros., 1968). McQueen was one of the five stars who formed the First Artists production company in 1969, along with Streisand, Paul Newman, Sidney Poitier, and Dustin Hoffman. (See **Part II, 15. Barbra Streisand as Movie Producer.**)

*   *   *

In 1990, while promoting his latest film, *Crossing the Line* (Miramax, 1991) actor **Liam Neeson** (born 1952) casually made reference to a new girlfriend. When a reporter asked him to describe her, he said, "She's a Bronx Jewess."

The Irish-born Neeson meant Streisand (a Brooklyn Jewess). The relationship started when Barbra invited Irish actor Peter Caffrey to her Malibu home for a private screening of *The Prince of Tides*. Caffrey invited Neeson to accompany him.

Caffrey later said, "Streisand was all over Liam like a raincoat. They slipped away at the end of the screening and didn't surface till late the next day. It was quite clear what she saw in Liam—and it wasn't just his acting potential." This is a reference to "the supposed enormity of his credentials . . . his wedding tackle" (Ingrid Miller. *Liam Neeson: The First Biography*. New York: St. Martin's Press, 1995).

*   *   *

Ryan O'Neal (born 1941) became a popular actor through his stint as the stud in the prime-time drama *Peyton Place* (1964–69), and in the megabuck movie hit *Love Story* (Paramount, 1970). He was also famous for his offscreen exploits, mainly in the bedroom.

Streisand and O'Neal began seeing each other in early 1971. Gossip had it that she had found herself a boy toy (though they were both twenty-nine), and that he was using the most powerful actress in Hollywood to further his career.

They costarred in the comedy romp *What's Up, Doc?* and were close off screen.

But then Ryan was visited on the set by TV actress Peggy Lipton, which angered Barbra. When O'Neal underwent surgery, it was the actor's estranged wife Leigh Taylor-Young who rushed to his bedside.

The romance between Barbra and Ryan cooled, but they remained friends. O'Neal was briefly considered for *The Way We Were* (Columbia, 1973). However, the ex-lovers did costar in *The Main Event* (Warner Bros., 1979).

"When Joan Collins' autobiography, *Past Imperfect* (1978), was released, Barbra read one passage aloud to friends, wherein Joan described Ryan O'Neal as the best lover she'd ever had. '*Wh-a-a-t!*" said Barbra, wounded. 'Ryan? The best she ever had? *I* went with Ryan.' It was like she felt cheated, that Ryan had been holding out on her," said a source who had heard the exchange (Shaun Considine, *Barbra Streisand: The Woman, The Myth, The Music*).

Considine also quotes Ryan O'Neal as saying, "I found her very sexy, a terrific girl, but I think she used me!"

*   *   *

Jon Peters (born 1945) has been usually seen as The Great Love Story of Her life—or at least until actor James Brolin came along in 1996. Jon Peters first came into Barbra's world in August of 1973, when he responded to her summons for a new wig for her upcoming film *For Pete's Sake* (Columbia, 1974). A few moments after they met he told her she had a great ass, and so they were off and running.

The dynamic Peters had first married at fifteen, and he had put himself through beauty school by boxing professionally. Later he turned the family's beauty business into a chain of salons. He married one of his clients, actress Lesley Ann Warren, in May 1967. They were separated at the time Peters and Barbra met. The 1975 divorce decree gave the Peters joint custody of their son Christopher.

Barbra later said that it was love at first sight for herself and Peters. They gradually became soulmates, feeling they had much in common. He'd dropped the "h" from "John" just as she'd dropped an "a" from "Barbara." Jon's father died when he was ten, Barbra's when she was fifteen months old. In addition, both had survived unloving stepfathers.

They became lovers four months after they met and openly discussed their sexual relationship (Barbra in *Playboy*, 1977; Jon in *Playboy*, 1978). Jon: "Good in bed means giving head."

After they met, Jon Peters sold his chain of beauty salons to devote himself full time to Barbra Streisand. He produced her album *ButterFly* (1974), which was damned by critics for its unprofessional quality (even Barbra would later admit she disliked it). Together they produced *A Star Is Born* (Warner Bros., 1976), which remains her most successful movie to date.

The lovers bought twenty-three acres of land in a secluded area of Malibu and built a fairy-tale kingdom with five dollhouse-like homes. They usually lived in separate houses on the Malibu spread, which might be one of the reasons the relationship lasted so long.

Bitten by the show biz bug, Peters set out to become a movie producer. "With undeniable and inestimable assistance from his girl-

28

friend Barbra, [Jon Peters] propelled himself to the ranks of movie producers in the 1970s, much to the salacious and drooling delight of Hollywood wags, who dubbed the couple a joke: the superstar and her shampoo boy. With his partner Peter Guber, Peters became something of a mogul in the eighties with, among other pictures, *Batman* (Warner Bros., 1989), the biggest grossing film in Warner history" (Randall Riese. *Her Name Is Barbra*. New York: Birch Lane, 1993).

Ironically, it was through his involvement with Barbra that Peters was able to become a producer . . . but now this meant he had little time for Barbra's projects. And, as everyone knows, she is a woman who demands 100 percent. Or else.

Peters moved out at the end of 1979. He sold Barbra his interest in the Malibu estate in 1984.

They remain close friends, and he still throws lavish birthday parties for her on his Beverly Hills estate. Barbra's godchild, Caleigh, Jon's adopted daughter, has become one of the most important people in her life.

*   *   *

In 1969 singing icon **Elvis Presley** (1935–1977) was to follow Barbra as the headliner at the International Hotel in Las Vegas. He was there for her opening, and during her performance she introduced him to the audience. Afterward . . . Barbra was alone in her dressing room when Elvis entered and said "Hi." Silence. He then picked up a bottle of nail polish, dropped to one knee, and silently painted Barbra's long fingernails. Stunned, she said, "Thanks."

Barbra supposedly told lover Jon Peters of this encounter . . . and he recounted it in an unpublished interview.

An associate of Elvis said that the intimacy didn't end with the fingernail job. Barbra and Elvis got together. "Not necessarily just a one-night stand, but probably no longer than two or three." (Spada, *Streisand: Her Life*).

Anne Edwards rebuts the Elvis story with a quote from Barbra, as told to friends: "When have you ever heard of a man painting a woman's fingernails as an ode to seduction? It would stick to *everything!*"

Barbra and Jon Peters wanted Elvis for *A Star Is Born* but he was already too far gone by then: "fat . . . lethargic, unfocused, out of it" (Spada, *Streisand: Her Life*).

29

*　　*　　*

Robert Redford (born 1937) had been the first choice for the blond, blue-eyed all-American hero of *The Way We Were*, but it took a lot of arm-twisting before he signed. That, and a salary that was $200,000 more than what Streisand was getting.

When *The Way We Were* became a major success, many theorized that it was due to the chemistry between the two superstars.

It was clear to cinematographer Harry Stradling that the chemistry between Streisand and Redford extended beyond their roles. "They were very close," Stradling said. "During the scene where they were both in bed, it was very arousing . . . more so than just actors acting" (Spada, *Streisand: Her Life*)

*　　*　　*

Roy Scott (born 1935) was a handsome member of Allan Miller's acting workshop in New York City back in 1958. Barbra was seen as just one of the girls available to Roy.

Roy himself said that they had deep feelings for each other. . . and that he was probably her first love.

*　　*　　*

Omar Sharif (born 1932) was a leading Egyptian movie star at the time he was cast in David Lean's *Lawrence of Arabia* (Columbia, 1962). His performance led to international stardom, which peaked early with the title role in *Doctor Zhivago* (MGM, 1965).

In the spring of 1967, Sharif was under contract to Columbia. He frequently saw director William Wyler in the studio commissary, and joked about playing Nick Arnstein in the upcoming *Funny Girl*. Wyler finally said, "Why not?" The bookkeepers, then, told him why not: Sharif was Egyptian, Streisand was Jewish, and the Arab-Israeli Six-Day War was still smoldering. The studio's decision to go with Sharif created much controversy. Barbra's films were forever banned in Arab-speaking countries.

The two stars created their own controversy by having an affair.

Said Sharif, "The first impression is that she's not very pretty. But after three days, I am honest, I found her physically beautiful, and I start lusting after this woman!" (*Life*, September 29, 1967).

Sharif had been married for twelve years but now he and his wife led separate lives. Barbra was still very much married, and Elliott Gould was hurt and angry. Their marriage was mortally wounded.

The affair ended when production on the movie wrapped. The two didn't meet again until 1974, when Sharif arrived to film his brief scenes as Nick Arnstein in *Funny Lady* (Columbia, 1975). This time, Barbra's jealous live-in lover, Jon Peters, was on the set, so it was business, not pleasure, as usual.

*   *   *

In April 1971 at The Crystal Palace in St. Louis, Barbra shared the bill with the Smothers Brothers, popular TV comedians of the sixties . . . and then briefly shared her bed with **Tommy Smothers** (born 1937).

*   *   *

Pierre Elliott Trudeau (born 1919), the prime minister of Canada, met Barbra Streisand in London on January 15, 1969, at a dinner party after the *Funny Girl* premiere. A year later, he flew to New York for a series of weekend dates. After finishing *The Owl and Pussycat* (Columbia, 1970), she flew to Ottawa, Canada, to see him. In Lawrence Grobel's *Playboy* interview (October 1977), Barbra admitted she "seriously contemplated" marrying Trudeau but he didn't ask.

In March of 1971, Trudeau married Margaret Sinclair, a young girl he had been wooing at the same time he was courting Streisand. The Trudeaus separated in 1977, by which time Margaret had become a familiar figure in jet set circles. She was romantically linked with the likes of Mick Jagger, King Hussein, Jack Nicholson—and Barbra's old flame Ryan O'Neal.

Streisand and Trudeau have remained friends. In 1984, he escorted her to a New York City reception in her honor given by the United Jewish Appeal.

*   *   *

Actor **Jon Voight** (born 1938) was seen with Barbra in 1995. In July, he was her date for a charity function in London as guests of Prince Charles. From there they flew to Saint-Tropez for another party.

31

Barbra prepares for the "His Love Makes Me Beautiful" Ziegfeld
Follies production number in *Funny Girl* (1968): as Fanny Brice, she
stops the show as a very pregnant bride.
PHOTO COURTESY OF PHOTOFEST

Randall Riese (*Her Name Is Barbra*) writes of Barbra reliving the childhood she never had through her attraction to younger men such as actor
Don Johnson, musician James Newton Howard, tennis star André
Agassi, and actor **Peter Weller** (born 1947). Weller, best known for playing *RoboCop* (Orion, 1987), was Streisand's boyfriend in the early 1990s.

*   *   *

32

And . . . there's also actor Gary Busey (who had third billing in *A Star Is Born*); Tina Sinatra's ex-husband, millionaire businessman Richard Cohen; Anthony Michael De Toth (son of film actress Veronica Lake and movie director André De Toth); actor Clint Eastwood; millionaire businessman Charles Evans (brother of millionaire movie producer Robert Evans); businessman Richard Greyson; British actor-singer Anthony Newley; and pianist Neil Wolfe. All of these notables are linked to Streisand in *Did She Or Didn't She? Behind the Bedroom Doors of 201 Famous Women* by Mart Martin (Secaucus, N.J.: Citadel/Carol, 1996). The men are listed under the heading "Lovers, Flings, or Just Friends?" without further comment or rumors or data to validate their being included on the list.

*   *   *

Now when Barbra wakes up in the morning, there's James Brolin!

James Brolin (born 1940) in Los Angeles, is six-foot-four, with green eyes and white hair. He began his acting career in television, going directly from college into the *Bus Stop* series (1961–62). He's known mainly for the long-running TV series *Marcus Welby, M.D.* (1969–76), for which he won an Emmy Award (Outstanding Performance by an Actor in a Supporting Role in a Drama), and for the television series *Hotel* (1983–88), which also starred Connie Sellecca and Anne Baxter.

Brolin entered movies in 1963 and has had a respectable, if unexceptional, career. Notably, he portrayed Clark Gable opposite Jill Clayburgh as Carole Lombard in *Gable and Lombard* (Universal, 1976); appeared with Barbra's ex-husband Elliott Gould and O. J. Simpson in *Capricorn One* (Warner Bros., 1978); was the head of the haunted household in the original *The Amityville Horror* (AIP/FWS, 1979); and played in a series of made-for-television movies (one of which, *Finish Line*, 1989, had his son, Josh, in a major supporting role), and forgettable feature films.

He's currently starring in the syndicated TV action series *Pensacola: Wings of Gold*, playing a Marine colonel who trains fighter pilots. He's executive producer of the series. Brolin also directed the feature film *My Brother's War* (1997), yet to be released, but which won a Best Feature award at the Hollywood Film Festival (whatever that is).

Brolin had been wed twice: to actress Jan Smithers (from the TV sit-com *WKRP in Cincinnati*, 1978–82), from 1986 until 1995; earlier, he had been married to Jane Cameron Agee (they have two children, actor Josh, twenty-nine, and Jess, twenty-five), from whom he was divorced in 1986 after twenty years of marriage. Jane accused Brolin of bigamy when he wed Jan, as their divorce was not yet final. Brolin declared that the ceremony had been merely symbolic and that they would apply for a marriage license after his divorce became final. Jane died in an auto accident in 1995.

Brolin was a blind date arranged by Barbra's friend Christine Peters (ex-wife of Jon Peters), who seated them together at a dinner party, July 1, 1996. Streisand's first words to him were "Who screwed up your hair?" (quoted on *The Rosie O'Donnell Show*, November 21, 1997).

Before the world knew what hit it, the media was covering the Streisand-Brolin relationship as the middle-age fairy tale of two who'd loved and lost before but had never given up on The Real Thing. After a year of it, much of the world was getting saturated with it.

Brolin nicknamed Barbra "Beezer." He said things like "I said to her the other day, 'I feel like I've been married to you since the day we met.' I wish I'd met her thirty years ago."

TV Guide, December 13, 1997, featured "The Year in Jeers," a light-hearted attack on "the silliness that pours out of our televisions." James Brolin was quoted as telling Barbra he didn't want to go to sleep because "then I'll miss you." Gong!

Columnists Marilyn Beck and Stacy Jenel Smith in their annual "Tacky Taste Awards" sent bouquets to the likes of Marv Albert, Mike Tyson, Jenny McCarthy, Ellen DeGeneres, et al., and to Barbra Streisand "for her stomach-churning performance, acting like a sex-starved teenybopper on the Barbara Walters show, fawning and paw-ing her current stud muffin, James Brolin, both of them nauseating everyone" (Los Angeles *Daily News*, November 27, 1997).

CHAPTER 4

The Wedding in White

After two years of rampant rumor and speculation, Barbra Streisand and James Brolin were wed on Wednesday, July 1, 1998—the second anniversary of their first date—in a sunset ceremony at her spectacular Malibu, California, compound overlooking the Pacific.

They were largely successful in keeping the ceremony a secret. Guests had been notified earlier by phone to keep the evening free for "a special celebration." Two days before the wedding, a huge white tent was erected on the lawn. This was the tip-off the media had been waiting for, and they made a mad dash for Malibu.

But the crazed paparazzi were held at bay by security forces, and could only watch helplessly from a distance as pickup trucks delivered food and flowers, and vans with tinted windows transported invited guests to the top of the bluff.

When Whoopi Goldberg married Lyle Trachtenberg in 1994 in nearby Pacific Palisades, Whoopi attached huge helium balloons to the roof to discourage the clattering helicopters from getting too close. Barbra went Whoopi one better by installing huge outdoor speakers and blasting White Zombie heavy-metal music toward the media to keep them from hearing any of the ceremony. (This also drove the neighbors insane, but tough, you know?)

Deborah Wald, a friend, was the only photographer allowed. *People* magazine supposedly paid Streisand a million dollars for exclusive rights to the photos, featured in its July 20 cover story.

It was a Jewish wedding but without the traditional huppah, the ceremonial canopy. Rabbi Leonard Beerman officiated. The couple exchanged plain gold wedding bands.

(It should be understood that all the names which follow should be preceded by "longtime friend" or "longtime associate.")

The wedding dress was by Donna Karan, an oyster-white floor-length gown with shimmering crystal beading and a fifteen-foot diaphanous veil. Barbra said it made her feel "like a princess." Brolin wore a double-breasted black tuxedo.

The music was supplied by a sixteen-piece orchestra led by Marvin Hamlisch. In addition to the "Wedding March" and an up-tempo "Here Comes the Bride" Barbra requested Andre Previn's "The Four Horsemen of the Apocalypse" music.

Barbra was given in marriage by her thirty-one-year-old son Jason Gould. Her half-sister Roslyn Kind, age forty-seven, was her bridesmaid. (Somehow Roslyn was left out of the family photo groupings in *People* magazine, as was sixty-five-year-old brother Sheldon.) Her eighty-nine-year-old mother Diane Kind wore a pink gown. The Brolin family was represented by his eighty-seven-year-old father Henry, his eighty-three-year-old mother Helen, his ten-year-old daughter Molly (who was ring bearer), his thirty-year-old son Josh (who acted as best man), and young grandchildren Eden (a flower girl) and Trevor, and twenty-six-year-old son Jess.

The hors d'oeuvres included sushi, vegetable wontons, smoked salmon on warm corn cakes, potato rostis, and ricotta-filled blintzes with cherry jam. The sit-down dinner, under the big tent, included soft-shell crabs, rotisserie-cooked baby chickens, and porcini ravioli.

Of the 105 guests, these also have been identified: actor John Travolta and wife Kelly Preston; actor Tom Hanks and wife Rita Wilson; jazz great Quincy Jones; film directors Steven Spielberg, Sydney Pollack, and Irwin Kershner; Barbra's assistant Renata Buser; songwriters Marilyn and Alan Bergman; Marge Tabankin of The Streisand Foundation; ice cream heir Richard Baskin; close friend Joanne Segel; Jon and Christine Peters and god-daughter Caleigh Peters; Evelyn and Mo Ostin; Irina and Mike Medavoy; Jeff Berg; Ellen Gilbert; agent Sue Mengers; manager Marty Erlichman; "First

Brother" Roger Clinton and wife Molly.

Since Barbra's aversion to singing before friends is well known, the highlight of the affair was probably when she sang two new love songs to Brolin, including "Just One Lifetime," written by Melissa Manchester and Tom Snow.

Those people who begrudge the happiness of others groaned over Brolin's published remark that "Every night is a new adventure. Sleeping is a waste of time. I can't wait to see her in the morning." He also said, "Every day that I wake up with her I thank the heavens for letting her into my life." They also felt it was a bit much for fifty-six-year-old Barbra to wear white. Others thought the gown showed too much cleavage. And there was speculation that she'd had cosmetic surgery under her eyes, after protesting for years that she never would.

The real party-poopers—the tabloids—checked in later with stories to wilt the flowers. The *Star* of July 21, 1998, claims that Barbra had Brolin sign an ironclad prenuptial agreement that, should they separate, would give him a $1-million payoff and $300,000 a year for every year they were married. Supposedly he'll get a $10-million-dollar bonus after ten years of marriage. And a gold watch!

[Barbra's first marriage, you'll remember, was in 1963 when she was the opening act for Liberace at Harrah's in Lake Tahoe. Impulsively, she and Elliott Gould drove to Carson City and exchanged vows in front of a Justice of the Peace. She had been advised to marry in Nevada because it has no community property laws.]

The *National Enquirer* of July 21 calls Streisand "the bride from hell," having temper tantrums all day because President Clinton wouldn't reschedule his trip to China so he could attend her wedding.

Most accounts report that the newlyweds winged to Barbados for their honeymoon. The *Enquirer* called that a smoke screen, and located them on a $5,000-a-day yacht off the coast of California.

The *Globe* of July 21 claims that the Brolins have set plans in motion to adopt a baby girl.

All in all, it was a fairy tale wedding for a couple way past the age of fairy tales—but with their kind of money they could sure try, couldn't they?

CHAPTER 5

Substitute Fathers and Stand-In Mothers

It's easy to practice pop psychology on Barbra Streisand because she keeps exposing her naked psyche in public.

She never knew her father, who died when she was only fifteen months old, and her mother was insensitive or indifferent or maybe just too busy.

It might be said that Barbra looks for father substitutes in her lovers and companions, with older men like businessman Sam Grossman, actor Omar Sharif, and Canadian prime minister Pierre Elliott Trudeau, whom she seriously contemplated marrying. Now she has white-haired actor James Brolin, who seems to embody everything Barbra wants in a lover, or a husband, or a father.

*   *   *

In addition she's found numerous mother figures. She speaks of her first doll, a hot-water bottle with its own sweater, in numerous interviews. It was made for her by a loving Austrian woman named Tobey Wander Borokow, a neighbor who would babysit the little girl until her mother came home from work. Six-year-old Irving Borokow was Barbra's first boyfriend. He remembers his mother: "She was very motherly to Barbara; she was probably in contact with her more than her own mother was. My mother became her mother, basically" (James Spada, *Streisand: Her Life*. New York: Crown, 1995).

39

*   *   *

From age eleven, Barbra worked in the Chinese restaurant of Jimmy and Muriel Choy across the street from her apartment building. The Choys became surrogate parents. It was Muriel Choy who explained the facts of life to the curious young girl. Also, it was under the Choys' influence that Streisand began growing her fingernails long.

*   *   *

At some point in the late 1950s, when Barbra was high on the possibilities of becoming an actress and thinking about maybe being a singer, she met Cis Corman in one of her acting classes. Corman was a dynamic, sophisticated would-be actress sixteen years older than Barbra, and married to a practicing analyst. The two women became best friends and remain so today.

When Streisand formed her own production company, Barwood, Cis Corman was named president. To date, Barwood has been associated with seven of Barbra's sixteen movies. For the first project, *Up the Sandbox* (National General, 1972), Cis Corman was casting director. The seventh film, *The Mirror Has Two Faces* (TriStar, 1996), lists Cis Corman as executive producer. One of Barwood's most recent projects, TV's *The Long Island Incident* (NBC, 1998), credits Corman and Streisand as executive producers, in that order.

Anne Edwards' Streisand biography has the most to say about Corman. "Cis was now involved in all her production plans. A born mediator, a woman of classic understanding, Cis had early on become a substitute maternal figure to Streisand, a totally nonjudgmental 'mommy' to whom she could reveal her worst feelings and fears, let everything hang out, so to speak, knowing that Cis would not castigate her for her honesty and would instead offer her some clearheaded guidance" (*Streisand: A Biography*. Boston: Little, Brown, 1997).

*   *   *

The November 1994 *Vanity Fair* cover story discusses two more of Streisand's older female friends: Evelyn Ostin, whose husband was the longtime head of Warner Bros. Records, and Joanne Segel, who is married to a retired entertainment business manager. The three friends are actively involved with the inner-life explorations labeled "New Age." Segal calls herself a psychospiritual therapist.

*   *   *

The mother substitute who may have meant the most to Barbra Streisand was Virginia Kelley, the mother of President Clinton. The two women met at the January 1993 inauguration gala and felt an immediate kinship.

"I called her my Southern mom," Streisand says. "She knew how to soothe with words. Virginia would say, 'Do you know how precious you are?' Every conversation, she'd say, 'I love you.' The way I was brought up, nobody ever used words like 'I love you.' I just wanted to take care of her. I was so looking forward to have her visit me out here. I wanted to take her shopping, because she was so appreciative of everything she was given" (Los Angeles *Daily News*, November 12, 1997).

Virginia Kelley died in 1994. Barbra attended her funeral and was deeply moved by the Southern spirituals sung there. Two years later, she released the album *Higher Ground*, a collection of inspirational songs. The album is dedicated to Virginia Kelley.

CHAPTER 6

Highlights of the Extraordinary Life and Career of Barbra Streisand: A Chronology

1942

April 24 — Barbara Joan Streisand is born to Diana and Emanuel Streisand in the Jewish Hospital of Brooklyn, New York. An older brother, Sheldon, had been born in 1935. The baby girl has sparkling blue eyes, but is bald until she's two years old.

Diana, age thirty-three, is one of four children of a Russian immigrant, a tailor who doubled as a cantor. She grew up wanting to be a singer. Emanuel ("Manny") is thirty-four, the son of an immigrant fish seller from Eastern Europe. He's a teacher, a man of learning.

1943

August 4 — When Barbara is only fifteen months old, her father dies suddenly from an improperly treated epileptic seizure:

Apparently, a doctor tries to stop the seizure with an injection of morphine, which creates an adverse reaction. The official cause of death is respiratory failure.

1947

Barbara begins school, attending the yeshiva on Willoughby Street in Brooklyn, where her father had taught.

1948, 1949

Summer — Her mother thinks Barbara is too thin, maybe anemic, and sends her to a health camp in upstate New York.

1950

September — From the fourth grade on, Barbara attends public schools, as her mother can no longer afford the yeshiva.

While attending P.S. 89, she becomes friends with twins Marilyn and Carolyn Bernstein; they form a singing group called Bobbie and the Bernsteins.

December 23 — Diana Streisand is scandalously eight-and-a-half months pregnant with the child of real estate dealer Louis Kind. (Barbra later dismisses him as "a car salesman or something.") Louis Kind marries the widow.

1951

January 9 — Barbara's half-sister Rosalind (later shortened to Roslyn) is born. The fifty-six-year-old Kind dotes on the new baby, but he has no use for Barbara, who, in turn, feels that he hates her. He refers to the two girls as Beauty and the Beast. (Roslyn later defends her father, suggesting that maybe Barbara was a rotten kid who provoked adults.)

1952

The family spends two weeks in South Fallsburg, in the Catskills, where the resort hotel has a talent show for the children. Ten-year-old Barbara sings and dances in the shows.

1953

At age ten, Barbara auditions for Metro-Goldwyn-Mayer, which is looking for child talent for upcoming movies. The scouts urge her to enter their training classes but Diana nixes the notion when she learns she's expected to pay for the lessons.

1954

Barbara auditions for Star Time, a school for child performers. She's there for four months, but then has to quit when there's no more money to pay for classes.

1955

September 12 — Barbara's first day of high school, at Erasmus Hall High School, at Flatbush and Church Avenues in Brooklyn.

On Sundays Barbara helps out at Choy's Chinese Restaurant on Nostrand Avenue, owned by the parents of her new friends Jimmy and Muriel Choy. The Choys become a second family to her. It's Muriel Choy who explains the facts of life to Barbara.

December 29 — Barbara's very first recording session, at the Nola Recording Studios, where one can make a record for a few dollars. Her mother Diana sings "One Kiss," then Barbara sings "You'll Never Know" and "Zing! Went the Strings of My Heart." (The last song is on the 1991 four-disc set *Just For the Record*.)

1956

April 22 — For Barbara's fourteenth birthday she goes with a friend to see the Broadway play *The Diary of Anne Frank*. She feels she could have played the role.

May 14 — Louis Kind packs up and moves out. In September, Diana takes him to court for legal separation and alimony payments.

1957

June — Barbara is accepted by the Malden Bridge Playhouse in Malden Bridge, New York, to spend the summer working in all aspects of the theater.

Fall — She auditions for an apprenticeship program at the Cherry Lane Theatre in Greenwich Village and is accepted. It's headed by acting teacher Allan Miller.

Barbara auditions for Lee Strasberg's Actors Studio but is not accepted. Maybe they found out she's only fifteen, not the required eighteen.

1958

Allan Miller accepts Barbara into his Theater Studio workshop on West Forty-Eighth Street in Manhattan in exchange for babysitting. As she learns and blossoms as an actress, Allan Miller becomes a surrogate parent.

Another summer of stock, at the Clinton Playhouse in Clinton, Connecticut: Barbara plays oversexed Ellie May in a play version of Erskine Caldwell's 1932 novel *Tobacco Road*. She becomes friends with

45

Warren Beatty, who performs major parts in most of the Playhouse productions.

Before Christmas, Barbara auditions for the play *Driftwood*, a vanity production presented in the attic of playwright Maurice Tei Dunn's apartment on Forty-Ninth Street at Third Avenue in New York City. Joan Rivers is also in the cast and writes of it in her book *Enter Talking* (New York: Delacorte, 1996), misremembering the details. The show runs for six weeks, playing to audiences of mostly families and friends.

1959

January 26 — Barbara graduates from Erasmus Hall High School half a semester early, fourth in her class.

Within weeks she and friend Susan Dworkowitz rent a tiny walkup apartment at 339 West Forty-Eighth Street in Manhattan, next door to Allan Miller's workshop. Soon thereafter, Susan moves back to Brooklyn and Marilyn Fried, another aspiring actress, becomes Streisand's new roommate.

June to September — Barbara spends another season in summer stock, at the Cecilwood Theatre in Fishkill, New York. She appears in Terence Rattigan's *Separate Tables* (1956).

1960

Friends insist that Barbara become a professional singer. She auditions for a touring company of *The Sound of Music* and the show's casting director also suggests that she try singing in clubs.

April — Barbara becomes friends with actor-singer Barry Dennen when they perform in Karel and Josef Capek's play *The Insect Comedy* (1921) at the Jan Hus Theatre on East Seventy-Fourth Street.

Barry Dennen recognizes Barbara's inherent musicality. He makes her see that "singing could be like acting, except I played all the parts myself." Dennen says "Barbra was my creation," but she never gave him credit.

June 6, 1960 (Carve it in stone!) — Eighteen-year-old Barbara enters the talent contest at The Lion, a gay bar at 62 West Ninth Street in Greenwich Village. She sings "A Sleepin' Bee" and "When Sunny Gets Blue." She wins. She gets to perform for two weeks, receiving fifty dollars a week and all the food and drink she wants. Says Barbra: "In those days I could be had for a baked potato!" (Shaun Considine,

Barbra Streisand: The Woman, The Myth, The Music. New York: Delacorte, 1985).

After her second week at The Lion, Barbara Joan Streisand becomes Barbra Streisand.

Barbra auditions at The Bon Soir at 40 West Eighth Street, "a fabled club owned and run by the Mafia" (James Gavin, *Intimate Nights: The Golden Age of New York Cabaret*. New York: Grove, 1991).

"Get that broad outta here!" yells boss Phil Pagano, but he's persuaded to give her a chance.

August 7 — Barbra appears as "a little extra surprise" at The Bon Soir and wows the audience.

September 9 — She begins a two-week engagement at The Bon Soir . . . which stretches into ten weeks. She earns $108 a week.

"The Bon Soir didn't make Streisand a star, it made her a happening" (Randall Riese, *Her Name Is Barbra*. New York: Birch Lane, 1993).

1961

March 2 to April 2; April 6–15 — Barbra appears at The Caucus Club in Detroit, the first time she's been out of the Northeast.

April 5 — Barbra makes her first television appearance, on NBC's late-night *Jack Paar Show* (which later becomes *The Tonight Show*). Actor friend Orson Bean is the substitute host that night. She sings "A Sleepin' Bee."

April 17 to May 8 — Barbra appears at The Crystal Palace in St. Louis. The comedy team of the Smothers Brothers share the bill.

May 9 to June 6 — Barbra begins her second engagement at The Bon Soir. Comedians Renee Taylor and Phil Leeds are also on the bill.

In the audience is Marty Erlichman, who had been the manager of blues singer Josh White. He also had discovered the folk group the Clancy Brothers but was still looking for "the big one." Mesmerized by this unusual girl from Brooklyn, he offers to work for her for a year without commission, to prove himself. (There's a rare photo of Marty Erlichman with Barbra on page 19 of Allison J. Waldman's *The Barbra Streisand Scrapbook*. New York: Citadel/Carroll, 1995.)

June 22 — Barbra makes her first appearance on Mike Wallace's *P.M. East* late-night East Coast talk-variety show. Between June 1961 and June 1962, she appears on the TV program a remarkable thirteen times. She becomes the show's "resident eccentric."

July 3–16 — Barbra is hired by The Town 'n' Country Club in Winnipeg, Ontario, Canada. She quickly antagonizes the club owner by the way she dresses and refuses to make concessions or to cooperate. She stalks off stage after singing four songs because the audience won't quiet down. She's fired after a week.

July 17 to August 12 — A return booking at Detroit's Caucus Club.

Second week in September — Barbra begins rehearsals for *Another Evening with Harry Stoones*, an off-Broadway revue with music, starring Diana Sands and Dom DeLuise, at the Gramercy Arts Theatre on East Twenty-Seventh Street. (The in-joke is that there was never a first evening with Harry.)

October 21 — *Another Evening with Harry Stoones* opens and . . . when the producers read the reviews . . . it closes.

Second week in November — Barbra is called upon as a one-night replacement (for comic Pat Harrington, Jr.) at the classy uptown nightspot The Blue Angel, at 152 East Fifty-Fifth Street near Third Avenue. Arthur Gelb of the *New York Times* is there to review singer Felicia Saunders—and is overwhelmed. Gelb thinks his piece was Barbra's first review in a major paper.

November 16 — The Blue Angel books Barbra for two weeks. She's a smash.

Same day — She auditions for David Merrick's new Broadway-bound musical *I Can Get It For You Wholesale*. She auditions five more times—they're just not sure—before she's signed for the role of the mousy garment district secretary Miss Marmelstein.

While *Wholesale* is in rehearsals, she returns to The Blue Angel as headliner.

Shortly after her *Wholesale* audition, writer Arthur Laurents, the director of *Wholesale*, urges Columbia Records president Goddard Lieberson (nicknamed "God"), to sign Barbra for records. Lieberson feels she is too "special," too eccentric.

1962

During the *Wholesale* rehearsals/tryouts in Philadelphia, Barbra, almost twenty, and leading man Elliott Gould, age twenty-three, become lovers.

March 22 — *I Can Get It For You Wholesale* opens at the Shubert Theatre on West Forty-Fourth Street. The cheering audience gives

48

Barbra a three-minute standing ovation after her "Miss Marmelstein" novelty-song number.

Elliott Gould moves in with Barbra in her Third Avenue apartment over a seafood store.

April 1 — The cast records *I Can Get It For You Wholesale* for Columbia Records.

Columbia records a twenty-fifth anniversary edition of Harold Rome's *Pins and Needles*, his first big Broadway success, and Rome insists that Barbra participate.

The New York Drama Critics Circle Award pick Barbra and Sandy Dennis (from *A Thousand Clowns*) in a tie as Best Supporting Actresses of 1962.

April 29 — Barbra's nominated for the Antoinette Perry Award (the Tony) for Best Supporting Actress in a Musical but loses to Phyllis Newman of *Subways Are For Sleeping*.

May 29 — Barbra appears on *The Garry Moore Show*, a CBS-TV variety hour, and sings "Happy Days Are Here Again." Her memorable interpretation of the evergreen song as the story of a woman who lost at love creates a sensation.

Spring — She appears five times on TV's *P.M. East* . . . and is heard by David Kapralik, director of artists and repertoire at Columbia Records. "She blew me away," he says.

May 10 — Four hundred "close" friends show up for Barbra's twentieth birthday party, held at midnight (after the *Wholesale* performance) at the classy Lichee Tree Restaurant on Eighth Street in Greenwich Village.

August 21 — Barbra debuts on NBC's *The Tonight Show*, with guest host Groucho Marx.

October 1 — Barbra signs a contract to record for Columbia Records. She demands, and gets, full creative control of her albums.

October 4 — She is a guest on *The Tonight Show Starring Johnny Carson* (which assumed that title just two nights earlier). Carson becomes an early Streisand enthusiast.

October 23–November 18 — She returns to The Bon Soir, to an ever-growing audience of loyal fans.

December 9 — The final performance of *Wholesale*.

December 16 — Barbra appears on *The Ed Sullivan Show* (CBS) singing "My Coloring Book" and "Lover, Come Back To Me."

1963 — "The Year of Barbra Streisand"

January 2 — Barbra makes her fourth appearance with Johnny Carson on *The Tonight Show.*

January 8–28 — The Blue Angel presents Barbra for three sold-out weeks.

January 23, 24, 25 — Barbra records *The Barbra Streisand Album* with innovative musical director and arranger Peter Matz. Like Barry Dennen, Matz understands that she's more of an actress than a singer and gives her a commercial sound that will help her recording success.

> Barbra goes on an incredible year-long nonstop tour to promote *The Barbra Streisand Album*, her first, to be released on February 25. She appears on *The Tonight Show* twice, *The Ed Sullivan Show* twice, *The Judy Garland Show*, *The Dinah Shore Show*, a *Bob Hope Comedy Special*, *The Irv Kupcinet Show*, and cohosts *The Mike Douglas Show* in Cleveland. She sings at The Frolics Club in Boston, the Eden Roc Hotel in Florida, and the hungry i in San Francisco. Booked for three weeks at Basin Street East, she opens for Benny Goodman and runs away with the show. She appears on the *Jerry Lewis Muscular Dystrophy Telethon*, the *March of Dimes Telethon*, and *The Keefe Brasselle Show*. She finds time to sing for President Kennedy *and* to marry Elliott Gould. (See **Part II: 9. Ladies and Gentlemen: Will You Welcome Now, Barbra Streisand—in Person** and **Part II: 11. Barbra on Television** for specific dates.)

March — Elliott Gould flies to England to star in a revival of *On the Town*. Barbra is offered a role in the musical but feels she can't interrupt her rapidly growing success story.

April 13 — *The Barbra Streisand Album* enters *Billboard* magazine's Top 100 Albums chart.

May 24 — Streisand takes a day off from Basin Street to sing for President John F. Kennedy at the annual Press Correspondents Dinner, where she asks the President for an autograph and tells him, "You're a doll." She puts the autograph down her dress, and loses it.

May 25 — She flies to London to see Elliott in *On the Town*. The production opens to indifferent reviews, with almost no mention of Gould.

The Barbra Streisand Album climbs to number eight on the *Billboard* chart, making her the best-selling female vocalist of the day.

July 2 to August 4 — Barbra appears at the Riviera Hotel in Las Vegas as the opening act for Liberace . . . and miscalculates the audiences. She dresses elegantly (choosing her own wardrobe) rather than in Vegas flash and sings ballads rather than Vegas bombast. Liberace suggests that her wardrobe could be a bit snazzier. "Like yours?" she snorts.

A Flashback

Early 1961 — Hollywood agent Ray Stark plans a Broadway musical about his mother-in-law, legendary entertainer Fanny Brice (1891–1951). He hires producer David Merrick, composer Jule Styne, and lyricist Stephen Sondheim. He sends the script to Mary Martin, who shows interest.

Sondheim points out that Martin's not Jewish. "You've got to have a *Jewish* girl," he tells Stark. "Or at least someone with a nose!"

Says Jule Styne, "*Where* are you gonna find a girl with a nose?"

July 25 — The producers of the upcoming Broadway musical *Funny Girl* announce that Barbra Streisand has been signed to play the leading role.

August 21–September 8 — She appears at The Cocoanut Grove club in the Ambassador Hotel in Los Angeles before an audience of Hollywood celebrities. She gets a standing ovation but won't do an encore.

Late August — *The Second Barbra Streisand Album* is released; it makes the Top Ten in a matter of weeks and is soon certified gold.

Barbra and Elliott rent a sumptuous duplex penthouse apartment on Central Park West that had once belonged to Lorenz Hart.

September 9 — Barbra has a two-week engagement singing at Harrah's club in Lake Tahoe, again opening for Liberace.

Friday, September 13 — Barbra and Elliott Gould drive to Carson

City, Nevada, and are married. She changes "Love, honor, and obey" to "Love, honor, and feed." Loyal manager Marty Erlichman is best man.

September 27 — *The Bob Hope Comedy Special* airs on NBC, with Streisand, Dean Martin, James Garner, and Tuesday Weld as guests.

October 4 — Barbra tapes her TV appearance on CBS's *The Judy Garland Show.*

October 5 — Her first engagement at the Hollywood Bowl is with Sammy Davis, Jr.

November 22 — President John F. Kennedy is assassinated in Dallas. Barbra remembers where she was: in a jewelry store buying her first important piece, a beautiful antique choker. "I never wear it," she says.

November 29 to December 7 — Barbra has one- and two-night stands in Chicago, Indianapolis, San Jose, Sacramento, San Francisco, and Los Angeles.

December 10 — Rehearsals begin in Manhattan for *Funny Girl.*

December 27 — *Cue* magazine presents Barbra with its "Entertainer of the Year" Award—though she has yet to star on Broadway, in movies, or on television. And she's only twenty-one, *fer crisssake!*

1964

January 13 — *Funny Girl* has its first tryout at the Shubert Theatre in Boston. It doesn't go well. Barbra requests that acting teacher Allan Miller be brought in to coach her.

February 4 — By the time the show reaches Philadelphia, Barbra and costar Sydney Chaplin are lovers. (He's the son of screen legend Charlie Chaplin and the comedian's second wife, actress Lita Grey.) There are rumors that Streisand is pregnant. However, by the time the company reaches New York, the affair is over.

February — *Barbra Streisand/The Third Album* is released; it goes gold within a year.

February — The *Funny Girl* cast album is number two on the *Billboard* chart within three weeks of its release—before the show opens!

March 26 — *Funny Girl* opens on Broadway and the acclaim is deafening.

April 10 — *Time* magazine puts Barbra on the cover.

July 12 — Barbra tries out material for a new album on the concert stage at the Forest Hills Music Festival in Queens.

October 31 — Five Streisand albums are listed on *Billboard*'s chart of the Top 100 Albums: *The Barbra Streisand Album, The Second Barbra Streisand Album, Barbra Streisand/The Third Album, Funny Girl*, and *People*.

In 1964 Barbra starts sessions with a therapist and will continue in therapy on and off for the next thirty years.

1965

January 18 — Barbra sings for President Lyndon B. Johnson's Inaugural Eve Gala in Washington, D.C. Columnist Dorothy Kilgallen says that she makes "People" sound almost as important as the National Anthem.

April — The Reverend Dr. Martin Luther King is in the audience of *Funny Girl* when Barbra takes part in a benefit to raise money for civil rights.

April 24 — Her twenty-third birthday. The cast of *Funny Girl* gives her a white miniature French poodle she names Sadie.

April 28 — *My Name Is Barbra*, her first television special, airs on CBS. It is a sixty-minute one-woman show with full orchestra but no guest stars. "She is so great it is shocking," writes the reviewer for United Press International.

Spring 1965 — French composer Michel Legrand (Oscar-nominated for *The Umbrellas of Cherbourg* [French, 1964] works on a new album with Barbra in the deserted theatre after *Funny Girl* performances.

May — *The Barbra Streisand Album* wins Grammy Awards for Album of the Year and Best Female Vocalist.

June 22 — CBS signs Barbra to a five-million-dollar, ten-year contract—the longest in television history. She's given artistic control over her projects. Barbra announces she will start with three specials over the next two years, but already seems rather bored by it all: "It's O.K., I guess. But you can live just as well on $50,000 as on $300,000—you know what I mean? I mean how many cars can you have?" (*Time*, July 2, 1964).

October 10 — Elliott Gould opens on Broadway in the expensively mounted musical *Drat! The Cat*. It looks like a hit—but there's a newspaper strike so no one hears about it. It closes after only five performances.

November 22, 24 — Composer Harold Arlen records the album

Harold Sings Arlen (With Friend) singing his own songs, and asks Barbra to join him. Her first three albums contain seven of his songs, and she says he's her favorite composer and a friend. However, she sings only one solo and a duet with Arlen, and still demands *half* the royalties for the entire album. Harold Arlen is stunned but agreeable.

December 26 — Barbra gives her last performance on Broadway as Fanny Brice. For the first time, as a favor to producer Ray Stark, she sings "My Man," Fanny Brice's signature song, which had been left out of the show. Mimi Hines replaces Streisand as Fanny Brice and the show runs for another year and a half.

1966

March — The new issue of *Vogue* magazine features Barbra on the cover with a flower in her mouth. Inside, she models the latest Paris fashions for photographer Richard Avedon.

March 30 — *Color Me Barbra*, her second CBS-TV special, is televised. It is another ratings champ, but the Sunday before the show the *New York Times* prints the Rex Reed interview that starts the Barbra-as-monster legend.

April 13 — A triumphant Barbra Streisand opens in *Funny Girl* in London, with the entire fourteen-week run already sold out. British movie actor Michael Craig is the new Nick Arnstein.

Immediately after the opening, Elliott Gould tells Barbra that she's pregnant (her doctor had told him).

July 16 — Barbra's 900th and last stage performance in *Funny Girl*.

July 18 — Back in America, pregnant Barbra cuts down her projected concert tour to just four cities: July 30 – Newport, Rhode Island. August 2 – Philadelphia. August 6 – Atlanta. August 9 – Chicago.

October — *Opera News* magazine features Streisand on its cover with super opera diva Joan Sutherland, thus saluting Barbra's "operatic" approach to popular music.

October — *Je M'appelle Barbra* is released. It becomes number five on the charts, but is the first Streisand album not to go gold.

December 29 — Jason Emanuel Gould is born in Mount Sinai Hospital, New York City, by cesarean section. He weighs seven pounds, three ounces. The New York *Daily News* headlines their story, "MILLION DOLLAR BABY!"

1967

February — *Simply Streisand*, an album of standards, is released.

May 2 — Barbra Streisand arrives in Hollywood to become a movie star. She has signed with Columbia Pictures to be *Funny Girl* (1968) . . . with Twentieth Century-Fox to do *Hello, Dolly!* (1969) . . . and with Paramount to headline *On a Clear Day You Can See Forever* (1970) — *without ever having faced a movie camera.*

The Hollywood community is soon antagonized by her rudeness and arrogance. Biographer James Spada says, "The bad feelings she stirred up during her first few months in Hollywood would haunt her for the rest of her career" (*Streisand, Her Life*. New York: Crown, 1995, p.189).

June 17 — On a three-day weekend during the *Funny Girl* shooting, Barbra appears in a free concert in Central Park, which is taped for a TV special—*A Happening in Central Park*; 60,000 people are expected . . . 135,000 show up.

Barbra receives a death threat, allegedly from the Palestine Liberation Organization (it's less than two weeks after the Arab-Israel "Six-Day War"). Barbra is terrified that the spotlight will make her a target. Twice she forgets song lyrics. The experience so unnerves her that it will be nearly twenty years before she sings in New York again.

July 9 — Fears confirmed? A man with a gun is arrested before a Streisand concert at the Hollywood Bowl.

August 7 — Photography begins on *Funny Girl*, directed by veteran William Wyler. Egyptian actor Omar Sharif is cast as the Jewish Nicky Arnstein.

A famous Hollywood quote comes out of the clash of wills between the first-time film star and veteran director William Wyler: "Willy shouldn't be so hard on her. After all, this is the first picture she's ever directed."

Elliott Gould is cast in the movie *The Night They Raided Minsky's* (United Artists, 1968), to be filmed in New York. Barbra feels deserted. She finds solace with thirty-five-year-old Omar Sharif. Elliott Gould learns of the affair and is humiliated; their marriage never recovers from this setback.

October 11 — CBS airs *The Belle of 14th Street*, Barbra's third TV special. It features black entertainer John Bubbles dressed as a chicken in a song-and-dance number which many see as racist and distasteful. No soundtrack album of this show is released.

October — Columbia Records signs Barbra to a new contract. It makes the headlines when it's learned that her royalty per album, at her demand, is one cent more than that paid to the Beatles.

1968

January 21 — At the Broadway for Peace 1968 rally-fundraiser Barbra announces her support for Eugene McCarthy, the antiwar Democratic Senator from Minnesota and presidential candidate.

Barbra options the screen rights to an Isaac Bashevis Singer story, "Yentl, the Yeshiva Boy," which had been sent to her by producer Valentine Sherry (a guy). Barbra tells agent Freddie Fields she wants to star in it as her next movie. Agent Sue Mengers says she shouldn't do another ethnic part so soon after playing Fanny Brice onscreen.

April 15 — Filming begins on *Hello, Dolly!* Costar Walter Matthau is immediately outraged by Barbra's behavior. He yells, "You haven't got the talent of a butterfly's fart!"

September 18 — *Funny Girl* premieres as a "road show" (reserved seat) attraction. "Barbra's motion picture debut turned out to be the most dazzling in show business history" (Spada, *Streisand: Her Life*) Other writers made other hyperbolic claims.

Swathed in Blackglama fur, Barbra poses for photographer Richard Avedon for the "What Becomes a Legend Most?" print ad campaign.

1969

January 6 — Filming begins on *On a Clear Day You Can See Forever*, costarring Yves Montand and directed by Vincente Minnelli. Montand later says, "When we commenced . . . I had the mistaken impression that I was the costar. I was Miss Streisand's first leading man who can sing, even though this was her third musical. I thought she was my leading lady, a partner. I doubt I shall ever choose to work again in Hollywood" (Edwards, *Streisand: A Biography*). He didn't. Montand's autobiography (*You See, I Haven't Forgotten*. New York: Knopf, 1992) makes only two passing references to Streisand, saying that his musical numbers had been "ruthlessly pruned."

January 15 — At the London premiere of *Funny Girl*, Barbra is attracted to Pierre Elliott Trudeau, fifty-year-old prime minister of Canada.

October 1968, a month after the premiere of *Funny Girl*, Barbra and husband Elliott Gould attend a party for Steve McQueen's *Bullitt*.
PHOTO COURTESY OF ARCHIVE PHOTOS/FOTOS INTERNATIONAL

January 17 — Maurice Chevalier escorts Barbra to the Paris premiere of *Funny Girl* at the Paris Opera House. There is a near riot as 150 paparazzi break through police lines and storm the Opera House.

February 11 — Through a press representative, Barbra and Elliott Gould make a joint announcement of their separation.

April 14 — "It's a tie!" gasps presenter Ingrid Bergman at the Fortieth Annual Academy Awards. Trophies for the Best Actress of 1968 go to Katharine Hepburn (for *The Lion in Winter*) and to Barbra Streisand. "Hello, gorgeous!" Streisand greets the shiny little man/statuette.

April 21 — Louis Kind, the mean stepfather, dies at age seventy-six in Manhattan. His will excludes second wife Diana and his step-daughter. Barbra skips the funeral.

April 24 — Barbra is twenty-seven. The cast and crew members of *Clear Day* throw a surprise birthday party for her—in the airplane bound for location filming in New York.

May 16 —The Friars (theatrical) Club pays tribute to Barbra Streisand as Entertainer of the Year—only the second woman to be so honored (Sophie Tucker was the first). At the festivities Barbra is ser-enaded by composers Harold Arlen, Jerry Herman, Jule Styne, Richard Rodgers, Harold Rome, Cy Coleman, and Burton Lane.

June 11 — Barbra, Paul Newman, and Sidney Poitier announce a new film production company, First Artists, to "create a new enter-prise, distinct from both major studio films and independent produc-tion companies, for the development and production of theatrical motion pictures," and, above all, to give them complete creative con-trol. Steve McQueen joins the company in 1971 and Dustin Hoffman is added a year later.

In early January 1979, the company is bought by an Australian firm—"a strong indication of how little First Artists meant to the stars them-selves. They were willing to sacrifice their autonomy—their ideal—for financial gain"—(Ed Holly, vice president of First Artists, quoted in Anne Edwards, *Streisand: A Biography*. Boston: Little, Brown, 1997).

July 2–30 — Barbra returns to Las Vegas as the inaugural attraction at the new International Hotel. She still doesn't understand the tastes and styles of Vegas; sometimes her audience is even hostile.

Elvis Presley is to follow Barbra at the International. One night after her show, he comes into her dressing room and paints her fin-gernails. (See **Part I: 3. The Men in the Life of Barbra Streisand.**)

July — Barbra buys a Mediterranean-style villa on Carolwood Drive in Holmby Hills (adjacent to Beverly Hills).

July — Columbia Records releases *What About Today?*, an attempt at more contemporary songs—but her choices have little to do with current issues. It's her poorest-selling studio album to date.

October 6 — Barbra seeks to change her screen image with *The Owl and the Pussycat* (Columbia, 1970), a raucous romantic comedy in which she plays a feisty prostitute. She films a topless scene but insists that the footage be "fogged" over before the film is released. Ten years later *High Society* magazine prints photos of bare-chested Barbra.

December 16 — *Hello, Dolly!* premieres in New York City. The *New York Times* critic Vincent Canby calls Barbra "a national treasure."

1970

Barbra announces she will star in the film *Masquerade* (known earlier as *Yentl*). She wants Czech director Ivan Passer to direct.

January — Nineteen-year-old Roslyn Kind (Barbra's stepsister) makes her nightclub singing debut at the Persian Room of Manhattan's Plaza Hotel. She *sounds* like Barbra but just isn't as good.

January 28 — Handsome Canadian prime minister Pierre Elliott Trudeau invites Barbra to Manitoba's centennial celebration. She apparently seriously thinks of marrying him. As it turns out, Trudeau is more in love with Margaret Sinclair, a much younger girl he has been wooing at the same time he is courting Streisand.

April 19 — An honorary Tony is awarded Barbra as Broadway's Star of the Decade.

June 9 — Whatever Bella wants: Barbra throws opens her new New York City home—a five-story, seventeen-room townhouse at 49 East Eightieth Street—for a political fundraiser for Democratic congressional hopeful Bella Abzug.

June 17 — *On a Clear Day You Can See Forever* opens with little publicity or promotion. Fifteen minutes have been cut, including two complete musical numbers and much of Jack Nicholson's part. Cecil Beaton's lavish costumes are singled out for praise.

October 30 — *The Owl and the Pussycat* is released to mostly favorable reviews. For the first time, Streisand is seen as a woman with sexual appeal. More importantly, the movie makes money.

November 27–December 10 — Barbra fulfills a commitment at the Riviera Hotel in Las Vegas, then does two weeks (December 13, 1970 to January 2, 1971) at the International Hotel (later renamed the Las Vegas Hilton).

1971

January 10 — Actor/hunk Ryan O'Neal, thirty and just separated from wife Leigh Taylor-Young, is Barbra's new off-camera companion. They have been keeping their relationship under wraps, but now they're featured in the tabloids.

February — *Stoney End*, another album attempt to make the transition into uptempo pop, is released to favorable reviews. The title song, written by Laura Nyro, becomes her biggest-selling single since "People" six years ago.

Barbra meets with Elliott Gould to discuss a possible reconciliation. He informs her that his girl friend Jenny Bogart (daughter of director Paul Bogart) is pregnant. Barbra asks him to file for divorce as soon as possible.

June 30 — A quickie seven-day divorce is obtained for Streisand and Gould in the Dominican Republic.

August 16 — Filming begins in San Francisco on *What's Up, Doc?* (Warner Bros., 1972), starring Barbra and Ryan O'Neal. This is an attempt by director Peter Bogdanovich to make a madcap comedy along the lines of *Bringing Up Baby* (RKO, 1938) and *The Lady Eve* (Paramount, 1941)—neither of which Barbra finds funny.

August — *Barbra Joan Streisand* album is released, another offering of contemporary pop and rock music. The success of this album and *Stoney End* proves that the singer has a new, younger group of fans. The old fans cry betrayal.

December 24, 1971 to January 13, 1972 — Two weeks at the Las Vegas Hilton. Observers feel Barbra is finally learning the knack of seeming to enjoy performing for a Las Vegas crowd. She pretends to get stoned on marijuana, but the audience doesn't get it.

1972

March 9 — *What's Up, Doc?* premieres at Radio City Music Hall to mostly rave reviews and becomes Barbra's biggest box office hit to date.

Filming begins on *Up the Sandbox* (National General, 1972), an attempt to make a movie *about* something.

April 15 — Warren Beatty persuades Barbra to perform at a fundraiser for Democratic front-runner George McGovern at the Los Angeles Forum.

May — *Up the Sandbox* goes up the river to Nairobi, Africa, to shoot a fantasy sequence. Barbra takes five-year-old Jason along for the ride.

Spring — Barbra's mother Diana and stepsister Roslyn move to California, into a two-bedroom condo in Beverly Hills that Barbra buys for them. One tabloid prints a photo of the back alley behind the apartment building to show what a dump the place is. Barbra has paid a million dollars for it.

September 18 — Filming begins on *The Way We Were* (Paramount, 1973), with Robert Redford.

Christmas — *Up the Sandbox* is released. Expecting a zany comedy, audiences are confused and disappointed by the very feminist-oriented content.

1973

February 19 — Nominations for the Forty-Sixth Academy Awards are announced: *The Way We Were* earns six, including Best Actress and Best Song. The movie wins for Best Song, "The Way We Were," but Glenda Jackson (for *A Touch of Class*) is named Best Actress.

Summer — Jon Peters, tough guy/hairstylist, age twenty-eight, answers Barbra's call for a new hairdo for her new film *For Pete's Sake* (Warner Bros., 1974). "You've got a great ass," he tells her—and a passionate relationship begins. They're lovers and business partners for nearly ten years, and good friends after that.

Jon Peters sells out his hairdressing empire, moves in with Barbra in Holmby Hills, and devotes his time and talent to learning and getting ahead in the film business.

October 16 — *The Way We Were* opens around the country and becomes a runaway hit.

November 2 — *Barbra Streisand . . . and Other Musical Instruments* airs on CBS. It's her last TV special under her contract, and the least successful. There is no soundtrack album.

Streisand agrees to star as *Funny Lady* (Columbia, 1975), the movie sequel to *Funny Girl*, saying, "Now I'm more of an actress and less of an ego."

1974

March — Barbra and Jon Peters, buying separate lots, purchase three acres in the secluded Ramirez Canyon area of Malibu, California. Within two years they buy another sixteen acres.

March — Columbia wants a new Streisand album for Christmas. Barbra insists that Jon Peters produce it, which causes problems.

June 26 — *For Pete's Sake* opens, advertising "Zany Barbra," but word of mouth and negative reviews keep receipts down.

Jon Peters talks Barbra into a remake of *A Star Is Born* (Warner Bros., 1976). He will produce; the movie will be made as a First Artists/Barwood production, with Barbra as executive producer.

Should Jon direct? Should Jon play the male lead? He tells Barbra, "You know, you're the only woman who has ever intimidated me."

October — The Streisand-Peters album is released. It's called *ButterFly*. It's judged one of the worst albums ever made by a major talent. Nevertheless . . . it also goes gold three months after its release!

December 1 — Jon and Barbra are shopping for a car in the Terry York Chevrolet lot in California's San Fernando Valley, over the hills from Los Angeles. A salesman becomes hostile to Barbra, telling her how much he hates her movies and her records and her looks. Jon attacks the salesman, injuring him so badly he can no longer work. The matter is settled out of court on December 12, 1977.

Christmas — Barbra celebrates Christmas in Malibu with son Jason, her lover Jon Peters, and his son Christopher—the first time she has celebrated the Christian holiday.

1975

January 24 — The cover story by Marie Brenner in today's *New Times* magazine ridicules Barbra's personal and professional relationship with Jon and dubs *A Star Is Born*, which Peters is producing and Barbra unofficially codirecting, "Hollywood's Biggest Joke." The cover illustration shows a bald-headed Barbra with the tag line "A Star Is Shorn: a Beverly Hills hairstylist started with Streisand's head—and is now taking over her image, her career, and her newest movie."

March 9 — *Funny Girl to Funny Lady*, a live, nationally televised concert to promote *Funny Lady* and to benefit the Special Olympics, is presented in front of Washington dignitaries (including President Gerald Ford). "People who tuned in to see Barbra Streisand were cheated. They sought entertainment, but what they received was plugola" (Frank Swertlow of UPI).

March 10 — *Funny Lady* premieres in New York City.

March 18 — At the royal command performance in London of *Funny Lady*, Barbra asks Queen Elizabeth: "Why do women have to wear gloves and not men?" The Queen flunks the quiz.

July 9 — Barbra agrees to appear on TV's *The Tonight Show Starring Johnny Carson* for the first time since March of 1963 . . . but changes her mind the day before. Once a champion of Streisand, Carson's now an enemy.

April — Barbra and singer-songwriter Rupert Holmes put together Barbra's thirtieth album, *Lazy Afternoon*, which restores her to the pop mainstream. "Shake Me, Wake Me" is a popular hit in dance clubs.

September 19 — Kris Kristofferson is signed as Streisand's co-lead in *A Star Is Born*.

1976

February 2 — Filming begins on *A Star Is Born*, with the participants trying to out-shout one another. Kris Kristofferson screams, "I ain't trusting my career to no Vegas singer and her hairdresser!" He tells Jon Peters, "If I want shit out of you, I'll squeeze your head!" Barbra confides to director Frank Pierson that the film's failure would end her relationship with Jon Peters.

April 24 — Barbra's thirty-fourth birthday and the wrap party for *A Star Is Born* are celebrated together.

November 15 — Frank Pierson writes "My Battles With Barbra and Jon" about his experiences with *A Star Is Born*. The article appears simultaneously in *New York* and *New West* magazines, November 15, 1976. "The piece was a startlingly intimate exposé that painted her as megalomaniacal, frightened, indecisive, rude, disruptive, and monstrously self-absorbed. Jon emerged as a brash hot dog, jumping up and down, threatening violence, full of 'mad schemes,' and incompetent." (Spada, *Streisand: Her Life*).

December 14 — Barbra agrees to be interviewed by CBS journalist Barbara Walters, *but demands final cut*. Walters agrees.

December 16 — Barbra is to put her handprints and footprints in the wet cement of the Chinese Theatre in Hollywood. At the same time, she is to have her star on the Hollywood Walk of Fame. Barbra cancels—without explanation or apology.

December 18 — *A Star Is Born* premieres in Westwood, one of the wealthier Los Angeles suburbs. Invited guests to the premiere party are instructed to wear white . . . because Barbra will be wearing black. The musical is a hit, mainly with young people. It remains Barbra's most successful movie to date. Barbra is now confident that she can direct a movie.

1977

The Malibu ranch provides rest and relaxation for Barbra for most of the next two years. She creates a lavish compound of five separate residences, each decorated in a distinct style: "All these houses are the dollhouses I never had."

Take a Tour of Barbra's Malibu Ranch

1. The eclectic and rustic main house, known as "the barn," Barbra's favorite, with lofts, stone fireplaces, stained glass, and a thirty-foot pitched ceiling.

2. "The Deco house," a cool, streamlined example of 1930s Moderne with chrome-and-glass fixtures, gray and red lacquer, and geometric patterns.

3. A post-and-beam neocraftsman-style house that might have been lifted right out of America's Colonial era.

4. "The peach house" (converted from a stable), a three-story Mediterranean-style villa built into the hillside, contains guest quarters, a huge screening room, and a gym.

5. A caretaker's cottage, which became the Barwood house (the name of Barbra's production company), used for offices.

February — *A Star Is Born* wins five Golden Globe awards in the Musical or Comedy category: Best Picture, Best Actress, Best Actor, Best Song, Best Score.

March 28 — The Academy Awards: Barbra and Paul Williams win Oscars for "Evergreen," chosen Best Song.

A few weeks later, at the Grammys, Streisand and Williams win for Song of the Year.

July/August — Roslyn Kind makes another attempt at show business, appearing at the Grand Finale in New York and at the Backlot in West Hollywood. She seems to be copying Barbra, wearing a similar hairdo and singing similar songs.

October 1977 — *Playboy* magazine features Lawrence Grobel's lengthy interview with Barbra. She is said to be the first actress ever featured on the magazine's cover (if you don't count Marilyn Monroe). Barbra poses in a *Playboy* bunny outfit, then chickens out and switches to skimpy white shorts and a Superman T-shirt.

1978

After fifteen years as Barbra's manager, Marty Erlichman decides there's no room for him with Jon Peters running the show.

May — Songbird, the first album under her new Columbia contract, is released. This LP features "You Don't Bring Me Flowers," which she records as a duet with Neil Diamond. This song becomes her biggest hit single.

After her opening at the Persian Room in the Plaza Hotel in January 1970, would-be singer Roslyn Kind (in the middle) poses with her mother, Diana, and her famous half-sister Barbra Streisand.
PHOTO COURTESY OF ARCHIVE PHOTOS

May — On the ABC television special *The Stars Salute Israel at 30*, Barbra sings four songs, including "Hativka," the Israeli national anthem. Via satellite, she schmoozes with prime minister Golda Meir in Tel Aviv.

October 2 — Production begins on the comedy *The Main Event* (Warner Bros., 1979), costarring old flame and friend Ryan O'Neal.

1979

June 22 —*The Main Event* opens to mainly negative reviews. However, once again, Barbra's popularity turns the comedy into a substantial hit.

October — Barbra records a duet with disco diva Donna Summer, "Enough Is Enough/No More Tears." *US* magazine votes Streisand and Summer the top female vocalists of the seventies.

November — *High Society* magazine features photos of topless Barbra from *The Owl and the Pussycat*, with the banner headline "Barbra Streisand Nude!" Barbra sues, and wins—the magazine is to be recalled, but it's already too late.

New Year's Eve — The battling lovers finally decide to split. Jon Peters moves back to Encino, to the wilds of the San Fernando Valley. Barbra retreats to her New York penthouse.

1980

January 5 — Jason Gould's bar mitzvah (his coming of age as a man) is held at the Pacific Jewish Center, a traditional synagogue in Venice, California.

Barbra struggles to get funding for her movie musical *Yentl* (MGM/United Artists, 1983).

May 13 — Universal Studios announces that Barbra will appear in the film *All Night Long* (1981), taking second billing to Gene Hackman. It's assumed that she's doing this as a favor to her longtime agent Sue Mengers, who is married to Jean-Claude Tramont, director of the feature film. For twenty-four days' work, Barbra is to receive $4 million plus 15 percent of gross profits, "making Cheryl Gibbons the most expensive supporting role in film history" (according to the press).

(Later, agent Mengers bills client Streisand for her cut of the $4 million, but Streisand says, no way!—I was doing you a favor, why should I give you a commission? The two former friends do not speak thereafter for a number of years.)

June 1 — The American Civil Liberties Union holds a fundraising concert at the Los Angeles Music Center honoring songwriters Marilyn and Alan Bergman. Barbra sings an all-Bergman program. Neil Diamond joins her for "You Don't Bring Me Flowers."

September — *The Guilty* album is released, with songs written by the

Bee Gees. Three singles: "Woman in Love," "Guilty," and "What Kind of Fool" make *Billboard*'s Top Ten chart.

1981

March 6 — All Night Long opens and is rejected by most critics. The *New York Times* story claims that audiences are not just indifferent to the film but "actively despise it."

April — The school of the Pacific Jewish Center in Santa Monica, California, is rededicated in honor of Barbra's late father. It's now called the Emanuel Streisand School in appreciation of Barbra's generous donation.

Barbra spends much of the year trying to launch *Yentl*. Marilyn and Alan Bergman convince her that it should be a musical. Barbra decides she will direct it but still no studio will finance it.

Orion Pictures finally gives *Yentl* the go-ahead—with Barbra writing, producing, directing, and starring—*if* it can be made for $13 million. However, after the big budget disaster of Michael Cimino's *Heaven's Gate* (United Artists, 1980), Orion backs out of *Yentl*.

Ex-lover Jon Peters and ex-admirer Peter Guber form PolyGram Pictures and agree to finance *Yentl* . . . but Barbra decides she needs to be independent, both personally and professionally.

Ex-agent David Begelman is made head of United Artists. Insisting upon strict terms, United Artists (now part of MGM) agrees to finance *Yentl*, at a budget of $14 million.

1982

April 14 — Production on *Yentl* begins in London with the shooting of the film's interior scenes.

An English tabloid claims there's trouble with *Yentl*'s cast and crew, who resent Barbra's arrogant style. The crew sends the newspaper a letter of rebuttal, signed by everyone: "She has captivated us all with her dedicated professionalism."

July — Exterior work on *Yentl* begins in Czechoslovakia in the threadbare village of Roztyly, two-and-a-half hours from Prague. Streisand cuts her trademark long fingernails to stubs and digs in.

1983

Fall — When Barbra returns to Malibu after eighteen months in Europe producing *Yentl*, her business relationship with Jon Peters finally has evaporated. He later sells her his part of the Malibu estate.

November 16 — *Yentl* premieres at the Cinerama Dome Theatre in Hollywood. The reviews are wildly mixed—it's called everything from masterpiece to disaster—but it does make money.

Christmas — Barbra meets Richard Baskin, age thirty-four, heir to the Baskin-Robbins ice cream fortune, at a party. He moves in with her the following February and stays for three years.

1984

January 28 — One of the highlights of her life—Barbra Streisand receives the Golden Globe award for Best Director, for *Yentl*.

February 8 — *Yentl* is mainly ignored in the nominations for the Academy Awards. This decision creates controversy. Does Hollywood really hate Streisand, or is it jealous of her success, or is it just sexist?

April 9 — At the Fifty-Sixth Annual Academy Awards, *Yentl* wins only one statuette, for Best Original Film Score.

1985

November — *The Broadway Album* is released. It's number one on the charts in just a matter of weeks.

With Jon Peters out of the picture, Barbra suggests to faithful Marty Erlichman that he resume acting as her agent.

Barbra establishes The Streisand Foundation, charged with distributing her charitable donations to help civil liberties, disarmament, and environmental concerns.

1986

January — Production begins on the dramatic movie *Nuts* (Warner Bros., 1987), but problems arise: Director Mark Rydell is replaced by Martin Ritt. Shooting is postponed until October in order to gain Richard Dreyfuss as her costar.

Spring — Barbra options *The Normal Heart*, Larry Kramer's acclaimed 1985 play about AIDS and the government's indifference to finding a cure for the disease.

From the beginning, Kramer worries about Streisand's plan to star in the project. After all, it is not the story of Dr. Emma Brookner (the only female member of the cast), it's about the men whose lives are in mortal jeopardy.

September 6 — Barbra goes public with her political interests, inviting the top names in politics, movies, and music to her *One Voice* concert under the stars at her Malibu ranch. Tickets are $5,000 a pair, refreshments included.

The concert raises $1.5 million, which goes to support the campaigns of six Democratic senatorial candidates. Five of the six win their congressional seats.

October 20 — Production finally begins on *Nuts*.

1987

February — At the Grammy Awards in Los Angeles, Barbra is introduced to blond actor Don Johnson, age thirty-eight, star of the popular TV cop show *Miami Vice*.

Fall — After three-and-a-half years with Richard Baskin, the affair cools down. He and Barbra become just friends.

November 20 — *Nuts* is released to negative reviews and negative box office.

Christmas is spent in Aspen, Colorado, with the Bergmans and other friends.

At a day-after-Christmas party, Don Johnson shows up and pulls Streisand off into a private corner. They leave together early.

1988

January–February — Streisand and Don Johnson take their affair public: They get cozy in a New York City restaurant; they attend the Holmes-Tyson prizefight in Atlantic City; they show up at the ShoWest Convention in Las Vegas.

March 18 — Barbra does a wordless walk-on in the TV series *Miami Vice*, for the episode called "Badge of Dishonor."

April 24 — Jon Peters throws a party at his Beverly Hills home for Barbra's forty-sixth birthday. Don can't come because he's shooting the movie *Dead-Bang* (Warner Bros., 1989) in Canada.

June — Twenty-one-year-old Jason Gould moves out of his mother's home and into a condo in West Hollywood, an area nicknamed "Boy's Town" for its large number of gay bars, dance clubs, gyms, and even all-gay apartment houses. Three years later, he buys a $345,000 home in the same area.

Mid-September — Barbra and Don record the duet "Till I Loved

You" from the unproduced pop opera *Goya . . . A Life*. This duet is included on Barbra's *Till I Loved You* album and also on Don Johnson's *Let It Roll* album (both 1988).

September 14 — Stevie Wonder performs at the Apollo Theatre in Harlem for a music video. Barbra joins him in an impromptu duet.

Early December — The romance with Don Johnson is over. Tabloid-style salacious reasons are suggested. (See **Part 1: 3. The Men in the Life of Barbra Streisand.**) Barbra is shocked when Johnson and his ex-wife Melanie Griffith announce they are to remarry.

October 6 — *Till I Loved You* is released. The critics find it unsatisfying, but it goes platinum in just a few weeks.

October 16 — Barbra sings at a Beverly Hills fundraiser for Democratic presidential candidate Michael Dukakis.

1989

April 9 — It's announced that Barbra will direct *The Prince of Tides* (Columbia, 1991) and also star. Robert Redford declines to costar, as he doesn't wish to be directed by Streisand. (His role is taken by Hollywood hunk Nick Nolte.)

When MGM/United Artists drops the project, Barbra turns once again to Jon Peters, now cochairman of Columbia Pictures.

1990

May 15 — The *Star* tabloid claims that Barbra's twenty-five-year-old son Jason is gay. Their headline: "Barbra Streisand Heartsick—Her Only Son Hangs Out at Gay Bars."

June 18 — *The Prince of Tides* begins production in Beaufort, South Carolina.

Early July — Barbra's mother has open-heart surgery in Los Angeles. Barbra remains in South Carolina.

September — John Barry, hired to write the score for *The Prince of Tides*, angrily quits over Barbra's total involvement in everything to do with the film, including the music. He is replaced by James Newton Howard . . . who is soon romantically involved with Barbra.

1991

July — There's another tabloid story about Jason. Alleges the *Globe*: "Barbra Weeps Over Gay Son's Wedding"; the tabloid says that Jason has "married" male model David Knight. Knight later tells biographer Randall Riese that he'd never met Jason. Biographer James Spada insists they were indeed involved.

Caryn James of the *New York Times*, in a preview of fall films, calls *The Prince of Tides* "a vanity production."

November 23 — Barbra appears on CBS's *60 Minutes*, answering questions from cohost Mike Wallace. She breaks down on camera while discussing her stepfather.

December 9 — Premiere of *The Prince of Tides* in New York. The reviews are good but her performance is consistently panned. Many feel it would have been a better film if she'd directed another woman in the leading role. It becomes Barbra's second most successful movie, after *A Star Is Born*.

Christmas — Barbra returns to Aspen, Colorado, where she first became involved with Don Johnson. This year she meets tennis star André Agassi, who is three years younger than her own son. Agassi is called the "King of Grunge," a scruffy antihero. Streisand defends him as being intelligent, sensitive, and evolved. She describes him as "an extraordinary human being. He plays like a Zen master." This pronouncement is widely quoted . . . but what the hell does it mean?

1992

January — Barbra becomes only the third woman ever nominated as Best Director by the Directors Guild of America.

February 18 — Barbra meets Diana, the Princess of Wales, at the London premiere of *The Prince of Tides*.

February 19 — *The Prince of Tides* wins seven Oscar nominations, including Best Picture, Best Actor (Nick Nolte), and Best Supporting Actress (Kate Nelligan), but omitting Barbra for Best Director.

The Golden Globe Awards: Nick Nolte wins as Best Actor in a Drama.

The Academy Awards: the money is on Nolte to win for Best Actor . . . but *The Silence of the Lambs* (Orion, 1991) grabs all five top awards. Bubkes for *The Prince of Tides*.

April 25 — For Barbra's fiftieth birthday Jon Peters produces a party at his Beverly Hills estate, inviting hundreds of leading industry figures.

Spring — Barbra and André Agassi begin serious dating . . . but the affair suddenly cools. Supposedly, Agassi's longtime girlfriend, who is his own age, objects.

A "Reincarnation Ball" to publicize *On a Clear Day You Can See Forever*: (1970) Barbra comes as Colette (1873-1954), one of her French heroines, the author of *Gigi*.
PHOTO COURTESY OF ARCHIVE PHOTOS/FOTOS INTERNATIONAL

September 16 — Barbra meets Bill and Hillary Rodham Clinton when she headlines a Beverly Hills fundraiser for his presidential campaign. She sings "On a Clear Day (You Can See Forever)" and "Happy Days Are Here Again."

November 18 — AIDS Project Los Angeles honors Streisand and recording mogul David Geffen with its Commitment to Life award. Streisand makes a speech in which she criticizes the government for its lack of action in fighting AIDS. She suggests that entertainers boycott areas where "the moral climate . . . is no longer acceptable"—such as Colorado, where voters had rescinded gay rights laws.

December 11 — The American Civil Liberties Union presents Barbra with its Bill of Rights award.

December 14 — Barbra signs a new contract with Sony (Columbia's new parent company), covering both records and films, that's worth sixty million dollars.

December — She says she can't afford to keep up the twenty-two-acre estate in Malibu . . . and she's unable to sell it. So she donates it to the Santa Monica Mountains Conservancy, a California state agency which will use the estate as an environmental research complex. Oh, and uh, by the way, Barbra takes a $15 million tax write-off.

1993

January 19 — Barbra sings at the inaugural gala for President Clinton. She wears a dark suit with a floor-length skirt slit up the side, for which she is criticized in a *New York Times* editorial.

It is at the inaugural that she's introduced to Virginia Kelby, the president's mother. "When they met, there was this profound magnetic connection between them," says Margery Tabankin (administrator of The Streisand Foundation), quoted in *George* magazine, November 1996. They would speak by phone several times a week until Virginia's death in January 1994. "Virginia brought very motherlike qualities to Barbra's life, and Barbra became the young woman that Virginia never got to raise."

March — Barbra quietly spends several nights in the White House. Later, in 1997, a miniscandal erupts when it is disclosed that President Clinton enticed potential campaign donors with offers of a night in the White House—the big spenders got to sleep in the historic Lincoln Bedroom. In Barbra's case there are rumors of an affair with the President.

April 24 — Donna Karan, Barbra's favorite fashion designer, hosts a party for her fifty-first birthday. Liza Minnelli stands up and sings . . . and her ease in front of an audience amazes Streisand. Streisand starts to question her own fear of live audiences. She thinks of returning to the concert stage.

May — As "Tinseltown's preeminent ambassador" to Washington (*People*, May 31, 1993), Barbra spends seven days in May in Washington, seeing and being seen.

May 1 — She attends the White House Press Correspondents Dinner with ex-boyfriend Richard Baskin. Among the other celebrities are Dana Delany, Michael Douglas, Richard Dreyfuss, Markie

Post, along with Bill and Hillary.

May 3 — Barbra has dinner with Attorney General Janet Reno, discussing women's issues.

May 4 — Barbra attends House Armed Services Committee hearings on gays in the military, and goes to a Democratic Congressional Dinner with Health and Human Services Secretary Donna Shalala.

The singer is attacked for her political involvement. The *Wall Street Journal* says that Streisand "finds herself cast as the presumptive leader of a flying wedge of glamorous nitwits, jetting in from the Coast to have their political credentials validated." *The New Republic* says, "The idea that these insulated and bubbleheaded people should help make policy is ridiculous. Hollywood actors are even more out of touch than elected politicians." (Did Barbra read this? She always cites *The New Republic* as a favorite magazine.)

June — Barbra flies to England to attend the Wimbledon tennis championships . . . to cheer on André Agassi. The press ridicules the twenty-eight-year age difference.

June 29 — *Back on Broadway*, her fiftieth album, is released. It enters the Billboard chart at number one.

The December *Architectural Digest* features Barbra on its cover along with her Tamara de Lempicka painting of *Adam et Eve*, one of the prizes of her Art Deco collection, which will be auctioned at Christie's in New York. An anonymous bidder, later revealed to be Madonna, buys it for two million dollars.

December 31, 1993 and January 1, 1994 — Barbra returns to the concert stage for the first time in twenty-two years when she appears at the opening of Kirk Kerkorian's MGM Grand Hotel in Las Vegas. She earns an estimated $8 million for the two-night live engagement.

1994

March 3–4 — Christie's New York auction house offers 535 of Barbra's collectibles—her thirty-year Art Deco collection, automobiles, clothing, and assorted tsatskes. Says Barbra: "I think I'm going through a period of shedding, of letting go of a lot of things: fears, houses, objects, material possessions." The Christie's sale brings in $5.3 million.

March 27 — Tickets go on sale for Barbra's first concert tour in twenty-eight years. In the American "leg" of the engagement she will appear in Washington, D.C., Detroit, Michigan; San Jose and Anaheim, California; and New York City. Top ticket price is $350. In *Daily Variety* (June 2) Todd Everett suggests that next time she perform "at prices more suited to the Democrats she supports than the Republicans she plays to." An unidentified newspaper dubs the high-profile tour "My Name Is Brazen."

April 20 — The concert tour begins in London, England, at Wembly Arena.

April 24 — Barbra celebrates her fifty-second birthday at Mimmo d'Ischia restaurant in London with friends Steven Spielberg, Carrie Fisher, Elton John, and Michael Caine and wife Shakira.

May 10 — The American part of the tour begins in Washington, D.C. *Newsweek* states, "For two hours of video recollections, thirty songs, and a liberal dose of liberal politicking, the First Voice ruled a senate's worth of congressmen, cabinet members, and judges."

May 15 — Detroit.

June 2 — Anaheim. A bad cold forces her to postpone four of the six play dates.

June 7 — At the San Jose arena outside San Francisco.

June 13 — Barbra attends a state dinner at the White House, escorted by TV news anchorman Peter Jennings . . . and accompanied by much publicity and many romance rumors.

June 20 — She appears at Madison Square Garden for the first of seven different appearances in this fabled New York arena and gets an overwhelming reception from her New York fans. It's estimated that the seven shows gross over $60 million.

July 18–24 — The tour's new finale, in Anaheim. The last two shows are taped for forthcoming television specials.

November — Prince Charles visits Los Angeles. He and Barbra talk just briefly, but an observer notes that they have terrific eye contact: "It was like POW!" They spend a private hour together in the secluded Bel-Air Hotel, off Sunset Boulevard in West Los Angeles. "The idea of Streisand and Charles ever being romantically involved seemed bizarre enough somehow to make sense," wrote Anne Edwards in *Streisand: A Biography* (Boston: Little, Brown, 1997).

1995

February 3 — Barbra appears at Harvard University at the John F. Kennedy School of Government to deliver a speech on "The Artist as Citizen." During the Q&A session, a young woman starts telling Barbra how wonderful she is but the star interrupts her with, "You've got a guy for me?"

February 6 — NBC airs *Serving in Silence: The Margarethe Cammermeyer Story*, the true story of the army nurse who admitted she was a lesbian. The film is produced by Barbra Streisand and her producing partner and close friend Cis Corman.

March — The National Academy of Recording Arts and Sciences votes to honor Barbra with a Lifetime Achievement Award at the annual Grammy Awards ceremony. Barbra doesn't show up at the presentation.

April 4 — Barbra buys a thirty-two-thousand-square-foot house in Malibu, California, on a bluff called "the Queen's Necklace" for the way homes sparkle at night around the curve of Santa Monica Bay.

May 21 — Brandeis University awards Barbra an honorary Doctorate of Humane Letters degree. She ends her thank-you speech with "I know my father would be proud, too."

Spring — Streisand announces that her next feature film will be *The Mirror Has Two Faces* (TriStar, 1996), based on a 1958 French movie. Playwright Larry Kramer is furious because an adaptation of his *The Normal Heart* was long supposed to be Barbra's next screen project.

July — Barbra flies to London with actor Jon Voight, age fifty-seven, to attend a charity function as guests of Prince Charles. Then there's a party for musician-producer Quincy Jones in Saint-Tropez.

August 13 — Barbra purchases two Malibu homes next to the one she bought in April: a ten-thousand-square-foot Georgian-style manor and a three-bedroom, two-thousand-square-foot abode. She is seen to be creating a three-home, three-acre personal compound for herself.

September 10 — At the Forty-Seventh Emmy Awards ceremony, Barbra wins two prizes for *Barbra: The Concert*: Best Individual Performance and Best Variety/Music Special.

Also, the TV movie *Serving in Silence: The Margarethe Cammermeyer Story*, which Barbra's Barwood company produced, wins Emmy awards for Best Actress (Glenn Close), Best Supporting Actress (Judy Davis), and Best Screenplay (Alison Cross).

1996

January 2 — Barbra allows her option on Larry Kramer's *The Normal Heart* to lapse—after ten years.

April 8 — Larry Kramer denounces Streisand in *Variety*: "She was all set to make *The Normal Heart* about a worldwide plague, and at the last minute she switches to a film about a woman who gets a facelift!" Barbra asserts that she *will* make the movie, after *The Mirror Has Two Faces*, but will only star and produce, and will find someone else to direct. Jason Gould contacts Larry Kramer and suggests himself as director . . . proving that he's inherited the Streisand chutzpah.

May 21 — Hello Gorgeous!, the world's first Barbra Streisand store/museum, opens on Castro Street in San Francisco.

July 1 — Friends arrange a blind date for Barbra with actor James Brolin, age fifty-five (a year older than she). They hit it off right away.

September 12 — Barbra sings at a Hollywood fundraiser for President Clinton's reelection campaign.

October 23 — ShowEast '96 awards Barbra their Cecil B. DeMille Filmmaker of the Year Award at the annual NATO/ShowEast convention in Atlantic City. Barbra sends a 35mm film acceptance speech.

November 15 — *The Mirror Has Two Faces* opens nationwide to overwhelmingly negative reviews, which is said to come as a terrible shock to the star-director.

November 25 — Barbra spends Thanksgiving week in Ireland, where James Brolin is filming a movie.

1997

March 24 — At the Academy Awards, Barbra makes a quick trip to the ladies room . . . and misses Celine Dion singing "I Finally Found Someone," Barbra's hit song from her non-hit movie *The Mirror Has Two Faces*. Lauren Bacall (who plays Streisand's mother in the film) seems a sure-thing winner for Best Supporting Actress, but the voters think otherwise, giving the award to Juliette Binoche of *The English Patient* (Miramax, 1996).

March 30 — The Holmby Hills mansion of eighteen years is put on the market. She's asking $7.5 million for this piece of California real estate.

September 9 — Streisand expands her entertainment empire by signing a TV production deal with King World Productions for two-hour television specials. She is reportedly offered a million-dollar signing bonus. King World distributes such TV fare as *Wheel of Fortune*, *Jeopardy*, and *The Oprah Winfrey Show*.

October 5 — Premiere of Showtime Cable's movie *Rescuers: Stories of Courage—Two Women*, from executive producers Barbra Streisand and Cis Corman.

November 11 — *The Higher Ground* album is released. It's a collection of inspirational songs, prompted by the moving music she heard at the funeral of Virginia Kelly Clinton, late mother of President Clinton.

November 21 — Barbra and James Brolin appear on TV's syndicated *The Rosie O'Donnell Show*. Rosie thinks ahead and changes the set's furniture so Barbra will be photographed from her favored left side. *Entertainment Weekly* is watching. It lists Barbra and Brolin in its "Hot Sheet," the topics the country's talking about: "Barbra Streisand . . . and James Brolin are making us all queasy with gooey interviews."

December 24, 1997 — Kevin Costner's new Warner Bros. film *The Postman* (Warner Bros., 1997)—which he produced, directed, and stars in—opens to devastating reviews and poor business. Stephen Holden's critique in the *New York Times* concludes, "As a bald-faced exercise in cinematic self-deification, *The Postman* makes Barbra Streisand's *Mirror Has Two Faces* seem almost modest."

1998

February 5 — Barbra and James Brolin attend a White House dinner for British prime minister Tony Blair. Streisand uses the occasion to verbalize her support for sex-scandal-plagued President Clinton: "It's no one's business what anyone does behind closed doors. What matters is what kind of job they do, and how well they're doing—whether you're a farmer or a doctor, a performer or a president of the United States" (*Los Angeles Times*, February 5, 1998).

Showing his understanding of the political situation, James Brolin tells the press, "He's the most fun president we've ever had—I think we can all agree about that" (*New York Times*, February 18, 1998).

February 19 — James Brolin shoves a New York *Daily News* photographer who's trying to catch Streisand and Brolin leaving a movie theatre. Brolin is charged with misdemeanor assault but it's down-graded to harassment because Brolin didn't shove his victim *that* hard.

February 24 — *The Globe* tabloid reports that "Stars Circle Wagons Around the Prez," as Hollywood's top stars rush to show their support. Barbra is pictured with Brolin, and also being hugged by the Prez.

February 25 — Barbra doesn't show up for the Fifty-Ninth Grammy Awards. Her doctor claims she has the flu, but the tabloids say she didn't want to perform with Celine Dion as scheduled because she's upset that the younger singer is taking away her crown as America's number one diva.

April 24 — Barbra is fifty-six years old.

May 3 — *The Long Island Incident* airs on NBC. Cis Corman and Barbra Streisand are executive producers for the film, which is based on the true story of housewife Carolyn McCarthy, whose husband was killed in 1993 by a crazed gunman on a commuter train on Long Island, New York. McCarthy was later elected to Congress on an antigun platform.

The made-for-TV movie receives favorable reviews, but is denounced in full-page newspaper ads signed by actor Charlton Heston as first vice president of the National Rifle Association. He accuses the movie of "profiteering on the back of a tragedy." He says Streisand pushed the film's antigun politics to win ratings during a sweeps week and to sell ads. He invites the actress-producer to a debate on the right to bear arms (*Los Angeles Times*, May 4, 1998).

Streisand declines, saying that she won't allow Heston to use her celebrity to attract attention to his cause. Columnist Maureen Dowd regrets that Yentl did not accept Moses' challenge, because she certainly would have beaten him (*New York Times*, May 6, 1998). Barbra's friend Rosie O'Donnell goes to bat for her: "Look Chuck [Charlton Heston]—I know you played Moses. I know you're a big guy in the big NRA [National Rifle Association]. Say one more thing about my friend Barbra, I'm gonna kick your butt! You have your beliefs, others have theirs. Leave her (Barbra) alone." (*National Enquirer*, May 23, 1998).

May 24 — Hello Gorgeous!, the Streisand museum/store on Castro Street in San Francisco, California, closes its doors for lack of foot traffic but will continue to sell Streisandiana through the mail.

Pundit Bob Mills reports that the site will be occupied by the Charlton Heston Museum called "Hello Gun Nut" (*Los Angeles Times*, May 17, 1998).

July 1 — Barbra Streisand and James Brolin are married in a flower-strewn ceremony at her Malibu compound. The 105 guests include many from Hollywood's A-List: Steven Spielberg, John Travolta, Mike Medavoy, Sue Mengers, plus Barbra's mother, brother, half-sister, and son. She is said to be angry that Bill and Hillary Clinton couldn't make it.

August 7 — Elliott Gould is doing publicity interviews for *Getting Personal*, his new show on Fox-TV. Asked to name one of his worst jobs, he quickly responds, "As you know, I was once married to Barbra Streisand!" (quoted in *Entertainment Weekly*).

And now you know why Elliott wasn't invited to the wedding.

August 20 — *Variety* columnist Army Archerd reports that Barbra's next CD will include the two love songs she sang to James Brolin at their July wedding.

August 28 — James Brolin is honored with a star on the Hollywood Walk of Fame. Brolin says he always wanted to be a part of Hollywood, "but I never dreamed I would be implanted in this sidewalk." About four hundred and fifty cheering spectators show up for the ceremony, most of them obviously Barbra's fans. She takes the microphone and says, "Jim, I'm delighted to be here as your wife. I'm very proud of you." Apparently the honor is all right for her husband but not good enough for her: In 1976 she ungraciously declined to be represented on the Hollywood Walk of Fame, or to leave her handprints and footprints at the Chinese Theatre. (See **A Chronology**, page 63.)

September 8 — According to today's *New York Post*, Barbra is talking with director Mike Nichols about staging her next (and final?) world concert tour.

CHAPTER 7

The Ultimate Barbra Trivia Quiz, Part One

1. What movie costarred both of Barbra's husbands?
2. "They're Beauty and the Beast!" said father/stepfather Louis Kind — referring to whom?
3. Who was "Streisand's Toy Boy Goy"?
4. Biographer and super-fan James Spada says Barbra was the first major star to say "F*** off!" in a movie. Which f***ing movie?
5. Pat Newcomb was Barbra's publicist on *Hello, Dolly!* (Twentieth Century-Fox, 1969) and *The Prince of Tides* (Columbia, 1991). Say . . . Pat Newcomb . . . where do you know that name from?
6. The first individual ever to win three Oscars in one night won two of them through his professional association with Barbra. Who and for what and for what year?
7. What living legend (now dead) said, "Streisand has the unmitigated gall to imitate me!"
8. Which actors appeared with Barbra in more than one film?
9. What Streisand movie project was earlier known as *A Secret Dream*?
10. When Barbra and Elliott Gould were expecting a child, they decided that if the baby was a boy, they'd name him Jason. If it was a girl, she'd be called _____.
11. Who is Barbra's favorite fashion designer?

81

12. What couturier created the sequined see-through black net jump-suit that Barbra wore to the 1969 Academy Awards?

13. Barbra became an active crusader for gay rights . . . yet was once involved with a guy who said, "I'm as happy as a faggot in a submarine!" Who?

14. This fellow once dated Barbra. Later, he became romantically involved with a blonde more famous than even Barbra . . . and he died just hours before the blonde did. Name him.

15. What do you know about Barbra's connection to a certain hot-water bottle?

16. The original male star of the Broadway musical *I Can Get It For You Wholesale* (1962) was British actor _____, who backed out, and so the role went to Elliott Gould.

17. Name a fictional character played by both Barbra Streisand and by older actress Ruth Gordon (1896–1985).

18. Listen to these names: understudy Lainie Kazan, chess whiz Bobby Fischer, Barbra Streisand, movie star Barbara Stanwyck, and restaurateur Muriel Choy. Which one did not attend Brooklyn's Erasmus Hall High School?

19. Barbra said, "The only happiness I know is real is the happiness I get from eating _____."

20. What is Barbra's lucky number?

21. In which film did Barbra star with a Phantom of the Opera?

22. Use these names to fill in the blanks below.
    * Edie Adams * Linda Gerrard * Mimi Hines * Lainie Kazan
    * Louise Lasser * Carol Lawrence * Lisa Shane
    a. _____ Barbra's understudy on Broadway in *Funny Girl* (1964).
    b. _____ replaced Barbra in the last ten weeks of the New York stage musical *I Can Get It For You Wholesale* (1962).
    c. _____ Barbra's understudy in the second year of *Funny Girl*, and actually played her stage role on occasional matinees.
    d. _____ replaced Barbra when she left *Funny Girl*.
    e. _____ Barbra's understudy in the London stage production of *Funny Girl* (1966).
    f. _____ and _____ both starred in summer stock productions of *Funny Girl*.

23. Barbra herself replaced which actress in the movie *All Night*

Long (Universal, 1981)?

24. How many times would you guess Barbra sang "My Man"—the song made famous by show business great Fanny Brice (1891–1951)—during the run of *Funny Girl*?

25. *A Glimpse of Tiger* was changed and rewritten and recast and jazzed up, and became which Streisand movie?

26. What did Streisand do to get on President Richard Nixon's list of "political enemies"?

27. Who was the only costar to receive more money from a feature film than Barbra did?

28. Who was Barbra's first choice of male lead for *The Way We Were* (Columbia, 1973)?

29. On what occasion did Barbra get together with Jonathan Kaplan, director of the Jodie Foster hit *The Accused* (Paramount, 1988)?

30. What did Barbra Streisand's movie stand-in, Marie Rhodes, have in common with Marlon Brando's stand-in?

ANSWERS TO TRIVIA QUIZ, Part 1

1. *Capricorn One* (Warner Bros., 1978), an implausible but fun action flick about a faked manned flight to Mars, starring Elliott Gould, James Brolin, Hal Holbrook, Sam Waterston, and O. J. Simpson.
2. "Beauty" was Louis Kind's daughter Roslyn, "Beast" was his step-child Streisand.
3. Don Johnson, as lampooned in Berke Breathed's syndicated comic strip *Bloom County*.
4. *The Owl and the Pussycat* (Columbia, 1970), in which Streisand plays a foul-mouthed hooker.
5. Pat Newcomb had also been Marilyn Monroe's longtime publicist.
6. Marvin Hamlisch, who won Oscars for Best Song, "Evergreen," and Best Original Score, *The Way We Were* (Columbia, 1973). He won his third Oscar that night for Best Score Adaptation for *The Sting* (Twentieth Century-Fox, 1973).
7. Mae West, quoted in *Playboy*, January 1971.
8. Omar Sharif: *Funny Girl* (Columbia, 1968) and *Funny Lady* Columbia, 1975); George Segal: *The Owl and the Pussycat* (Columbia, 1970) and *The Mirror Has Two Faces* (TriStar, 1996); Ryan O'Neal: *What's Up, Doc?* (Warner Bros., 1972) and *The Main Event* (Warner Bros., 1979).
9. *Yentl* (MGM/United Artists, 1983).
10. Samantha.
11. Donna Karan.
12. Arnold Scaasi, who insists the outfit was not see-through, that it was underlined with nude-colored georgette crepe. When the flash-bulbs went off, the lights "eliminated" the black net covering and made it appear that you were seeing Barbra's naked butt.
13. André Agassi, the tennis player.
14. Dodi Fayed, the Arab playboy who died in the 1997 Paris car crash that killed Princess Diana. He'd spent time in Hollywood dating pretty girls and thinking about being a movie producer.
15. The only doll Barbra had as a child was a hot-water bottle dressed in one of her old sweaters.
16. Laurence Harvey.
17. Dolly Levi. Ruth Gordon starred as Dolly in Thornton Wilder's play *The Matchmaker* (1955). The musical version, *Hello, Dolly!*,

debuted on Broadway in 1964 with Carol Channing. Streisand starred in the 1969 Hollywood movie.

18. Muriel Choy, who ran the restaurant where Barbra once worked.
19. Coffee ice cream.
20. Twenty-four. It's the number of the tugboat in *Funny Girl*. It's part of Pierre Trudeau's address. She gave birth to Jason when she was twenty-four. And so on.
21. *Hello, Dolly!* (Twentieth Century-Fox, 1969) with Michael Crawford as the juvenile lead Cornelius Hackl.
22. a. Lainie Kazan
    b. Louise Lasser
    c. Linda Gerrard
    d. Mimi Hines
    e. Lisa Shane
    f. Edie Adams and Carol Lawrence
23. Lisa Eichhorn.
24. Just once, at Barbra's last performance of *Funny Girl* on Broadway at the Winter Garden Theatre on December 26, 1965. It was never *in* the show because composer Jule Styne felt that it made Fanny Brice—a strong woman—seem too vulnerable. Barbra sang it that one time as a favor to producer Ray Stark.
25. *What's Up, Doc?* (Warner Bros., 1972).
26. She participated in a Los Angeles fundraiser for Democratic front-runner George McGovern, April 15, 1972.
27. Robert Redford. Producer Ray Stark paid Redford's huge asking price because he felt so strongly in the potential of a Streisand-Redford on-camera pairing.
28. Ryan O'Neal.
29. Jonathan Kaplan directed Barbra's first music video *Left in the Dark* (1984).
30. They are the same person—Marie Rhodes, the only woman known to have doubled for a major male star and a major female star.

PART 2

THE
CAREER

CHAPTER 8

Barbra Streisand on Stage

All things being equal, Barbra Streisand might just as well have become America's greatest Shakespearean actress—given what we know about her drive and determination, her boundless ego, her remarkable talent. She maintained for a long time that she *was* an actress, not a singer, and that her ambition was to play Juliet and Cleopatra and Lady Macbeth and Medea—you know, nonsinging roles.

However, Shakespeare has never really found a home in America. So Barbra probably wouldn't be working that often, and she certainly wouldn't have been able to afford multiple mansions overlooking the Pacific. No, singing was the right decision for her.

Barbra's theatrical career encompasses four sessions of summer stock, offbeat endeavors off-Broadway, and two big Broadway hits. The American Theater Wing thought enough of her skill to award her its first "On-Stage Hall of Fame Award" in 1970 as Star of the Decade.

Summer Stock

[dates in parentheses are of the original Broadway productions]

Malden Bridge Playhouse, Malden Bridge, New York. Summer 1957.
   Teahouse of the August Moon (1953) by John Patrick. Barbra plays one of the Japanese children.

Desk Set (1955) by William Marchant. Barbra is Elsa, the sexy secretary. *Picnic* (1953) by William Inge. Barbra is Millie Owens, the tomboy sister played in the 1955 Columbia movie by Susan Strasberg.

Clinton Playhouse, Clinton, Connecticut. Summer 1958.
   Tobacco Road (1933) by Erskine Caldwell and Jack Kirkland. Barbra is oversexed Ellie May, who'll do anything for a turnip.

Cecilwood Theatre, Fishkill, New York. Summer 1959.
   Separate Tables (1956) by Terence Rattigan. Barbra is one of the numerous characters in this British drama of love and loneliness set in the dining room of a British seaside resort hotel.

Cecilwood Theatre, Fishkill, New York. August 16–30, 1960.
   The Boy Friend (1954) by Sandy Wilson. Barbra plays Hortense the French maid and sings on stage for the first time.

At the "Reincarnation Ball" in 1970 with Fred Glaser, her hairdresser, and Sue Mengers, her sometime agent
(she urged Barbra not to make *Yentl*).
PHOTO COURTESY ARCHIVE PHOTOS/FOTOS INTERNATIONAL

Off-Broadway

Cherry Lane Theatre, New York City. Winter, 1957–58.
Purple Dust (1940) by Sean O'Casey. Barbra is the understudy to Avril, and the assistant stage manager.

Garret Theatre, New York City. January–February, 1959.
Driftwood (1954) by Maurice Tei Dunn. Barbra plays Lorna, who turns out to be not only the Woman in Black but also the Chief! (You had to be there.) Joan Rivers (born 1933) is also in the cast.

Jan Hus Theatre, New York City. May 8–10, 1960.
The Insect Comedy (1923) by Karel and Josef Capek. Barbra appears as various insects in this avant-garde look at the human condition. Future lover-mentor Barry Dennen is also in the cast.

Gramercy Arts Theatre, New York City. October 21, 1961.
(One performance—the show opens on a Sunday night, and the Monday morning reviews kill it.)
Another Evening with Harry Stoones, an off-Broadway revue with music and lyrics by Jeff Harris. Streisand has two solos: "Jersey" and "Value" (a.k.a. "I'm in Love with Harold Mengert"). Other newcomers in the cast are comic Dom DeLuise (born 1933) and African American actress Diana Sands (1934–1973).

There are some favorable notices but they appear too late. Says *Variety*, "Barbra Streisand is a slim, offbeat, deadpan comedienne with an excellent flair for dropping a dour blackout gag, and she belts across a musical apostrophe to New Jersey with facile intensity."

Broadway

Shubert Theatre, New York City.
Opened: March 22, 1962.
Closed: December 9, 1962 (300 performances).
I Can Get It for You Wholesale, a musical of life in the "rag trade" (the garment industry), based on the 1937 novel by Jerome Weidman. Music and lyrics by Harold Rome. Choreography by Herb Ross. Directed by Arthur Laurents. Produced by David Merrick.

Featuring Elliott Gould (as Harry Bogen) in his first starring role, Lillian Roth (Mrs. Bogen), Marilyn Cooper (Ruthie Rivkin), Jack Kruschen (Maurice Pulvermacher), and Sheree North (Martha Mills) as a hooker.

Barbra Streisand plays the put-upon, efficient secretary Yetta Marmelstein. She stops the show every night singing "Miss Marmelstein" while whizzing around the stage seated in a typing chair on rollers.

The show in general gets indifferent reviews but it runs for nine months, mainly because of the ecstatic notices given Barbra and the excitement she creates. This is from critic Whitney Bolton (New

---

"Born in Madagascar and Reared in Rangoon . . . "

The cast members of *I Can Get It for You Wholesale* were asked to compose their own brief biographies for the *Playbill* program. Barbra sees this as an opportunity to get audiences interested in her even before the curtain goes up, so she writes:

"Barbra Streisand is nineteen, was born in Madagascar and reared in Rangoon, educated at Erasmus Hall High School in Brooklyn and appeared off Broadway in a one-nighter called *Another Evening with Harry Stoones. Wholesale* is her first Broadway show, although she has appeared at New York's two best-known supper clubs, The Bon Soir and The Blue Angel. She also has appeared eight times on Mike Wallace's *P.M. East* and twice on the [Jack] Paar show. She is not a member of Actors Studio."

She later changes it to: "Barbra Streisand is twenty, was born in Zanzibar and reared in Aruba. . . . "

Finally, three months into the run, she provides a straight version of her resumé: "Barbra Streisand is twenty, was born and reared in Brooklyn, New York, educated at Erasmus Hall. . . ."

Thirty-five years later, on TV's *The Rosie O'Donnell Show*, Barbra is kidded about her *Playbill* bio. Rosie asks just where exactly Rangoon is, and Barbra waves it aside as "near Africa." All those who know it's in Burma, raise your hand.

York *Morning Telegraph*, March 23, 1962): "Especially to be noted . . . a shriek-voiced new comedienne who probably won't be out of work for the next eight years. Her name is Barbra Streisand, who is 19 years old and has packed 38 years of poise and professionalism into her still-young life. Miss Streisand, singing or talking, burbling or walking, screaming or whispering, is a great, good friend to *I Can Get It for You Wholesale*."

Winter Garden Theatre, New York City.
Opened: March 26, 1964.
Streisand gives her last performance on Broadway on December 26, 1965. Mimi Hines replaces her as Fanny Brice and the show runs for another year and a half, finally closing on July 1, 1967 (after 1,348 performances).
Funny Girl, a musical about the life and loves of beloved entertainer Fanny Brice (1891–1951), is based on her tape-recorded memories. Music by Jule Styne, lyrics by Bob Merrill. Choreography by Carol Haney. Book by Isobel Lennart (and others, uncredited). Directed by Garson Kanin. Production supervisor, Jerome Robbins. Produced by Ray Stark.
With Sydney Chaplin (*Nick Arnstein*), Kay Medford (*Mrs. Brice*), Danny Meehan (*Eddie Ryan*), Jean Stapleton (*Mrs. Strakosh*), and Lainie Kazan (*Vera*, and also understudy to Streisand).
The Broadway opening of *Funny Girl* is spectacularly successful. *Life* (May 22, 1964) calls it "unquestionably the single biggest personal triumph show business has seen in years."
Writes *Time* (April 10, 1964): "If New York were Paris, Broadway could temporarily consider itself the Rue Streisand. Some stars merely brighten up a marquee; Barbra Streisand sets an entire theater ablaze. . . . Actress, songstress, comedienne, mimic, clown—she is the theater's new girl for all seasons."

London

Prince of Wales Theatre, London.
Opened: April 13, 1966.
Closed: July 16, 1966.
Funny Girl, the London production, directed by Lawrence Kasha.

Michael Craig replaces Sydney Chaplin as Nick Arnstein. Husband Elliott Gould could have had the part at Barbra's request, but he turns it down as a matter of pride.

The Role She Never Played

In interviews over the years, Barbra speaks frequently of wanting to portray Juliet in Shakespeare's *Romeo and Juliet*. In 1969, when she wins her special Tony as Broadway Star of the Decade, she talks of playing Juliet while she is still young enough.

In a *New York Times* interview (January 21, 1973) she discusses doing repertory theater: "I've always wanted to play Juliet. And L'Aiglon and Camille and Medea. I'd also like to play Shaw's Cleopatra, and—when I'm older—Shakespeare's Cleopatra. It's challenging to take a role people have seen played many times and bring it alive again. I like comparison, I *enjoy* risks."

She finally does play Juliet, in 1975, and thinks it the best thing she's done. "It wasn't until she was thirty-three that she had the nerve to direct herself for Lee Strasberg in her version of a scene from *Romeo and Juliet* at the Actors Studio. 'See, I had written letters to [acting teacher and guru] Lee Strasberg when I was riding on the IRT subway ever since I was fourteen or fifteen years old and never mailed them to him,' she says. 'One of my treasured possessions . . . is his tape after my performance, because he had no criticisms. He really got what I was doing. I played her like a spoiled brat. I wasn't this 'fancy' Juliet with her family in court as the proper girl of Verona. But also what she was like when she was in the chamber with the nurse—played by Sally Kirkland—who was her friend. It was very spoiled, really bratty" (*Vanity Fair*, September 1991).

Encouraged by Strasberg's approval, she has her agent ask the networks if they were interested in a TV special. "They weren't! They said, 'Does she sing in it? Who's playing Romeo?' How big a star do you have to be before you can play *Romeo and Juliet* on TV? I was so discouraged" (*Playboy*, October 1977).

Barbra Streisand *did* play Shakespeare on television, in her 1967 CBS special *The Belle of 14th Street*, in which she and guest star Jason Robards performed a scene from *The Tempest*. Neither viewers nor reviewers were very impressed.

In the mid-1980s, there is talk of Barbra Streisand and Marlon Brando costarring in a big-screen rendition of *Macbeth* . . . but it is all Hollywood sound and fury, signifying nothing.

Special Guest Appearances
by Elliott Gould and Lainie Kazan

In the Hong Kong–style action flick *The Big Hit* (TriStar, 1998), Mark Wahlberg is a contract killer juggling two women: a foxy black mistress who takes his money and cheats on him, and his fiancée, a Jewish American Princess who treats him worse—she invites her parents for the weekend!

The dreaded pair arrive and, no surprise, they're a nightmare. Overweight, overbearing Mom thinks plastic surgery is keeping her beautiful, and dad is a lush. But, nice surprise, they're played by Lainie Kazan and Elliott Gould—two who could really tell you some stories about Barbra Streisand.

*   *   *

Elliott Gould and Barbra Streisand both grew up in New York City's great middle-class melting pot called Brooklyn: Barbra in Williamsburg and Elliott in the Bensonhurst section. Elliott had a doting mother who sent him to a show business school for kids, thinking it would help him relax. Barbra pleaded to attend a show business school, but there was no money for such luxury.

I Can Get It for You Wholesale was the breakthrough for both of them. Elliott auditioned for lead understudy in this 1962 Broadway musical, and Barbra auditioned for the small role of the secretary. Elliott got the understudy job and then was hired as leading man. Barbra got the role of Miss Marmelstein. Then they got each other. (Some gossip has it that she got him, that she was determined to marry a star.) But then Streisand came close to being kicked out of the show because she was late so often, flagrantly keeping the company waiting (she was officially reprimanded by Actors Equity). Elliott, on the other hand, was almost replaced because he perspired—he sweated freely, constantly, and noticeably in the stylish suits he wore on stage. He was nearly replaced by Michael Callan but Nora Kaye Ross, wife of the show's choreographer Herbert Ross, fought to keep him.

* * *

The **Lainie Kazan** story:

Two years later, in January 1964, the Broadway-bound musical *Funny Girl* was trying out in Boston with unknown, unproved star Barbra Streisand, and the nervous early reports were not good. Among those auditioned as possible replacements for Streisand was the beautiful Lainie Kazan (born 1940). The show's producers decided to stick with Streisand. Lainie was later hired as her understudy.

Fast forward to 1965 and Barbra is fabulously successful as Funny Girl. But on February second, she calls in sick with laryngitis. The stage manager notifies Lainie Kazan that she is going on . . . and Lainie notifies her newspaper friends. Streisand hears of this, and drags herself to the theater. The newspapers print stories of the sick star who'll do anything to keep others out of her spotlight. But Streisand is even sicker the next day, and Lainie does go on. Barbra sends her congratulations, but privately insists that Kazan be fired.

Depending on who you ask, Lainie was fired . . . or else left on her own because of the new offers she was receiving.

CHAPTER 9

Ladies and Gentlemen: Will You Welcome Now, Barbra Streisand —in Person!

In the beginning Barbra Streisand insisted that she was an actress, not a singer. When she started telling herself she was *acting* out the songs, that each one was a minidrama, she became one of the great singers.

She often had trouble establishing a rapport with her audiences, probably from her own self-image syndrome and from problems with audiences who often couldn't get past their image of this unusual-looking character with the prominent nose. Add to that her stage fright, which only increased over the decades, and the fear that she might be shot by some wacko while performing. (A telephone threat against Streisand *was* received. A man with a gun *was* arrested.)

So her public appearances have been few and far between. Streisand the singer reached god(dess)hood mainly through her recordings, a few of the better movies and television appearances, and a few fundraisers. Fans who've seen an in-the-flesh performance by Streisand speak of it with the awe of those who have taken joy rides in flying saucers, or who have won Publishers Clearing House Sweepstakes.

The list that follows may be more substantial than one might reasonably expect, but it should be noted that it covers nearly forty years. So don't say you never had a chance—what were you doing that was more important?

97

Mink-swathed Barbra—don't tell me it's dyed rabbit— makes a point to costar George Segal, who prepares to defend himself from the killer fingernails. It's at a party for *The Owl and the Pussycat* (1970).
PHOTO COURTESY OF J. C. ARCHIVES

June 6–June 27, 1960—Eighteen-year-old Barbara enters a talent contest at The Lion, a Greenwich Village gay bar. She says she didn't realize it was a gay bar; surprise! she wins. She sings there for a month. After the second week, Barbara becomes Barbra.

August 7, 1960—Barbra appears as "a little extra surprise" at the more upscale Bon Soir club on Manhattan's Eighth Street.

September 9–November 20, 1960—She begins a two-week engagement at The Bon Soir . . . that stretches into ten weeks, at $108 a week.

March 2–April 2; April 6–15, 1961—Barbra appears at The Caucus Club in Detroit, the first time she's been out of the Northeast.

April 17–May 8, 1961—At the Crystal Palace in St. Louis she shares the spotlight with the Smothers Brothers.

May 9–June 6, 1961—Back to The Bon Soir, sharing the bill with comedians Renee Taylor and Phil Leeds.

July 3–16, 1961—The Town 'n Country club in Winnipeg, Manitoba, Canada.

July 17–August 12, 1961—A one-month return booking at Detroit's Caucus Club.

November 16–December 13, 1961—Moving up, up, uptown in the world, Barbra opens a two-week engagement at The Blue Angel, a classy Big Apple nightspot on Fifty-Fifth Street at Third Avenue. She'd been there several weeks earlier as a one-night replacement for comic Pat Harrington.

   During this period she's rehearsing during the day for the Broadway-bound musical *I Can Get It for You Wholesale* (1962). At night she is a headliner at The Blue Angel.

May 22–June 3, 1962—By popular request: back to The Bon Soir.

July 16–August 17, 1962—By overwhelming demand: back to The Blue Angel.

October 23–November 18, 1962—The Bon Soir.

January 8–28, 1963—The Blue Angel.

Barbra Goes on Tour to Promote
The Barbra Streisand Album, Her First

February 5, 1963—The Revere Beach Frolics Club, Boston, Massachusetts.

February—The Chateau, in Lakewood, Ohio.

March 19–23, 25–26—Eden Roc Hotel, Miami Beach, Florida.

March 27–April 20—the hungry i, San Francisco.

May 13–June 1—Basin Street East, New York City. She opens for veteran big band leader and clarinetist Benny Goodman and "runs away with the show" (Jack Thompson, New York *Daily Mirror*, May 15, 1963).

May 24—The White House Correspondents Association Dinner, at the Washington Hilton.

June 11–30—Mr. Kelly's, a Chicago club.

July 2–August 4—Riviera Hotel, Las Vegas, opening for Liberace.

August 9—Lido Country Club, Long Island, New York.

August 10—Concord Hotel, Lake Kiamesha, New York.

August 21–September 8—The Cocoanut Grove, Ambassador

Hotel, Los Angeles. Many Hollywood celebrities show up to see what the shouting's about. This is Streisand's most important booking to date.

September 9–22—Harrah's, Lake Tahoe, Nevada. Again opening for Liberace (Whose idea is this? Liberace's!)

October 5—The Hollywood Bowl, Los Angeles, with Sammy Davis, Jr.

Not part of the record tour:

November—A benefit for Leonard Goldenman at the Harmony Club in New York City.

November 29–30—The Arie Crown Theatre, Chicago.

December 1—Clowes Memorial Hall of Butler University, Indianapolis.

December 2—Concert Hall, Indiana State University in Terre Haute.

December 4—San Jose Civic Auditorium, San Jose, California.

December 5—Civic Auditorium, Sacramento, California.

December 6—San Francisco Masonic Auditorium.

December 7—The Shrine Auditorium, Los Angeles.

July 12, 1964—Barbra auditions material for a new record album at the Forest Hills Music Festival in Queens, New York.

August 1964—The Democratic National Convention in Atlantic City, New Jersey.

January 8, 1965—Barbra sings at the Inaugural Eve Gala for President Lyndon B. Johnson in Washington, D.C.

April 4, 1965—The Rev. Martin Luther King is in the audience when Barbra sings in a civil rights benefit concert, *Salute to Selma*, in New York City.

August 8, 1965—The Forest Hills Music Festival, Queens, New York.

June 12, 1966—A concert for the Festival of American Arts at the United States Embassy in London. She sings songs from the George Gershwin opera *Porgy and Bess* (1935).

July 21, 1966—At the Columbia Records convention in Las Vegas, Barbra makes an appearance as the label's reigning pop star. She sings selections from her *Je M'Appelle Barbra* album, which Columbia is nervous about.

Summer, 1966—Barbra is pregnant, so she cuts back on a projected concert tour. She'll sing in just four cities:

July 30—The Festival Field in Newport, Rhode Island.

August 2—John F. Kennedy Stadium in Philadelphia.

August 6—Fulton County Stadium in Atlanta.

August 9—Soldiers Field in Chicago.

June 11, 1967—The *Rally for Israel's Survival* at the Hollywood Bowl in Los Angeles.

June 17, 1967—On a three-day weekend during the *Funny Girl* (Columbia, 1968) shooting, Barbra appears in a free concert in New York's Central Park. Though 60,000 people are expected, 135,000 show up!

July 9, 1967—The Hollywood Bowl, Los Angeles.

January 21, 1968—The *Broadway for Peace 1968* fundraiser at Philharmonic Hall in New York City.

June 26, 1968—Benefit performance in New York City for Democratic presidential candidate Eugene McCarthy.

July 17, 1968—Harry Belafonte, Barbra Streisand, and Bill Cosby in a benefit performance at the Hollywood Bowl.

October 17, 1968—Israeli Bond luncheon at the Hollywood Palladium.

July 2–30,1969—Barbra is the inaugural attraction at the new Las Vegas International Hotel. For the four-week engagement she receives salary plus hotel stock worth $1 million. (Who needs the Publishers Clearing House Sweepstakes?)

October 11, 1969—Evening for John Lindsay, liberal Republican candidate for mayor of New York, at the Felt Forum in New York City.

November 1, 1970—*Broadway for Bella* (Abzug), liberal Democratic congressional hopeful, at the Felt Forum in New York City.

November 27–December 10, 1970—Two weeks at the Las Vegas Riviera.

December 13, 1970–January 2, 1971—Back in Las Vegas at the Hilton (formerly the International). Observers note that Barbra finally *seems* to enjoy performing in front of a Las Vegas crowd.

December 24, 1971–January 13, 1972—And so, after three weeks at the Hilton, it's goodbye to Las Vegas . . . until 1993.

April 15 1972—Another fundraiser: 4 For McGovern, the Democratic front-runner, at the Los Angeles Forum. The other three performers: Carole King, James Taylor, and Quincy Jones and orchestra.

April 7, 1973—Fundraiser for political activist Daniel Ellsberg, sponsored by the ACLU, in Beverly Hills.

March 9, 1975—*Funny Girl to Funny Lady*: a concert in Washington, D.C., to promote Barbra's new movie *Funny Lady* and to benefit the Special Olympics. In the audience are President Gerald R. Ford and Senator Edward M. Kennedy. The concert is televised on CBS.

March 20, 1976—To create a receptive audience for a sequence in her movie *A Star Is Born* (Warner Bros., 1976), a concert is held at the Sun Devil Stadium in Phoenix, Arizona, during which Barbra and the film's costar Kris Kristofferson perform.

June 1, 1980—The American Civil Liberties Union holds a fundraising concert honoring songwriters Marilyn and Alan Bergman at the Dorothy Chandler Pavilion in downtown Los Angeles. Barbra sings an all-Bergman program. Neil Diamond joins her for "You Don't Bring Me Flowers."

September 6, 1986—The *One Voice* concert. Barbra seeks to raise money for Democratic senatorial candidates. She invites four hundred guests—top names in politics, movies, and music—to her concert under the stars on her Wonderland ranch in Malibu, California.

Viva, Las Vegas!
The Complete Itinerary

The Riviera Hotel
July 2–August 4, 1963
Las Vegas International Hotel (later the Hilton)
July 2–July 30, 1969
The Riviera
November 27–December 10, 1970
Las Vegas Hilton
December 13, 1970–January 2, 1971
Las Vegas Hilton
December 24, 1971–January 13, 1972
MGM Grand Hotel
December 31, 1993–January 1, 1994

October 16, 1988—More politics: Barbra sings at the Beverly Hills *Voices for Change* fundraiser for Michael Dukakis, Democratic presidential candidate.

July 1, 1992—*Women for a Change* fundraiser at the Beverly Wilshire Hotel in Beverly Hills.

September 16, 1992—Still an ardent Democrat, Barbra headlines the *Voices for Change* fundraiser in Beverly Hills for presidential nominee Bill Clinton.

November 18, 1992—AIDS Project Los Angeles honors Streisand and recording mogul David Geffen with its Commitment to Life Award. At the awards ceremony, held at the Universal Amphitheatre in Universal City (just over the hill from Hollywood), featured performers sing selections from *West Side Story*. For the finale, Barbra and Johnny Mathis duet on "One Hand, One Heart" and "I Have a Love."

January 19, 1993—Barbra headlines the inaugural gala for the winner — President Bill Clinton.

December 31, 1993 and January 1, 1994—Barbra returns to the concert stage for the first time in twenty-two years when she appears at the opening of Kirk Kerkorian's MGM Grand Hotel in Las Vegas. For Barbra, something happens—something clicks. A light bulb goes on. Barbra sends out an announcement: She's found the Las Vegas concerts "such a lovely experience" that she's decided to do a limited tour "to express my appreciation for the love and support I have received for such a long time."

March 27, 1994—Tickets go on sale for Barbra's first concert tour in twenty-eight years. Top seat price is $350, and ticket scalping is rampant.

The Appreciation Tour

April 20, 25, 27, 29, 1994—The tour debuts in London, at Wembley Arena.

May 10, 12—The American trek begins at the USAir Arena, Landover, Maryland, outside Washington, D.C.

May 15, 17, 19—The Palace of Auburn Hills, in Auburn Hills, Michigan, near Detroit.

June 2, 4—Arrowhead Pond of Anaheim, near Disneyland in Southern California . . . but a bad cold forces the star to postpone four of the six scheduled play dates.

June 7, 9—The San Jose Arena, not far from San Francisco.

June 20, 23, 26, 28, 30; July 10, 12—Appearing at Madison Square Garden. Her New York fans give her an overwhelming reception. The shows gross an estimated $60 million.

July 18, 20, 22, 24—Back to Anaheim for the postponed engagements. The last two performances are taped for HBO and CBS television specials.

*   *   *

September 12, 1996—Barbra sings at a Beverly Hills fundraiser for President Clinton's reelection campaign.

CHAPTER 10

The Complete Streisand Discography

The Albums

From 1958 to 1974, when a record or album made one million dollars in *wholesale* revenues, it was declared a gold record. In 1975, the basis was changed to 500,000 units sold in addition to the one million dollars wholesale revenues.

The platinum record, conceived in 1976, is one that sells a million units and totals at least two million dollars in revenues. Double platinum, triple platinum, and quadruple platinum mean, incredibly, just what you think they mean.

Over the years, each time that a new playback format (eight-track, cassette, CD, and so on) is marketed to the general public, the Barbra Streisand catalog is usually among the first to be reissued. This accounts for the delayed platinum designation for some of her album titles.

Chart position refers to the highest number on the popularity scale the album reached. Unless otherwise indicated (as with the original-cast recordings and movie soundtracks), Barbra is doing all the singing on all these albums.

I Can Get It for You Wholesale
Columbia 53020. April 1962. Original cast recording of the 1962 Broadway musical.
Chart position: No. 125.

Songs: Barbra sings "Miss Marmelstein" and joins in on three other songs: "I'm Not a Well Man," "Ballad of the Garment Trade," and "What Are They Doing to Us Now?"

Pins and Needles
Columbia, 57380. May 1962. Twenty-fifth anniversary edition (a studio recording of the 1936 Broadway hit).
Chart position: did not make the Top 200.
   Songs: Barbra sings five solos: "Doing the Reactionary," "Nobody Makes a Pass at Me," "Not Cricket to Picket," "Status Quo," and "What Good Is Love?", and is heard on a sixth song, "Four Little Angels of Peace."

For the record:
The first solo album Barbra recorded was never released. She was taped at The Bon Soir club in New York City on November 5, 6, and 7, 1962, to capture the excitement of a live performance. The tapes were judged inferior, and the album was not released. Eight songs from The Bon Soir sessions turn up on the 1989 Streisand collection, *Just for the Record*.

The Barbra Streisand Album
Columbia 57374. February 1963.
Chart position: No. 8; certified gold.
Grammy Awards: Album of the Year; Best Female Vocal Performance; Best Album Cover. "Happy Days Are Here Again" was nominated for Record of the Year.
   Songs: "Cry Me a River," "My Honey's Loving Arms," "I'll Tell the Man in the Street," "A Taste of Honey," "Who's Afraid of the Big, Bad Wolf?", "Soon It's Gonna Rain," "Happy Days Are Here Again," "Keepin' out of Mischief Now," "Much More," "Come to the Supermarket (in Old Peking)," and "A Sleepin' Bee."

The Second Barbra Streisand Album
Columbia 57378. August 1963.
Chart position: No. 2; certified gold.
   Songs: "Any Place I Hang My Hat Is Home," "Right as the Rain," "Down with Love," "Who Will Buy?", "When the Sun Comes Out," "Gotta Move," "My Coloring Book," "I Don't Care Much," "Lover,

Come Back to Me," "I Stayed Too Long at the Fair," and "Like a Straw in the Wind."

For the record:
"Barbra Streisand—Live, 1963"
(also known as *Live at the hungry i*)
A bootleg album that surfaced in 1985 of a performance at the hungry i club in San Francisco. Barbra brought legal action and the album was soon withdrawn.

Barbra Streisand/The Third Album
Columbia 57379. February 1964.
Chart position: No. 5; certified gold.
   Songs: "My Melancholy Baby," "Just in Time," "Taking a Chance on Love," "Bewitched (Bothered and Bewildered)," "Never Will I Marry," "As Time Goes By," "Draw Me a Circle," "It Had to Be You," "Make Believe," and "I Had Myself a True Love."

Funny Girl
Capitol 64681. April 1964. Original cast recording of the Broadway musical.
Chart position: No. 2; certified gold.
Grammy Award: Best Broadway Cast Album.
   Songs: Overture, "If a Girl Isn't Pretty" [sung by friends of Fanny's mother], "I'm the Greatest Star," "Cornet Man," "Who Taught Her Everything?" [Kay Medord and Danny Meehan], "His Love Makes Me Beautiful," "I Want to Be Seen with You Tonight," "Henry Street," "People," "You Are Woman" [with Sydney Chaplin], "Don't Rain on My Parade," "Sadie, Sadie," "Find Yourself a Man," "Rat-tat-tat-tat," "Who Are You Now?", "The Music That Makes Me Dance," and "Don't Rain on My Parade" [reprise].

People
Columbia 9015. September 1964.
Chart position: No. 1; certified gold.
Grammy Awards: Best Female Vocal Performance; Best Album Cover. Also nominated for Album of the Year and Record and Song of the Year ("People").
   Songs: "Absent-Minded Me," "When in Rome (I Do as the Romans Do)," "Fine and Dandy," "Supper Time," "Will He Like Me?", "How

Does the Wine Taste," "I'm All Smiles," "Autumn," "My Lord and Master," "Love Is a Bore," "Don't Like Goodbyes," and "People."

My Name Is Barbra
Columbia 9136. May 1965. Soundtrack of the 1965 CBS special.
Chart position: No. 2; certified gold.
Grammy Award: Best Female Vocal Performance. Also nominated for Album of the Year and Best Album Cover.
    Songs: "My Name Is Barbra," "A Kid Again"/"I'm Five," "Jenny Rebecca," "My Pa," "Sweet Zoo," "Where Is the Wonder?", "I Can See It," "Someone to Watch over Me," "I've Got No Strings," "If You Were the Only Boy in the World," "Why Did I Choose You," and "My Man."

My Name Is Barbra, Two
Columbia 9209. October 1965.
Chart position: No. 2; certified gold, 1966; platinum, 1986.
    Songs: "He Touched Me," "The Shadow of Your Smile," "Quiet Night," "I Got Plenty of Nothin'," "How Much of the Dream Comes True," "Second Hand Rose," "The Kind of Man a Woman Needs," "All That I Want," "Where's That Rainbow," "No More Songs for Me," medley: "Second Hand Rose"/"Give Me the Simple Life"/"I Got Plenty of Nothin' "/"Brother, Can You Spare a Dime?"/"Nobody Knows You When You're Down and Out"/"Second Hand Rose"/"The Best Things in Life Are Free."

Color Me Barbra
Columbia 19278. March 1966. Soundtrack of the 1966 CBS special.
Chart position: No. 3; certified gold.
Grammy nominations: Album of the Year, Best Female Vocal Performance, and Best Album Cover.
    Songs: "Yesterdays," "One Kiss," "The Minute Waltz," "Gotta Move," "Non, C'est Rien," "Where or When," medley: "Animal Crackers in My Soup"/"Funny Face"/"That Face"/"They Didn't Believe Me"/"Were Thine That Special Face"/"I've Grown Accustomed to Her Face"/"Let's Face the Music and Dance"/"Sam, You Made the Pants Too Long"/"What's New, Pussycat?"/"Small World"/"I Love You"/"I Stayed Too Long at the Fair"/"Look at That Face," "C'est Si Bon," "Where Am I Going?", and "Starting Here, Starting Now."

Harold Sings Arlen (With Friend)
Columbia 12920. March 1966.
Chart position: did not make the Top 200.
Barbra sings "Ding Dong! The Witch Is Dead" with composer Arlen and the solo "House of Flowers."

For the record:
July 1966: While performing *Funny Girl* in London, Barbra sang for a special Independence Day celebration at the American Embassy. The performance was taped by Columbia Records, but never released.

For the record:
Also in London, Barbra recorded four Christmas songs for inclusion in an album of various artists. The album was released in November 1966, by the American Premiums Division of Columbia and was a giveaway by the Goodyear Rubber Company for gas stations.

Je M'Appelle Barbra
Columbia 19347. October 1966.
Chart position: No. 5.
  Songs: "Free Again," "Autumn Leaves," "What Now, My Love?", "My Premiere Chanson," "Clopin Clopant," "Le Mur," "I Wish You Love," "Speak to Me of Love," "Love and Learn," "Once Upon a Summertime," "Martina," and "I've Been Here."

For the record:
There was no soundtrack album released of the 1967 CBS special *The Belle of 14th Street* because of the negative reception the show received.

Simply Streisand
Columbia 19482. October 1967.
Chart position: No. 12.
  Songs: "My Funny Valentine," "The Nearness of You," "When Sunny Gets Blue," "Make the Man Love Me," "Lover Man," "More Than You Know," "I'll Know," "All the Things You Are," "The Boy Next Door," and "Stout-Hearted Men."

A Christmas Album
Columbia 9557. October 1967.
Chart position: No. 1 (on chart of seasonal albums); certified gold, 1996; triple platinum, 1997.
   Songs: "Jingle Bells," "Have Yourself a Merry Little Christmas," "The Christmas Song (Chestnuts Roasting on an Open Fire)," "White Christmas," "My Favorite Things," "The Best Gift," "Sleep in Heavenly Peace (Silent Night)," Charles Gounod's "Ave Maria," "O Little Town of Bethlehem," "I Wonder as I Wander," and "The Lord's Prayer."

Funny Girl
Columbia 3220. July 1968. Soundtrack of the 1968 Columbia motion picture.
Chart position: No. 12; certified gold, 1968; platinum, 1986.
Grammy nomination: Best Female Contemporary Pop Vocal Performance.
   Songs: "I'm the Greatest Star," "If a Girl Isn't Pretty" [sung by friends of Fanny's mother], "Roller Skate Rag" [ensemble], "I'd Rather Be Blue Over You (Than Happy with Somebody Else)," "His Love Makes Me Beautiful" [with the Ziegfeld Girls], "People," "You Are Woman, I Am Man" [duet with Omar Sharif], "Don't Rain on My Parade," "Sadie, Sadie," "The Swan," "Funny Girl," and "My Man."

A Happening in Central Park
Columbia 19710. September 1968. Soundtrack of the 1968 CBS special.
Chart position: No. 30; certified gold.
   Songs: "I Can See It," "New Love Is Like a Newborn Child," folk monologue/"Value," "Cry Me a River," "People," "He Touched Me," "Marty the Martian," "Natural Sounds," "Second Hand Rose," "Sleep in Heavenly Peace," and "Happy Days Are Here Again."

What About Today?
Columbia 47014. July 1969.
Chart position: No. 31.
   Songs: "What About Today?", "Ask Yourself Why," "Honey Pie," "Punky's Dilemma," "Until It's Time for You to Go," "That's a Fine Kind of Freedom," "Little Tin Soldier," "With a Little Help from My Friends," "Alfie," "The Morning After," and "Goodnight."

Hello, Dolly!
Polygram 10368. December 1969. Soundtrack of the 1969 Twentieth Century-Fox motion picture.
Chart position: No. 49.

Songs: "Just Leave Everything to Me," "It Takes a Woman" [Walter Matthau], "It Takes a Woman" [Streisand], "Put on Your Sunday Clothes" [ensemble], "Ribbons Down My Back" [Marianne McAndrew], "Dancing," "Before the Parade Passes By," "Elegance" [ensemble], "Love Is Only Love," "Hello, Dolly!" [with the Harmonia Gardens waiters and then Louis Armstrong], "It Only Takes a Moment" [Michael Crawford and Marianne McAndrew], "So Long, Dearie," and finale [ensemble].

Barbra Streisand's Greatest Hits
Columbia 9968. December 1969.
Chart position: No. 32; certified gold, 1971; double platinum, 1986.

Songs: "People," "Second Hand Rose," "Why Did I Choose You?", "He Touched Me," "Free Again," "Don't Rain on My Parade," "My Coloring Book," "Sam, You Made the Pants Too Long," "My Man," "Gotta Move," and "Happy Days Are Here Again."

On a Clear Day You Can See Forever
Columbia 57377. July 1970. Soundtrack of the 1970 Paramount motion picture.
Chart position: No. 108.

Songs: "Hurry, It's Lovely Up Here!", "On a Clear Day (You Can See Forever)," "Love with All the Trimmings," "Melinda," "Go to Sleep" [a duet sung by two Streisands], "He Isn't You," "What Did I Have That I Don't Have Now?", "Come Back to Me," "On a Clear Day" (Yves Montand), and "On a Clear Day" (Streisand).

The Owl and the Pussycat
Columbia 30401. December 1970. Dialogue and incidental music from the soundtrack of the 1970 Columbia motion picture; Barbra does not sing.
Chart position: No. 186.
Not available on compact disc.

Stoney End
Columbia 30378. February 1971.

Chart position: No. 10; certified gold, 1971; platinum, 1986.

Songs: "I Don't Know Where I Stand," "Hands off the Man (Flim Flam Man)," "If You Could Read My Mind," "Just a Little Lovin'," "Let Me Go," "Stoney End," "No Easy Way Down," "Time and Love," "Maybe," "Free the People," and "I'll Be Home."

Barbra Joan Streisand
Columbia 30792. August 1971.
Chart position: No. 11; certified gold.

Songs: "Beautiful," "Love," "Where You Lead," "I Never Meant to Hurt You," "One Less Bell to Answer"/"A House Is Not a Home," "Space Captain," "Since I Fell for You," "Mother," "The Summer Knows," "I Mean to Shine," and "You've Got a Friend."

Live Concert at the Forum
Columbia 31760. October 1972.
Chart position: No. 19; certified gold, 1973; platinum, 1986.
Grammy nominations: Best Female Pop Vocal Performance for "Sweet Inspiration"/"Where You Lead."

Songs: "Sing"/"Make Your Own Kind of Music," "Starting Here, Starting Now," "Don't Rain on My Parade," "On a Clear Day (You Can See Forever)," "Sweet Inspiration"/"Where You Lead," "Didn't We," "My Man," "Stoney End," "Sing"/"Happy Days Are Here Again," and "People."

Barbra Streisand . . . and Other Musical Instruments
Columbia 132655. October 1973. Soundtrack of the 1973 CBS special.
Chart position: No. 64.

Songs: "Piano Practicing," "I've Got Rhythm," "Johnny One Note"/"One Note Samba," "Glad to Be Unhappy," "People," "Second Hand Rose," "Don't Rain on My Parade," "Don't Ever Leave Me," monologue/"By Myself," "Come Back to Me," "I Never Have Seen Snow," "Auf dem Wasser zu Singen," "The World Is a Concerto"/"Make Your Own Kind of Music," and "The Sweetest Sounds."

On the TV special, guest star Ray Charles sang "Look What They've Done to My Song," then he and Barbra performed "Cryin' Time." These two songs are not included on the album.

The Streisand-Charles duet shows up on the 1991 *Just for the Record* four-disc set.

Barbra Streisand featuring "The Way We Were" and "All in Love Is Fair"
Columbia 32801. January 1974.
Chart position: No. 1: certified gold, 1974; platinum, 1986.
Grammy Award: Song of the Year ("The Way We Were").
 Songs: "Being at War with Each Other," "Something So Right," "The Best Things You've Ever Done," "The Way We Were," "All in Love Is Fair," "What Are You Doing the Rest of Your Life?", "Summer Me, Winter Me," "Pieces of Dreams," "I've Never Been a Woman Before," and "My Buddy"/"How About Me?"

The Way We Were
Columbia 57381. January 1974. Soundtrack of the 1974 Columbia motion picture.
Chart position: No. 20.
Grammy Awards: Song of the Year and Best Original Motion Picture Score.
 Songs: Barbra sings two versions of "The Way We Were," the one song from the movie.

ButterFly
Columbia 133005. October 1974.
Chart position: No. 13; certified gold.
 Songs: "Love in the Afternoon," "Guava Jelly," "Grandma's Hands," "I Won't Last a Day without You," "Jubilation," "Simple Man," "Life on Mars," "Since I Don't Have You," "Crying Time," and "Let the Good Times Roll."

Funny Lady
Arista 9004. March 1975. Soundtrack of the 1975 Columbia motion picture.
Chart position: No. 6; certified gold.
 Songs: "Blind Date," "More Than You Know," "I Like Him/Her" [with James Caan], "I Found a Million Dollar Baby in a Five and Ten Cent Store," "So Long, Honey Lamb" [with Ben Vereen], "I Got a Code in My Doze," "Clap Hands, Here Comes Charley" [Ben Vereen], "Great Day," "How Lucky Can You Get?", "Isn't This Better?", "Me and My Shadow" [musical interlude for Aquacade], "If I Love Again," and "Let's Hear It for Me."

Lazy Afternoon
Columbia 133815. October 1975.
Chart position: No. 12; certified gold.
  Songs: "Lazy Afternoon," "My Father's Song," "By the Way," "Shake Me, Wake Me," "I Never Had It So Good," "Letters That Cross in the Mail," "You and I," "Moanin' Low," "A Child Is Born," and "Widescreen."

Classical Barbra
Columbia 33452. February 1976.
Chart position: No. 46.
Grammy nominations: Best Classical Vocal Soloist Performance.
  Songs: "Beau Soir," "Brezairola," "Verschwiegene Liebe," "Pavane," "Apres un Reve," "In Trutina," "Laschia ch'io pianga," "Mondnacht," "Dank sie Dir, Herr," and "I Loved You."

A Star Is Born
Columbia 34403. November 1976. Soundtrack of the 1976 Columbia motion picture.
Chart position: No. 1; certified gold, 1976; quadruple platinum, 1984.
Grammy Awards: Song of the Year and Best Female Pop Vocal ("Evergreen").
Grammy nominations: Record of the Year ("Evergreen") and Best Original Film Score.
  Songs: "Watch Closely Now" [Kris Kristofferson], "Queen Bee" [with the Oreos], "Everything," "Lost Inside of You," "Hellacious Acres," "Evergreen," "Woman in the Moon," "I Believe in Love," "Crippled Crow," "With One More Look at You"/"Watch Closely Now," and "Evergreen" [reprise].

Streisand Superman
Columbia 134830. June 1977
Chart position: No. 3; certified gold, 1977; double platinum, 1994.
  Songs: "Superman," "Don't Believe What You Read," "Baby Me, Baby," "I Found You Love," "Answer Me," "My Heart Belongs to Me," "Cabin Fever," "Love Comes from Unexpected Places," "New York State of Mind," and "Lullaby for Myself."

Songbird
Columbia 135375. May 1978.

Chart position: No. 12; certified gold, May 1978; platinum, August 1978. *Grammy nominations:* Best Female Pop Vocal Performance and Song of the Year ("You Don't Bring Me Flowers").

Songs: "Tomorrow," "A Man I Loved," "I Don't Break Easily," "Love Breakdown," "You Don't Bring Me Flowers" [solo], "Honey, Can I Put Your Clothes On?", "One More Night," "Deep in the Night," and "Songbird."

NOTE: "You Don't Bring Me Flowers" on this album is a solo. It was after the release of this album that a Louisville disc jockey created an illegal Streisand-Diamond duet. Columbia put the two singers together and created a real duet, a single that created a sensation. The duet is on the *Greatest Hits, Volume 2* album.

Eyes of Laura Mars

Columbia 35487. July 1978. Soundtrack of the 1978 Columbia motion picture. *Chart position:* No. 125; not available on compact disc.

Song: Barbra sings the theme song "Prisoner" [as a favor to lover Jon Peters, producer of the film].

Barbra Streisand's Greatest Hits, Volume 2

Columbia 35679. November 1978. [Volume 1 was in 1969] *Chart position:* No. 1; certified gold, 1978; quintuple platinum, 1994. *Grammy nominations:* Record of the Year and Best Pop Vocal Performance by a Duo and Group ("You Don't Bring Me Flowers").

Songs: "Evergreen," "Prisoner," "My Heart Belongs to Me," "Songbird," "You Don't Bring Me Flowers" [duet with Neil Diamond], "The Way We Were," "Sweet Inspiration"/"Where You Lead," "All in Love Is Fair," "Superman," and "Stoney End."

The Main Event

Columbia 36115. June 1979. Soundtrack of the 1979 Warner Bros. motion picture. *Chart position:* No. 20; certified gold.

Songs: Barbra sings three different versions of the title song.

Wet

Columbia 236258. October 1979. *Chart position:* No. 7; certified gold, 1980; platinum, 1986.

Songs: "Wet," "Come Rain or Come Shine," "Splish Splash," "On Rainy Afternoons," "After the Rain," No More Tears"/"Enough Is

115

Enough" [duet with Donna Summer], "Niagara," "I Ain't Gonna Cry Tonight," and "Kiss Me in the Rain."

Guilty
Columbia 36750. September 1980.
Chart position: No. 1; certified gold, 1980; quintuple platinum, 1989.
Grammy Award: Best Pop Vocal by Duo or Group (with Barry Gibb).
Grammy nominations: Album of the Year, Record and Song of the Year ("Woman in Love"), Best Female Pop Vocal Performance ("Woman in Love").
   Songs: "Guilty" [duet with Barry Gibb], "Woman in Love," "Run Wild," "Promises," "The Love Inside," "What Kind of Fool" [duet with Barry Gibb], "Life Story," "Never Give Up," and "Make It Like a Memory."

Memories
Columbia 37678. November 1981.
Chart position: No. 6; certified gold, 1982; quadruple platinum, 1991.
   Songs: "Memory," "You Don't Bring Me Flowers" [duet with Neil Diamond], "My Heart Belongs to Me," "New York State of Mind," "No More Tears"/"Enough Is Enough" [duet with Donna Summer], "Comin' In and Out of Your Life," "Evergreen," "Lost Inside of You," "The Love Inside," and "The Way We Were."

Yentl
Columbia 39152. November 1983. Soundtrack of the 1983 MGM/United Artists motion picture.
Chart position: No. 9; certified gold, 1983; platinum, 1983.
Grammy nomination: Best Original Score for a Motion Picture.
   Songs: "Where Is It Written?", "Papa, Can You Hear Me?", "This Is One of Those Moments," "No Wonder," "The Way He Makes Me Feel," "No Wonder" [reprise], "Tomorrow Night," "Will Someone Ever Look at Me That Way?", "No Matter What Happens," "No Wonder" [reprise], "A Piece of Sky," "The Way He Makes Me Feel" [studio version], and "No Matter What Happens" [studio version].

For the record:
The Legend of Barbra Streisand: The Woman and Her Music in Her Own Words

Columbia. 1983. A two-LP set with a one-hour interview—a promotional set to publicize *Yentl*, available only for radio play.

Emotion
Columbia 39480. October 1984.
Chart position: No. 19; certified gold, 1985; platinum, 1987.
  Songs: "Emotion," "Make No Mistake," "He's Mine" [duet with Kim Carnes], "Time Machine," "Best I Could," "Life in the Dark," "Heart Don't Change My Mind," "When I Dream," "You're a Step in the Right Direction," "Clear Sailing," and "Here We Are at Last."

The Broadway Album
Columbia 40092. November 1985.
Chart position: No. 1; certified gold, 1986; quadruple platinum, 1995.
Grammy Awards: Best Female Pop Vocal and Best Arrangement Accompanying Vocal.
Grammy nomination: Album of the Year.
  Songs: "Putting It Together," "If I Loved You," "Something's Coming," "Not While I'm Around," "Being Alive," "I Have Dreamed"/"We Kiss in a Shadow"/"Something Wonderful," "Adelaide's Lament," "Send in the Clowns," "Pretty Woman"/"The Ladies Who Lunch," "Can't Help Lovin' Dat Man," "I Loves You, Porgy"/"Bess, You Is My Woman," and "Somewhere."

One Voice
Columbia 40788. April 1987.
Chart position: No. 9; Awards: platinum.
Grammy nominations: Best Female Pop Vocal Performance, Best Instrumental Arrangement Accompanying Vocal, and Best Performance in a Music Video.
  Songs: "Somewhere," "Evergreen," "Something's Coming," "People," "Send in the Clowns," "Over the Rainbow," "Guilty" [duet with Barry Gibb], "What Kind of Fool" [duet with Barry Gibb], "Papa, Can You Hear Me?", "The Way We Were," "It's a New World," "Happy Days Are Here Again," and "America the Beautiful."

Nuts
Columbia 4087. November 1987. Soundtrack of the 1987 Warner Bros. motion picture.

Streisand rejected the music that had been commissioned and composed the score herself—her first attempt at film music. Columbia put together thirteen minutes of the five main themes and released it as a mini-CD soundtrack.

Till I Loved You.
Columbia 40880. November 1988.
Chart position: No. 10; certified gold, 1989; platinum, 1991.
   Songs: "The Places You Find Love," "On My Way to You," "Till I Loved You" [duet with Don Johnson], "Love Fight," "All I Ask of You," "You and Me for Always," "Why Let It Go?", "Two People," "What Were We Thinking of?", "Some Good Things Never Last," and "One More Time Around."

A Collection . . . Greatest Hits and More
Columbia 45369. October 1989.
Chart position: No. 26; certified gold, 1989; double platinum, 1994.
   Songs: "We're Not Makin' Love Anymore," "Woman In Love," "All I Ask of You," "Comin' In and Out of Your Life," "What Kind of Fool" [duet with Barry Gibb], "The Main Event"/"Fight," Someone That I Used to Love," "By the Way," "Guilty" [duet with Barry Gibb], "Memory," "The Way He Makes Me Feel," and "Somewhere."

Just for the Record . . .
Columbia 44111. September 1991. A four-disc boxed set.
Chart position: No. 38; certified gold, 1991; platinum, 1992.
Grammy nominations: Best Traditional Pop Vocal Performance ("Warm All Over"), and Best Package Design.
   Songs:
Disc one: "You'll Never Know" [Barbra's first amateur recording: a homemade tape recorded when she was thirteen years old], "A Sleepin' Bee," "Moon River," "Miss Marmelstein," "Happy Days Are Here Again." Eight songs, previously unreleased, recorded at The Bon Soir club in 1962: "Keepin' Out of Mischief Now," "I Hate Music," "Nobody's Heart (Belongs to Me)," "Value," "Cry Me a River," "Who's Afraid of the Big Bad Wolf?", ("I Had Myself a) True Love," and "Lover Come Back to Me;" "Spring Can Really Hang You Up the Most," "My Honey's Lovin' Arms," "Any Place I Hang My Hat Is Home," "When the Sun Comes Out," "Be My Guest" [with Judy Garland and Ethel Merman]; and the medleys from TV's *The*

Judy Garland Show of October 20, 1963: "Hooray For Love"/"After You've Gone"/"By Myself"/"'S Wonderful"/"(I Like New York in June) How About You?"/"Lover, Come Back to Me"/"You and the Night and the Music"/"It All Depends on You"/"Get Happy"/"Happy Days Are Here Again."

Disc two: "I'm the Greatest Star," "My Man," and "Auld Lang Syne" [from the December 26, 1966, closing night of *Funny Girl* on Broadway]; "People," "Second Hand Rose" [sung by Barbra's mother], "Second Hand Rose" [sung by Barbra], "He Touched Me," "You Wanna Bet," "House of Flowers"/"Ding, Dong! The Witch Is Dead!," "(Have I Stayed) Too Long at the Fair"/"Look at That Face"/"Starting Here, Starting Now," "A Good Man Is Hard to Find," "Some of These Days," "I'm Always Chasing Rainbows," "Sleep in Heavenly Peace (Silent Night)," "Don't Rain on My Parade," "Funny Girl," "Hello, Dolly," "On a Clear Day (You Can See Forever)," "When You Gotta Go," and "In the Wee Small Hours of the Morning."

Disc three, mainly unreleased tracks: "The Singer," "I Can Do It," "Stoney End," "(They Long To Be) Close to You," "We've Only Just Begun," "Since I Fell For You," "You're the Top" [with Ryan O'Neal], "What Are You Doing the Rest of Your Life?", "If I Close My Eyes," "Between Yesterday and Tomorrow," "Can You Tell the Moment?", "The Way We Were," "Cryin' Time," "God Bless the Child," "A Quiet Thing"/"There Won't Be Trumpets," "Lost Inside of You," "Evergreen," and "Hatikvah."

Disc four: "You Don't Bring Me Flowers" [with Neil Diamond], "The Way We Weren't"/"The Way We Were," "Guilty," "Papa, Can You Hear Me?", "The Moon and I," "A Piece of Sky" [audition tape], "A Piece of Sky" [*Yentl* soundtrack], "I Know Him So Well," "If I Loved You," "Putting It Together," "Over the Rainbow," the theme from the 1987 movie *Nuts* [composed by Barbra], "Here We Are At Last," "Warm All Over," and "You'll Never Know."

The Prince of Tides
Columbia 48627. December 1991. Soundtrack of the 1991 Columbia motion picture.
Chart position: No. 84.
   Songs: "For All We Know" and "Places That Belong to You."

Back to Broadway
Columbia 44189. July 1993.
Chart position: No. 1; certified gold, 1993; double platinum, 1994.
Grammy nominations: Best Traditional Pop Vocal Performance, Best Pop Performance by a Duo or Group ("Music of the Night," with Michael Crawford), and Best Arrangement Accompanying a Vocal ("Luck, Be a Lady," "Some Enchanted Evening").
  Songs: "Some Enchanted Evening," "Everybody Says Don't," "The Music of the Night" [duet with Michael Crawford], "Speak Low," "As If We Never Said Goodbye," "Children Will Listen," and "I Have a Love"/"One Hand, One Heart" [duet with Johnny Mathis], "I've Never Been in Love Before," "Luck Be a Lady," "With One Look," "The Man I Love," and "Move On."

Duets (a Frank Sinatra album)
Capitol 89611. October 1993.
  Sinatra and Streisand sing Gershwin's "I've Got a Crush on You." Others performing in tandem with Sinatra: Kenny G, Gloria Estefan, Bono (of the U2 Group), Tony Bennett, Aretha Franklin. All the tracks were recorded separately, with the duets created in the studio.

Barbra: The Concert
Columbia 66109. September 1994.
Chart position: No. 10; certified gold, 1994; triple platinum, 1997.
Grammy nominations: Best Female Pop Vocal Performance ("Ordinary Miracles") and Best Traditional Pop Vocal Performance (for the album).
Special honor: Lifetime Achievement Award to Barbra Streisand.
  Songs:
Disc one: "As If We Never Said Goodbye," "I'm Still Here"/"Everybody Says Don't"/"Don't Rain on My Parade," "Can't Help Lovin' Dat Man," "I'll Know," "People," "Lover Man," "Will He Like Me?", "He Touched Me," "Evergreen," "The Man That Got Away," and "On a Clear Day (You Can See Forever)."
Disc two: "The Way We Were," "You Don't Bring Me Flowers," "Lazy Afternoon," medley: "Once Upon a Dream"/"When You Wish Upon a Star"/"Someday My Prince Will Come," "Not While I'm Around," "Ordinary Miracles," medley: "Where Is It

120

Written?"/"Papa, Can You Hear Me?"/"Will Someone Ever Look at Me That Way?"/"A Piece of Sky," "Happy Days Are Here Again," "For All We Know," and "Somewhere."

The Mirror Has Two Faces
Columbia 1996. Soundtrack of the 1996 TriStar motion picture.
Chart position: No. 7; certified gold, 1996; platinum, 1997.
Song: "I Finally Found Someone" [with Bryan Adams]. This song was nominated for a Grammy Award on January 6, 1998.

Higher Ground
Columbia 66181. November 1997
Chart position: No. 1; certified gold, 1997; platinum, 1997; double platinum, 1997.
Songs: "I Believe"/"You'll Never Walk Alone," "Higher Ground," "At the Same Time," "Tell Him" [duet with Celine Dion] [Note: The song was nominated for a Grammy Award on January 6, 1998], "On Holy Ground," "If I Could," "Circle," "The Water Is Wide"/"Deep River," "Leading With Your Heart," "Lessons to Be Learned," "Everything Must Change," and "Avinu Malkeinu."

Barbra's Number One Albums to Date
as charted by Billboard's *"The Top Five"*

- *People*—week of October 31, 1964 (five weeks).
- *The Way We Were*—week of March 16, 1974 (two weeks).
- *A Star Is Born*—week of February 12, 1977 (six weeks).
- *Barbra Streisand's Greatest Hits, Volume 2*—week of January 6, 1979 (three weeks).
- *Guilty*—week of October 25, 1980 (three weeks, nonconsecutive).
- *The Broadway Album*—week of January 25, 1986 (three weeks).
- *Back to Broadway*—week of July 17, 1993 (one week).

THE SINGLES

Billboard began in 1894 as a publication for poster printers, bill

121

posters, advertising agents, and secretaries of fairs. Along the way it evolved into a trade paper devoted to music and home entertainment. On July 20, 1949, *Billboard* introduced its Music Popularity Chart, reporting on the best-selling records in America. (The first number one record reported was Frank Sinatra singing Tommy Dorsey's "I'll Never Smile Again.")

The number one record for the week of July 9, 1955, was "Rock Around the Clock" by Bill Haley and the Comets, signaling the arrival of a new era in popular music: the age of rock. On August 4, 1958, *Billboard* began its Hot 100. Forty years later it's still one of the definitive industry charts to what America is buying.

Barbra Streisand has had these number one hits to date:
- *"The Way We Were"*—February 2, 1974.
- *"Evergreen"* (The love theme from *A Star Is Born*)—March 5, 1977.
- *"You Don't Bring Me Flowers,"* duet with Neil Diamond — December 2, 1978.
- *"No More Tears (Enough Is Enough),"* duet with Donna Summer—November 24, 1979.
- *"Woman In Love"*—October 25, 1980.
- *"Guilty,"* duet with Barry Gibb—November 15, 1980

The Singles *Not* on Albums

Barbra Streisand has recorded many singles never on her albums, including a version of "Funny Girl" that was dropped from the 1964 Broadway musical and differs from the rendition in the 1968 movie. The list here includes alternate versions and songs that never made it to an album.

1962 — "Happy Days Are Here Again" and "When the Sun Comes Out"
    — "Lover Come Back to Me" and "My Coloring Book"
1963 — "Happy Days Are Here Again" and "My Coloring Book"
1964 — "I Am Woman"
    — "Funny Girl"
1965 — "My Love"
    — "I Like Him"
1966 — "Les Enfants Qui Pleurant" and "La Mur"
1967 — "Stout-Hearted Men" and "Look"

Two notable profiles: Barbra with Ryan O'Neal in *What's Up, Doc?* (1972), Peter Bogdanovich's largely successful attempt to make a Thirties screwball comedy.

PHOTO COURTESY OF PHOTOFEST

1968 — "Our Corner of the Night" and "He Could Show Me"
— "Funny Girl" and "I'd Rather Be Blue Over You"
— "Don't Rain on My Parade"
1969 — "Frank Mills"
— "Before the Parade Passes By"
1970 — "The Best Thing You've Ever Done"
1971 — "Time and Love"
— "The Best Thing You've Ever Done"
— "Time and Love"
1973 — "The Way We Were"
1974 — "The Way We Were" [different version]
1975 — "How Lucky Can You Get"
1976 — "De Reve en Reverie" ["Evergreen" in French]
— "Sempreverde" ["Evergreen" in Italian]
— "Tema de Amor de 'Nace una Estrella' " ["Evergreen" in Spanish]
1979 — "No More Tears (Enough Is Enough)" with Donna Summer

123

1981 — "Promises" and "Make It Like a Memory"
1984 — "Papa, Can You Hear Me?"
1985 — "Emotion"
1987 — "Promises"
1989 — "We're Not Makin' Love Anymore"
1993 — "Children Will Listen"
1994 — "Ordinary Miracles" [studio] and "Ordinary Miracles" [live]
1996 — "Evergreen" [Spanish version]
1997 — "Tell Him" with Celine Dion [radio edit]

The Songs Never Released

Allison J. Waldman's *Barbra Streisand Scrapbook* (Secaucus, N.J.: Citadel/Carol, 1995) has a list of over fifty songs Barbra has recorded but never released in any form to date. The reasons usually cited are that she was unhappy with the quality of her voice or not satisfied with her own performance.

THE DUETS
WITH LOVERS AND OTHER FRIENDS
[in chronological order]

Judy Garland—Barbra guests on the October 20, 1963, *Judy Garland Show* on CBS-TV. She and Garland perform duets of "Be My Guest," a medley of "Happy Days Are Here Again" and "Get Happy," and then a lengthy medley of "Love" songs. Finally, they team with Ethel Merman for "There's No Business Like Show Business." These are included in *Just For the Record* . . . and on *The Garland Duets* album.

Sydney Chaplin— costar of Broadway's *Funny Girl*. He and Barbra sing "I Want to Be Seen with You" and "You Are Woman." These are on the 1964 original-cast album.

Harold Arlen—Barbra sings "Ding Dong! The Witch Is Dead" with composer Arlen on his 1966 *Harold Sings Arlen (With Friend)* album.

Louis Armstrong—"Hello, Dolly!" The two render a joyous version of the title song in the Harmonia Gardens restaurant/club sequence on the 1969 Twentieth Century-Fox soundtrack of the motion picture.

Burt Bacharach—Barbra appears on his 1971 CBS special. The two of them sing "(They Long to Be) Close to You" and other Bacharach-Hal David songs.

Ray Charles—guest stars on her 1973 CBS-TV special *Barbra Streisand . . . and Other Musical Instruments*. He sings "Look What They've Done To My Song," and he and Barbra join for "Cryin' Time Again."

Neil Diamond—"You Don't Bring Me Flowers" is included on *Barbra Streisand's Greatest Hits, Volume 2* (1978), *Memories* (1981), and *Just for the Record . . .* (1991).

Donna Summer—"No More Tears (Enough Is Enough)," which is on the 1979 *Wet* album and also the 1981 *Memories* disc. It's also on Donna Summer's *On the Radio: Greatest Hits, Volumes 1 & 2*.

Barry Gibb—"What Kind of Fool Am I?" and "Guilty," on the albums *Guilty* (1980), *One Voice* (1987), and *A Collection . . . Greatest Hits and More* (1989).

Kim Carnes—"Make No Mistake, He's Mine," on 1984 *Emotion* album.

Don Johnson—"Till I Loved You," on Barbra's 1988 album of the same name. It's also on Don Johnson's *Let It Roll* album.

The 1991 *Just for the Record . . .* four-disc set includes the duets with Judy Garland, Ray Charles, Harold Arlen, Neil Diamond, Barry Gibb, Burt Bacharach, and Louis Armstrong. It also features "You're the Top" with Ryan O'Neal, from the 1972 Warner Bros. film *What's Up, Doc?*

Michael Crawford—"The Music of the Night," included on the 1993 *Back to Broadway* album.

Johnny Mathis—"I Have a Love"/"One Hand, One Heart" on the 1993 *Back to Broadway* album.

Frank Sinatra—"I've Got a Crush on You" on Frank's 1993 *Duet* album.

Marlon Brando—"I'll Know." On her 1994 concert tour, Barbra sang a fabricated duet with Brando, shown in a film clip from the 1955 MGM/United Artists movie *Guys and Dolls*. Included on the *Barbra: The Concert* album.

Bryan Adams—"I Finally Found Someone." Featured on the 1996 *The Mirror Has Two Faces* album.

Celine Dion—"Tell Him." The duet appeared on the 1997 albums of both stars: Streisand's *Higher Ground*, Dion's *Let's Talk About Love*.

THE MUSIC VIDEOS

1977—*My Heart Belongs to Me*
1980—*Woman in Love*
1982—*Memory*
1983—*The Way He Makes Me Feel*
1983—*Papa, Can You Hear Me?* [film clip from the 1983
      MGM/United Artists motion picture *Yentl*]
1984—*Left in the Dark*
1985—*Emotion*
1985—*Somewhere*
1988—*Till I Loved You*
1989—*We're Not Makin' Love Anymore*
1991—*Places That Belong to You*
1991—*For All We Know*
1994—*As If We Never Said Goodbye*
1994—*Evergreen*
1996—*I Finally Found Someone* [duet with Bryan Adams]
1997—*Tell Him* [duet with Celine Dion]

CHAPTER 11

Barbra
on Television

GUEST APPEARANCES
[in chronological order]

The Jack Paar Show [which would become ***The Tonight Show***] (NBC, April 5, 1961) 60 minutes

Barbra's network television debut. She sings "A Sleepin' Bee."

Guest Host: Orson Bean, while Jack Paar is on vacation. The other guests are writer Gore Vidal and comedian Phyllis Diller.

"Miss Streisand credits her first television appearance to Orson Bean. 'I had worked with him in a nightclub. He asked me to appear on *The Jack Paar Show* while he was the substitute host. If it weren't for him, I might never have gotten any television program" (CBS press release for *My Name Is Barbra*, October 11, 1965).

The Jack Paar Show (NBC, May 22, 1961) 60 minutes

Again with guest host Orson Bean. She sings "Much More" and "I Stayed Too Long at the Fair." *TV Guide* lists her as "Barbara Strysand."

P.M. East (Group W Television) 60 minutes

Host: Mike Wallace.

This was an East Coast late-night talk-variety show—you never knew who was going to show up or what they'd do or say. In other words, it was tailor-made for this kooky Brooklyn girl with the incredible voice. She would sing, she would talk about whatever was on her mind. "Mike Wallace made her the semiresident nut," said *Time* (April 10, 1964). "In each [appearance she] seemed to be straining a little harder to live up to her own axiom of eccentricity. 'I scare you, don't I?' she said to guest David Susskind, the TV producer, one night. 'I'm so far out I'm in'."

The most detailed account of Barbra's *P.M. East* appearances is in Randall Riese's *Her Name Is Barbra* (New York: Birch Lane/Carol, 1993). "I like the fact that you're provoking," Barbra tells Mike Wallace. "Just don't provoke me!"

James Spada's *Streisand: The Woman and the Legend* (Garden City, New York: Dolphin/Doubleday, 1981) has a rare photo of Barbra with Mike Douglas; she's wearing fur-topped boots and a blonde Goldilocks wig (p. 52).

Barbra does six shows in 1961: June 22, July 12, October 13, November 27, December 1, December 21; and seven shows in 1962: January 2, April 6, April 20, May 1, May 4, May 15, and June 1.

Manhattan gay bars offer a two-for-one drink special the nights Barbra Streisand appears on *P.M. East*.

The Joe Franklin Show [a.k.a. ***Memory Lane with Joe Franklin***] (WOR, New York City) 60 minutes
Barbra haunted Joe Franklin's Times Square office with a vengeance, eager to be on his local TV talk show. "I was all set to actually wonder how much she'd charge to haunt a house," said Franklin (Riese, *Her Name Is Barbra*)—until he hears her sing.

Barbra appears on this late-night show three times in autumn of 1961.

The Garry Moore Show (CBS, May 29, 1962) 60 minutes
A Tuesday night primetime variety series. A regular feature was a musical salute to "That Wonderful Year 19—" (with a different year featured each week). Streisand's year was 1929, the year of the stock market crash. Barbra sings for the first time her stunning new interpretation of "Happy Days Are Here Again"—turning a song associated with political rallies into one of sarcasm and pain. There was imme-

diate interest from RCA Records . . . who then convinced themselves that she was uncommercial.

The other guests that night are Robert Goulet and comedians Allen and Rossi.

The Tonight Show (NBC, August 21, 1962) 90 minutes
Groucho Marx is the guest host. Barbra sings "Much More."

The Tonight Show Starring Johnny Carson (NBC, October 4, 1962) 90 minutes
This was Barbra's first appearance with Johnny Carson. They seem to hit it off right away. In a wonderful show of his support, Carson takes the unprecedented step of inviting her back regularly. Barbra appears on November 2, 1962; December 3, 1962; January 2, 1963; February 1, 1963; February 22, 1963; and March 5, 1963.

Twelve years later, Johnny becomes a bitter enemy.

Barbra agrees to appear on the July 9, 1975 *Tonight Show* to promote *Funny Lady* (Columbia, 1975) . . . but changes her mind the day before, without explanation and without apology. Carson tells the audience not to get mad at him but at Barbra: "Streisand will not be here Wednesday night—nor will she be here in the future."

The Ed Sullivan Show (CBS, December 16, 1962) 60 minutes
For her first appearance on the long-running variety showcase, Barbra sings "My Coloring Book" and "Lover, Come Back to Me."

The other guests are Liberace, Xavier Cugat, and Abbe Lane. In addition, Barbra appears on the following dates:
• **March 24, 1963**
   Barbra sings "Cry Me a River." The other guests are Totie Fields, Chubby Checker, and Woody Herman.
• **June 9, 1963**
   Barbra sings "When the Sun Comes Out." The other guests are the McGuire Sisters, Neil Sedaka, and Rip Taylor.
• **April 28, 1969**
• **September 28, 1969**
   Barbra sings a medley from *Hello, Dolly!*: "Hello, Dolly!" "Before the Parade Passes By," and "So Long, Dearie!", all of this from footage that had been taped in July in Las Vegas.
• **September 20, 1970**

129

The Dinah Shore Show (NBC, May 12, 1963) 60 minutes

For the last telecast of this popular variety series (after seven seasons), Dinah's guest stars are Georgia Brown, The Chad Mitchell Trio, Sam Fletcher, and Barbra Streisand.

The Keefe Brasselle Show (aka **Keefe Brasselle's Variety Garden**) (CBS, June 25, 1963) 60 minutes

The premiere is probably the highlight of this four-month series: Barbra sings "Soon It's Gonna Rain" from *The Fantastiks* (1960), and "A Taste of Honey."

Chrysler Presents a Bob Hope Comedy Special (NBC, September 27, 1963) 60 minutes

Barbra, Dean Martin, and Bob Hope appear in a comedy sketch as seedy-looking folk singers. (There's a full-page photo in James Spada's *Streisand: The Woman and the Legend*, p. 51.)

"Straight musical offerings were highlighted by the high voltage performance of Miss Streisand. Her renditions of 'Anywhere I Hang My Hat Is Home' and 'I'm Gonna Find a New Man' were marked by the dramatic intensity which has made this songstress a new hot property" (*Variety*, October 2, 1963).

The Judy Garland Show (CBS, October 20, 1963) 60 minutes

Guest stars: Ethel Merman, the Smothers Brothers, and Barbra Streisand.

Barbra's solos are "Down With Love" and "Bewitched." She and Garland sing rousing duets of "Be My Guest," a medley of "Happy Days Are Here Again" and "Get Happy"; and then a lengthy medley of love songs: "Lover Come Back," "Hooray for Love," etc. Finally, Judy and Barbra team with bombastic Ethel Merman for a brassy "There's No Business Like Show Business."

"There was an extremely harmonic play and a sympatico feeling between [Garland and Streisand]. When sitting on a pair of stools and bantering tunes back and forth, it was a true delight. It provided a vocal highlight of the season even though the current annum is only two weeks old" (*Variety*, October 9, 1963).

"I was always amazed over how she [Judy Garland] mentally rated guests on the show. If she liked and/or respected a given artist, or conversely, if she felt threatened by a performer's immense talent (the

Barbra Streisand guest shot comes to mind), she would pull out all the stops and meet any challenge—real or imagined—head on" (Mel Tormé, *It Wasn't All Velvet, An Autobiography.* New York: Viking, 1988).

What's My Line? (CBS, April 25, 1965) 30 minutes
Barbra appears as the "Mystery Guest," responding in Italian to questions from panelists Tony Randall, Arlene Francis, Bennett Cerf, Dorothy Kilgallen. When Streisand signs in she plugs her upcoming TV special, boldly writing "My Name Is Barbra" on the blackboard.

For the record:

"What Is ———— Really Like?" (WABC-TV, to have aired October 12, 1967)
A story in *Variety* from October 4, 1967, discusses this new TV program, which is to be hosted by Barry Farber. The story indicates that there are problems with the three current subjects—Senator Robert F. Kennedy, Frank Sinatra, and Barbra Streisand. Managers, lawyers, and friends are protesting the shows because of negative or unfriendly remarks by guests. There is no evidence that the shows ever aired.

The Kraft Music Hall: "Don Rickles' Brooklyn" (NBC, September 18, 1968) 60 minutes
Born-in-Brooklyn talent in "an innocuous and sometimes interesting session" (*Variety*, September 25, 1968), with Steve Lawrence, Eydie Gormé, Robert Merrill, and a remote report from Streisand and New York's Mayor John V. Lindsay from that night's premiere of the movie *Funny Girl* (Columbia, 1968).

The Fortieth Annual Academy Awards (ABC, April 10, 1968) 180 minutes
Barbra's first appearance, presenting the Oscar for Best Song to Sammy Davis, Jr., who is accepting for winner Leslie Bricusse ("Talk to the Animals").

The Forty-Second Annual Academy Awards (ABC, April 7, 1970) 180 minutes
Barbra is one of seventeen "Friends of Oscar." She presents the Academy Award for Best Actor to John Wayne for *True Grit* (Paramount, 1969).

131

The Tony Awards (NBC, April 19, 1970) 120 minutes

In 1962, Streisand had been nominated for the Antoinette Perry Award (the Tony) as Best Supporting Actress for *I Can Get It for You Wholesale*, but lost to Phyllis Newman for *Subways Are for Sleeping*.

On this night, Barbra accepts a special Tony award as Star of the Decade.

A World of Love (CBS, December 22, 1970) 60 minutes

Hosts: Bill Cosby, Shirley MacLaine.

A salute to children, in Christmas songs . . . and a pitch for the United Nations Children's Fund. The guests are Julie Andrews, Harry Belafonte, Richard Burton, Florence Henderson, Audrey Hepburn, and Barbra Streisand, who sings "The Best Gift."

Singer Presents Burt Bacharach (CBS, March 14, 1971) 60 minutes

Guest stars: Tom Jones, Rudolf Nureyev, and Barbra Streisand.

Barbra sings a "One Less Bell"/"House Is Not a Home" medley and premieres a new Bacharach song, "Be Aware." She and Bacharach sing "(They Long to Be) Close to You" and other Bacharach-Hal David favorites.

This show won the Emmy Award for 1971's Outstanding Single Program—Variety or Musical (Gary Smith and Dwight Hemion, producers).

Dick Cavett Special: "Funny Girl to Funny Lady." (CBS, March 9, 1975) 60 minutes

Guest stars: Barbra Streisand, James Caan, Muhammad Ali, Frank Gifford, and Eunice Shriver.

Songs: "The Way We Were," "Don't Rain on My Parade," "My Man," "The Man I Love" [duet with James Caan from *Funny Lady*], "It's Only a Paper Moon," "I Like Him (Her)," and "How Lucky Can You Get."

"Live television? What's that? What you saw last night . . . when Barbra Streisand turned a Special Olympics benefit for mentally retarded children . . . into a super, sensational plug for her new movie, *Funny Lady*. Any benefit has to benefit from Miss Streisand's singing, even if one cringes at the promoting of a movie along with such a worthy cause. But in all honesty, looking at Streisand film clips and hearing her sing is a slice of good entertainment" (Kay Gardella, New York *Daily News*, May 10, 1975).

"People who tuned in to see Barbra Streisand were cheated. They sought entertainment, but what they received was plugola" (Frank Swertlow of UPI).

The American Film Institute Salute to William Wyler (CBS, March 14, 1976) 120 minutes

Barbra is one of many participating celebrities. She pays tribute to the veteran director who guided her through her first Hollywood feature film, *Funny Girl* (Columbia, 1968).

The Forty-Ninth Annual Academy Awards (ABC, March 28, 1977) 180 minutes

Barbra's first appearance as a performer on an Oscar show. She sings one of the nominated songs, her own "Evergreen"—which wins for Best Song.

The Entertainer of the Year Awards (CBS, January 18, 1978) 120 minutes

Barbra is one of many celebrities who perform.

The Twenty-Second Grammy Awards (CBS, February 27, 1980) 120 minutes

Barbra sings "You Don't Bring Me Flowers" with Neil Diamond. The song doesn't win anything, but their live performance stops the show—generating a bigger ovation than a rare appearance by Bob Dylan.

I Love Liberty (ABC, March 21, 1982) 120 minutes

A two-hour special sponsored by People for the American Way, an organization founded by TV producer Norman Lear to help counteract the influence of right wing pressure groups.

Barbra tapes her segment in London, where she is working on *Yentl* (MGM/United Artists, 1983), singing a stirring rendition of "America" with the U.S. Air Force band. She is clearly lip-synching the song . . . as she is *out* of synch.

The other participants include Jane Fonda, Mary Tyler Moore, Walter Matthau, Kenny Rogers, and Melissa Manchester.

Funny, You Don't Look 200! (ABC, October 12, 1987) 60 minutes

Host: Richard Dreyfuss.

A variety show: a series of sketches on the effects of the U.S. Constitution on our daily lives. Barbra is one of eighteen guests.

133

Miami Vice (NBC, March 18, 1988) 60 minutes
Barbra does a wordless walk-on in the episode "Badge of Dishonor."
This is done as a favor, or a gag (maybe she needs the money), for the
show's star Don Johnson, her current boyfriend.

Sinatra 75: The Best Is Yet to Come (CBS, December 16, 1990) 120
minutes
Barbra is one of seventeen guests on this marathon two-hour special.

Saturday Night Live (NBC, February 22, 1992) 90 minutes
Barbra stops by NBC in New York City to say hello to the show's
producer, Lorne Michaels, and is persuaded to make a surprise
appearance in the middle of comedian Mike Myers' "Coffee Talk"
segment. No one is more surprised than the announced guests
Madonna and Roseanne.

The Thirty-Fourth Annual Grammy Awards (CBS, February 25,
1992) 120 minutes
Barbra receives a special Grammy Legend Award recognizing her
lifetime achievement as an entertainer.

*An American Reunion: The Fifty-Second Presidential Inaugural
Gala* (CBS, January 19, 1993) 120 minutes
Barbra performs an extended set of songs including the broadcast
premier of her own rendition of "God Bless America," and introduces
President-elect Bill Clinton.
Other celebrities include Bill Cosby, July Collins, Jack Lemmon, and
Kenny Rogers.

SPECIALS

My Name Is Barbra (CBS, April 28, 1965) 60 minutes
Directed by Dwight Hemion. Conception and choreography by Joe
Layton. Music arranged and conducted by Peter Matz.
The one-woman show, boldly omitting the traditional guest stars,
featured Barbra in three acts: as Alice in Wonderful; romping through
the expensive goodies of Bergdorf Goodman's department store while
singing of the simple life; and ending with Barbra in concert.
Songs, Act 1: "My Name Is Barbara," "Much More," "I'm Late,"

"Make Believe," How Does the Wine Taste?", "A Kid Again"/"I'm Five," "Jenny Rebecca," "My Pa," "Sweet Zoo," "Where Is the Wonder?", and "People."

Songs, Act 2: medley: "Second Hand Rose"/"Give Me the Simple Life"/"I Got Plenty of Nothin'"/"Brother, Can You Spare a Dime?"/"Nobody Knows You When You're Down and Out"/"The Best Things in Life Are Free."

Songs, Act 3: "When the Sun Comes Out," "Why Did I Choose You?", "Lover, Come Back to Me," "I Am Woman," "Don't Rain on My Parade," "The Music That Makes Me Dance," "My Man," and "Happy Days Are Here Again."

"The most enchanting, tingling TV hour of the season" (*Time*, April 30, 1965).

"She has the force of a bulldozer and, at times, the stridency of an ambulance siren" (Ben Gross, New York *Daily News*, April 29, 1965).

"The off-beat, perverse quality of this funny little girl with a big voice was caught by TV cameras while Miss Streisand, cool, confident and understandably pleased with her hour—and it was a triumph for her—proved that she can shine on television" (Paul Gardner, *New York Times*, April 29, 1965).

[The title is derived from a Leonard Bernstein song, "My Name Is Barbara," written in 1943 as part of a song cycle titled "I Hate Music."]

Color Me Barbra (CBS, March 30, 1966) 60 minutes

Produced by Dwight Hemion. Directed by Joe Layton. Music arranged and conducted by Peter Matz.

A second one-woman show, again using the three-act format: singing to animals in a circus dream sequence, wandering through the masterpieces of the Philadelphia Museum of Art, and ending with Barbra in concert.

Songs, Act 1: "Draw Me a Circle," "Yesterdays," "One Kiss," "The Minute Waltz," "Gotta Move," "Non, C'est Rien," and "Where or When."

Songs, Act 2: medley: "Animal Crackers in My Soup"/"Funny Face"/"That Face"/"They Didn't Believe Me"/"Were Thine That Special Face"/"I've Grown Accustomed to Her Face"/"Let's Face the Music and Dance"/"Sam, You Made the Pants Too Long"/"What's New, Pussycat?"/"Who's Afraid of the Big Bad Wolf?"/"Small World"/"Try

135

to Remember"/"Spring Again"/"(Have I Stayed) Too Long at the Fair"/"Look at That Face."

Songs, Act 3: "Any Place I Hang My Hat Is Home," "It Had to Be You," "C'est Si Bon," "Where Am I Going?", and "Starting Here, Starting Now."

"Campier and even more ambitious than her TV debut. Streisand's skits can be distracting, but her gall in presenting herself at age twenty-four as a museum piece startles, even while her voice offers all the evidence she needs" (Jim Farber, New York *Daily News*, June 20, 1994, reviewing the video release of the show).

"The most inventive and skillfully produced hour of the TV season" (Bob Williams, *New York Post*, March 31, 1966).

"She did variations on the formula of her first show and, if anything, topped herself" (John S. Wilson, *New York Times*, March 31, 1966).

"A one-woman tour de force of song and sex appeal" (*Newsweek*, March 28, 1966).

The Belle of 14th Street (CBS, October 11, 1967) 60 minutes
Produced by Dwight Hemion. Directed by Joe Layton. Music arranged and conducted by Peter Matz.

Costars: Jason Robards, Jr., John Bubbles, Lee Allen, and the Beef Trust Girls.

Songs: "I Don't Care," "Alice Blue Gown," "We're Two (Three, Four, Five) Americans" [with Robards and Allen], "Liebestraum," "Mother Machree," "Hark! I Hear Them" [adapted from Shakespeare's *The Tempest*], "My Melancholy Baby," "Everybody Loves My Baby (But My Baby Don't Love Nobody But Me)," "A Good Man Is Hard to Find," "Some of These Days," "How About Me?", "I'm Always Chasing Rainbows," "My Buddy," and "Put Your Arms Around Me, Honey."

Also: "You're the Apple of My Eye" and "I'm Going South" [sung by others].

Going for something different, Barbra's third TV special is a re-creation of a turn-of-the-century vaudeville revue. She sings favorites like "Alice Blue Gown" and the operatic "Leibestraum." She and Robards do a scene from Shakespeare's *The Tempest* (which many viewers found tiresome). John Bubbles appears in rooster feathers and chicken feet (which most viewers found racist).

The *New York Times* thought the show was "an embarrassing outing, a concoction of deranged productions" (October 12, 1967).

"In the show's latter half, it was Streisand solo lining out the music hall oldies as la Belle of 14th Street, and it was this sequence in which the production—and its star—came off best. It's something of a show just digging the closeups on that personalized Streisand mug. At least part of the admiration is for the fact that she's resisted all that nose bob advice" (*Variety*, October 4, 1967).

Barbra Streisand: A Happening in Central Park (CBS, September 15, 1968) [taped live on June 17, 1967—the airing of this performance was held up by CBS to coincide with the opening of Barbra's film of *Funny Girl* in 1968] 60 minutes

Produced by Robert Shereer. Music director: Mort Lindsay. Costumes by Irene Sharaff.

Songs: "The Nearness of You," "Down with Love," "Love Is Like a Newborn Child," "Cry Me a River," "I Can See It," "Love Is a Bore," "He Touched Me," "I'm All Smiles," "Value," "Marty the Martian," "Natural Sounds," "Second Hand Rose," "People," "Sleep in Heavenly Peace (Silent Night)," and "Happy Days Are Here Again."

Barbra performs in a free concert that attracts 135,000 people to the famed Manhattan Park. She's apprehensive, if not terrified, because someone's called in a death threat. (It's less than two weeks after the Arab-Israeli "Six-Day War" and here she is making a movie, *Funny Girl*, with Egyptian actor Omar Sharif.) She forgets lyrics. This is the last time she'll sing in public for nearly twenty years.

"Against the immensity of the great outdoors with those skyline and treetop backdrops, the one-of-a-kind stylist, slim as she is, seems to overpower that environment at times" (*Variety*, September 10, 1968).

"Undeniably, Miss Streisand is an electric individual for those eager to meet her more than halfway, but when it comes to really raising the house, the requisite drive and personality have not yet come to the fore. In time these qualities no doubt will emerge, and they will not be unimportant. . . . That she can display continuing growth amid all the burdens of immediate stardom is an encouraging omen" (Jack Gould, *New York Times*, September 16, 1968).

Barbra Streisand . . . and Other Musical Instruments (CBS, November 2, 1973) 60 minutes

Guest stars: Ray Charles, Dominic Savage. Concept by Ken and Mitzie Welch. Directed by Dwight Hemion.

Songs: "Piano Practicing," "I've Got Rhythm," "Johnny One Note"/"One Note Samba," "Glad to Be Unhappy," medley: "People"/"Second Hand Rose"/"Don't Rain on My Parade," "Don't Ever Leave Me," monologue/"By Myself," "Come Back to Me," "I Never Have Seen Snow," "Auf dem Wasser zu Singen," "The World Is a Concerto"/"Make Your Own Kind of Music," "The Sweetest Sounds," "Look What They've Done to My Song," and "Cryin' Time Again."

Barbra's fifth TV special and the last under her CBS network pact. She has 150 musicians from around the world, playing an amazing variety of instruments, but this is seen as little more than a gimmick. She is joined by Ray Charles for two numbers. She ends with a "Concerto for Voice and Appliances," finding music in household appliances.

"Barbra makes a big stretch—playing music from around the world—and plotzes bad" (Jim Farber, New York *Daily News*, June 20, 1994). "While it would be difficult to fault Streisand's voice, it is less difficult to fault her human quality—it is sorely lacking. She turns herself on, but she manipulates a song rather than sings it" (*Variety*, November 14, 1973).

"[The program] is overproduced, over-orchestrated and overbearing to the point of esthetic nausea. The effect prompted thoughts of a meal consisting entirely of whipped cream or, more precisely, a synthetic 'substitute topping'" (John J. O'Connor, *New York Times*, November 2, 1973).

"The only time her singing warmed up was in 'Cryin' Time' with Ray Charles, and during that song there was a moment when he was singing and she was harmonizing, listening to him too charmingly, her fingers busily toying on the piano—dear God, she was stealing scenes from a blind man" (Pauline Kael, *The New Yorker*, March 17, 1975).

The Stars Salute Israel at 30 (ABC, Los Angeles. May 8, 1978) 120 minutes

Host: Barbra Streisand.

Accompanied by Zubin Mehta and the Los Angeles Philharmonic, Barbra sings "People," "Tomorrow," and "Happy Days Are Here Again." She also performs "Hatikvah," the Israeli national anthem, and interviews Israeli Prime Minister Golda Meir via telephone and satellite.

Other guests include Mikhail Baryshnikov, Henry Fonda, Gene Kelly, Dean Martin, Paul Newman, and Joanne Woodward.

Putting It Together—The Making of the Broadway Album (HBO, January 11, 1986) 60 minutes

Interviewer: William Friedkin. *Guest artists:* Sydney Pollack, David Geffen, and Ken Sylk. *Executive producer:* Barbra Streisand. Produced by Joni Rosen. Music arranged and conducted by Peter Matz.

"A ludicrous indulgence. Babs restages her supposed battles with recent company 'suits' over releasing her Broadway record (as if that posed a commercial risk). A puffy Q & A session with the singer should sicken all but Linda Richmond styles" (Jim Farber, New York *Daily News,* June 20, 1994).

Streisand comments during the program: "I consider myself an actress. I don't sing a song I can't act."

Barbra Streisand: One Voice (HBO, December 27, 1986) [taped September 6, 1986] 60 minutes

Guest stars: Robin Williams and Barry Gibb.

Executive producer: Marilyn Bergman. *Director:* Dwight Hemion. *Musical producer:* Richard Baskin. *Musical director and conductor:* Randy Kerber.

Songs: "Somewhere," "Evergreen," "Something's Coming," "People," "Send in the Clowns," "Over the Rainbow," "Guilty" [duet with Barry Gibb], "What Kind of Fool" [duet with Barry Gibb], "Papa, Can You Hear Me?", "The Way We Were," "It's a New World," "Happy Days Are Here Again," and "America the Beautiful."

A benefit concert filmed on her Malibu, California, estate to raise money for Democratic congressional candidates. In between songs, she talks about the environment and other political issues.

Barbra Streisand: The Tour of the Century (E! Entertainment, April 20, 1994) 60 minutes

Host: Steve Kmetko of E! News Daily.

A cable special featuring both backstage and onstage footage as Streisand prepares for her kick-off concert in London, the opening of her 1994 world concert tour. Also included are scenes from the 1993 New Year's Eve concert in Las Vegas.

Barbra: The Concert (HBO, August 21, 1994) 150 minutes

Production conceived and directed by Barbra Streisand. Produced for television by Streisand and Dwight Hemion. Directed for television by Hemion. Written by Alan and Marilyn Bergman. Music arranged and conducted by Marvin Hamlisch.

Songs: "As If We Never Said Goodbye," medley: "I'm Still Here"/"Everybody Says Don't"/"Don't Rain on My Parade," "Can't Help Lovin' Dat Man," "I'll Know," "People," "Lover Man," "Will He Like Me?", "He Touched Me," "Evergreen," "That Man That Got Away," "On a Clear Day (You Can See Forever)," "The Way We Were," "You Don't Bring Me Flowers," "Lazy Afternoon," Disney medley: "Once Upon a Dream"/"When You Wish Upon a Star"/"Someday My Prince Will Come," "Not While I'm Around," "Ordinary Miracles," medley: "Where Is It Written?"/"Papa, Can You Hear Me?"/"Will Someone Ever Look at Me That Way?"/"A Piece of Sky," "Happy Days Are Here Again," "For All We Know," "Somewhere," and "What Are You Doing the Rest of Your Life."

"One of the super-duper TV events of the decade. An enthralling record of the live event" (Tom Shales, *Washington Post*, August 22, 1964).

"A flawless transition of a taut live performance into an equally compelling TV show" (*Daily Variety*, August 21, 1964).

Barbra's Specials on Videocassette

The following TV specials are available on home video:

My Name Is Barbra, CBS/Fox Music Video (1965)

Color Me Barbra, CBS/Fox Music Video (1966)

A *Happening in Central Park*, CBS/Fox Music Video (1968)

Putting It Together: The Making of the Broadway Album,
  CBS/Fox Music Video (1986)

One Voice, CBS/Fox Music Video (1986)

Barbra: The Concert (the video release is *Barbra the Concert/Live at the Arrowhead Pond*), Columbia Music Video (1994)

INTERVIEWS

The Today Show (NBC) 120 minutes
- April 4, 1962
- February 21–22, 1975. Interviewed by Barbara Walters.
- December 5–9, 1983
- September 15–17, 1986. A three-part interview with feminist and *Ms.* magazine editor Gloria Steinem sitting in for cohost Jane Pauley.
- November 18–20, 1987
- December 16–18, 1991
- November 12–13, 1996

For the record:

Talk show host David Frost taped a ninety-minute interview with Streisand in 1970 that never aired. The problem was that Frost's show was on the Metromedia network. CBS pointed out that Barbra was under contract to them, so the interview unfortunately was shelved.

The Barbara Walters Special (ABC, December 14, 1976) 60 minutes

The debut of Walters celebrity interview program. Timed to coincide with the opening of *A Star Is Born* (Warner Bros., 1976). Walters interviews Barbra and lover and coproducer Jon Peters, and President-elect Jimmy Carter and wife Roslyn.

Before agreeing to this appearance, Barbra demanded final cut. Walters agreed but later swore she would never again give control to a guest.

"It seemed strange that Barbara Walters would ask the same questions of a movie queen and her consort as she did of a President-elect and his wife, but the banality was dispensed equally" (*Variety*, December 17, 1976).

20/20: "Papa, Watch Me Fly" (ABC, November 17, 1983) 60 minutes

A one-hour interview with correspondent Geraldo Rivera, timed to the release of *Yentl* (MGM/United Artists, 1983).

In *TV Guide* (November 12, 1983), Rivera promises there will be no ground rules, that "[Barbra] was ready and willing to answer questions as tough as any I might ask for . . . [in] one of my investigative reports."

Tom Shales of the *Washington Post* (November 17, 1983) wasn't impressed with Geraldo's announced toughness. He wrote: "Rivera . . .

goes from groveling obsequity to a state of high unctuousness in the course of the program. Streisand merits so much attention because 'she is much more than a show business star,' she is 'a significant part of our country's cultural history.' In fact, the hour may be the longest movie plug in our cultural history."

Tough guy Geraldo neglects to mention that he and Barbra have the same manager—Jon Peters (Shaun Considine: *Barbra Streisand: The Woman, The Myth, The Music.* New York: Delacorte, 1985).

Scenes of Barbra at work on the film make up the best part of the show.

The Barbara Walters Special (ABC, September 13, 1985) 60 minutes

Nine years after her first Walters interview, the two talk about *Yentl* and her breakup with Jon Peters.

60 Minutes (CBS, November 24, 1991) 60 minutes

Mike Wallace produces an unexpected emotional response from Streisand as he asks about the early days of her career and her relationship with her parents.

Her stepfather? "This was not a nice man," she tells Wallace, fighting tears. She's tearful again when Wallace quotes a comment Streisand's mother made about her: "She hasn't time to be close to anyone."

Mike recalls when Barbra was a guest on his *P.M. East* show back in the 1960s.

Mike: "I really didn't like you back thirty years ago, and I don't think you liked me either."

Barbra: "I thought you were mean, very mean."

Mike: "You were totally self-absorbed."

Barbra: "Wait, wait, wait, I resent this. I resent this."

The *Washington Post* (November 23, 1991) described the interview as "a very compelling confrontation between two egomaniacs."

Larry King Live (CNN, February 6, 1992) 60 minutes

Barbra appears to promote her new film *The Prince of Tides* (Columbia, 1991).

20/20 (ABC, November 19, 1993) 60 minutes

An interview with Barbara Walters. In response to whether she is hard on herself and on others in her desire to get things right, Streisand says: "I have a long way to go. I have a lot to learn. I want to

142

Striking a pose for *Barbra Streisand . . . and Other Musical Instruments* (1973), her fifth and final and least successful CBS-TV special. Here she sings "One Note Samba" with East Indian instruments.
PHOTO COURTESY OF PHOTOFEST

feel like I— I've got to help better the world in some way. I've got to be of service, because this enriches my soul . . . it makes me feel good. But I also wish I were more compassionate, that I were more loving."

The Late Show with David Letterman (CBS, June 28, 1994) 60 minutes
David complains about how difficult it is to get tickets to Barbra's show at Madison Square Garden . . . when Barbra suddenly appears

with a pair of tickets for Dave. He later gives them to a woman in the front row of the audience.

Larry King Live (CNN, June 6, 1995) 60 minutes

An hour interview, mainly discussing her political interests. She criticizes Republican senator and presidential aspirant Bob Dole and the Republicans who attack Hollywood. She denies that she'll run for office, saying people "confuse my political passion and my political ambition." Why do people call her tough and controlling? "There's a need to discredit the accomplishments of strong, competent women."

Postscript: It's amazing that, in this day of inflated multimillion dollar movie budgets, no one has picked up on Streisand's comment about making *Yentl*: "I wanted the actors and actresses to have beautiful underwear. So, even though the audiences don't see it, they feel it—a sense of the period."

The Oprah Winfrey Show (CBS, November 11, 1996) 60 minutes

Streisand appears in order to talk about her new movie, *The Mirror Has Two Faces* (TriStar, 1996). It was a smart decision, as Oprah doesn't shut up about the movie—she shows clips, she raves about it to Barbra, she practically begs viewers to go see it.

This show gives Oprah her highest ratings since 1994, when her guest was John F. Kennedy, Jr.

Dateline NBC (NBC, November 12, 1996) 60 minutes

Jane Pauley asks the usual questions about Barbra's early success, perfectionism, not remarrying, etc. Barbra: "Jane, I swear to God, why don't you ask me about my movie? Why don't you talk about *The Mirror Has Two Faces*? It gets too personal, this stuff!"

20/20 (ABC, November 14, 1997) 60 minutes

Barbara Walters is awarded the first interview with Barbra and James (at long last love!) Brolin. "For the first time in my life I'm not afraid to love," says fifty-five-year-old Streisand.

The Rosie O'Donnell Show (Syndicated, November 21, 1997) 60 minutes

The Streisand-Brolin Road Show spends the full hour onstage with Rosie, who is emotionally overcome. Rosie has had the set's furniture rearranged so Barbra will be photographed from her favored left side. O'Donnell's ratings for this show are huge.

CHAPTER 12

A Hymn to Her: The Films of Barbra Streisand

*"Well, honestly, it's a little too much of you
—they don't want you in every scene."*
—Joe Gillis evaluating Norma Desmond's *Salome* screenplay in
Sunset Boulevard (Paramount, 1950)

THE FILMS

Funny Girl (Columbia Pictures, 1968) 155 minutes, G-rated
   Credits: A Rastar Productions Picture. Producer, Ray Stark; director, William Wyler; musical numbers directed by Herbert Ross; screenplay, Isobel Lennart; based on the play with music by Jule Styne, lyrics by Bob Merrill, book by Isobel Lennart; production design, Gene Callahan; set decoration, William Kiernan; costume design, Irene Sharaff; hairstyling, Vivienne Walker, Virginia Darcy; sound supervisor, Charles J. Rice; sound, Arthur Piantadosi, Jack Solomon; cinematography, Harry Stradling; supervising film editor, Robert Swink; editors, Maury Winetrobe, William Sands.
   Cast: Barbra Streisand (*Fanny Brice*); Omar Sharif (*Nick Arnstein*); Kay Medford (*Rose Brice*); Anne Francis (*Georgia James*); Walter Pidgeon (*Florenz Ziegfeld*); Lee Allen (*Eddie Ryan*); Mae Questel (*Mrs. Strakosh*); Gerald Mohr (*Branca*); Frank Faylen (*Keeney*).

Music: Jule Styne; lyrics, Bob Merrill. "My Man" music by Maurice Yvain; "Second Hand Rose" by James F. Hanley and Grant Clarke; "I'd Rather Be Blue" by Fred Fisher and Billy Rose.

Songs: "I'm the Greatest Star," "If a Girl Isn't Pretty" [sung by friends of Franny's mother], "Roller Skate Rag," "I'd Rather Be Blue Over You (Than Happy with Somebody Else)," "His Love Makes Me Beautiful," "People," "You Are Woman, I Am Man" [with Omar Sharif], "Don't Rain on My Parade," "Sadie, Sadie," "The Swan," "Funny Girl," and "My Man."

The Story: The rise to stardom of Fanny Brice (1891–1951), legendary entertainer who can stop shows both with her broad vaudeville comedy and her torch songs of lost love. Fanny loves dashing gambler Nick Arnstein, knowing it can never work.

Review (Pro): "Miss Streisand has matured into a complete performer and delivered the most accomplished, original and enjoyable musical-comedy performance that has ever been captured on film." — Joseph Morgenstern (*Newsweek*, September 30, 1968)

Review (Con): "As I watched the film go to pieces and crumble around Miss Streisand's shapely legs in the second half, I felt sorry both for Miss Streisand and for the audience. We were both being cheated. We are presented with an overblown, irritatingly fake Hollywood production." — Donald J. Mayerson (*The Villager*, October 10, 1968)

Of Note: The show's composer, Jule Styne (1905–1994), felt this was the best movie ever made from one of his musicals, but objected to the inclusion of "My Man." When she sang it at the end, said Styne, it made the character seem weak and self-pitying—which Fanny Brice never was.

Financial Statement: Rentals from *Funny Girl* were $26,325,000.

[Note: Statistics here, and in all further entries, are from *Variety*'s "All-Time Film Rental Champions" chart. Film rentals are monies paid to the distributor (not box-office grosses), for United States and Canada rentals. The *Variety* chart lists only those feature films paying four million dollars or more in domestic rentals.]

Hello, Dolly! (Twentieth Century-Fox, 1969) 146 minutes, G-rated
Credits: A Chenault Productions, Inc., Picture. Producer, Ernest

Lehman; director, Gene Kelly; associate producer, Roger Edens; dance and musical numbers staged by Michael Kidd; screenplay, Ernest Lehman; based on the musical written by Michael Stewart, which was based on the play by Thornton Wilder; production design, John De Cuir; art direction, Jack Martin Smith, Herman Blumenthal; set decoration, Walter M. Scott, George Hopkins, Raphael Bretton; costumes, Irene Sharaff; hairstyling, Edith Lindon; sound supervisor, James Corcoran; cinematography, Harry Stradling; editor, William Reynolds.

Cast: Barbra Streisand (*Dolly Levi*); Walter Matthau (*Horace Vandergelder*); Michael Crawford (*Cornelius Hackl*); Louis Armstrong (*orchestra leader*); Marianne McAndrew (*Irene Malloy*); E. J. Peaker (*Minnie Fay*); Danny Lockin (*Barnaby Tucker*); Joyce Ames (*Ermengarde*); Tommy Tune (*Ambrose Kemper*); Fritz Feld (*Fritz*).

Music and Lyrics: Jerry Herman; music scored and conducted by Lennie Hayton, Lionel Newman.

Songs: "Just Leave Everything to Me," "It Takes a Woman" [Walter Matthau], "It Takes a Woman" [Streisand], "Put on Your Sunday Clothes" [ensemble], "Ribbons Down My Back" [Marianne McAndrew], "Dancing," "Before the Parade Passes By," "Elegance" [ensemble], "Love Is Only Love," "Hello, Dolly!" [with the Harmonia Gardens waiters and then Louis Armstrong], "It Only Takes a Moment" [Michael Crawford and Marianne McAndrew], "So Long, Dearie," and finale [ensemble].

The Story: In Yonkers, New York, in the late 1800s, matchmaker Dolly Levi is hired to find a pretty wife for the wealthy merchant Horace Vandergelder . . . but then decides she wants him for herself.

Reviews (Pro): "Barbra Streisand, the umpteenth Dolly, is magnificent as always in a role that apparently brings out the best in those who attempt it. And the best of Barbra Streisand has got to be the best there is." — Joe Rosen (*New York Morning Telegraph*, December 17, 1969)

"One shudders to think where Hollywood musicals would be at this moment without Barbra Streisand." — Gary Arnold (*Washington Post*, December 20, 1969)

Review (Con): "The star, a fine if limited comedienne, impersonates Dolly as a teen-age Mae West, circling around the role and finding laughs occasionally, but never quite committing herself to it." — Vincent Canby (*New York Times*, December 17, 1969)

147

Of Note: A number of actresses were considered for the secondary but important role of Irene Molloy, among them Phyllis Newman, Yvette Mimieux, and Ann-Margret. The unknown Marianne McAndrew was chosen.

When Streisand was signed to play Dolly, there was widespread alarm that, at twenty-five, she was far too young for the role. Ironically, when Carol Channing was contracted to star in the original 1964 Broadway musical, there was concern that, at forty-three, she was too young! The musical role had been written with fifty-six-year-old Ethel Merman in mind.

Financial Statement: Rentals from *Hello, Dolly!* were $15,200,000.

On a Clear Day You Can See Forever (Paramount Pictures, 1970)
129 minutes, G-rated

Credits: Producer, Howard W. Koch; director, Vincente Minnelli; screenplay, Alan Jay Lerner; based on the musical play with lyrics and book by Alan Jay Lerner; choreography, Howard Jeffrey; production design, John De Cuir; set decoration, George Hopkins, Ralph Bretton; contemporary costumes by Arnold Scaasi; period costumes by Cecil Beaton; hairstyling, Frederick Glaser; sound, Benjamin Winkler, Elden Ruberg; cinematography, Harry Stradling; editor, David Bretherton.

Cast: Barbra Streisand (*Daisy Gamble/Melinda Tentrees*); Yves Montand (*Dr. Marc Chabot*); Bob Newhart (*Dr. Mason Hume*); Larry Blyden (*Warren Pratt*); Simon Oakland (*Dr. Conrad Fuller*); Jack Nicholson (*Tad Pringle*); John Richardson (*Robert Tentrees*); Pamela Brown (*Mrs. Fitzherbert*).

Music: Burton Lane; lyrics, Alan Jay Lerner; music supervised, arranged, and conducted by Nelson Riddle.

Songs: "Hurry, It's Lovely Up Here!", "On a Clear Day (You Can See Forever)," "Love With All the Trimmings," "Melinda," "Go to Sleep," "He Isn't You," "What Did I Have That I Don't Have?", "Come Back to Me," "On a Clear Day" [Montand], and "On a Clear Day" [Streisand].

Story: In present-day New York City, Daisy Gamble goes to a psychology professor who uses hypnosis to stop her cigarette smoking. Under hypnosis Daisy regresses to nineteenth-century England, where she is the elegant Melinda Tentrees. The

From Act II, scene two, of the 1962 Broadway musical *I Can Get It for You Wholesale*, Barbra sings "Miss Marmelstein."

Photo courtesy of Photofest

Streisand poses with a soulmate—Queen Nefertiti of Egypt—in the Philadelphia Museum of Art. This is from her second CBS-TV special, *Color Me Barbra* (1966).

Photo courtesy of Photofest

Barbra relaxes (if that's possible) on the circus set of *Color Me Barbra* (1966). She sings "Sam, You Made the Pants Too Long" to penguins, and poses as Nefertiti.

Photo courtesy of The Everett Collection

Barbra as "The Belle of 14th Street" in her 1967 TV special of the same name. Viewers like this re-creation of a vaudeville revue best when she just stands and sings old favorites.

Photo courtesy of Photofest

From the movie *Funny Girl* (1968), Streisand as Fanny Brice, a Jewish waif on New York City's Lower East Side —with two-inch Mandarin fingernails which she refused to trim.

Photo courtesy of Photofest

In *Funny Girl* (1968), Fanny
Brice (Streisand) takes Nick
Arnstein (Omar Sharif) to a
block party in her old neighborhood. A few minutes after this,
they'll sing "People."

Photo courtesy of
The Everett Collection

Auditioning for
Keeney's Music Hall
in *Funny Girl* (1968),
Barbra as Fanny Brice
proclaims "I'm the
Greatest Star!"
Photo courtesy of
The Everett Collection

At a 1968 free concert in New York City before 135,000 people, what they didn't see was that Barbra was terrified—someone had called in a death threat. Gown by Irene Sharaff.

Photo courtesy of Photofest

Barbra as Melinda Tentrees in one of Cecil Beaton's sumptuous gowns for *On a Clear Day You Can See Forever* (1970), the first known musical about reincarnation.

Photo courtesy of Photofest

An offcamera photo from *On a Clear Day You Can See Forever* (1970). The film made millions despite negative reviews.

Photo courtesy of
The Everett Collection

Barbra models one of her costumes from the African fantasy sequence in *Up the Sandbox* (1972), most of which ended up on the cutting room floor.
Photo courtesy of The Everett Collection

The profile that launched a thousand quips. Barbra is an older and wiser Fanny Brice in *Funny Lady* (1975)—but her mind was on lover Jon Peters.
Photo courtesy of Photofest

An understandably pensive Barbra watches over *A Star Is Born* (1976). She's the star, executive producer, contributing composer, and is credited with "musical concepts" and for providing her own clothes.

Photo courtesy of Photofest

Some viewers felt Barbra was just mooning around in *The Main Event* (1979). Others felt her butt slowed the movie down. (See chapter 12 for the critical response.)

Photo courtesy of Photofest

Barbra performs at the January 19, 1993, inauguration gala, then lets President-elect Clinton have the microphone. It's on this occasion that Streisand meets Clinton's mother, Virginia Kelly. They became very close.

Photo courtesy of Reuters Amy Sancetta/Archive Photos

Barbra's first concert tour in twenty-eight years begins on May 10, 1994, at the USAir Arena in Landover, Maryland, near Washington, D.C. Top ticket price is $350. Someone dubs the tour "My Name Is Brazen."

Photo courtesy of Reuters Stephen Jaffe/Archive Photos

Barbra defends the role of entertainers as political activists in a 1995 speech at Harvard University. She became furious with newsman Peter Jennings when he wouldn't deny rumors that he helped write her speech.

Photo courtesy of Reuters
Jim Bourg/Archive Photos

Barbra and James Brolin arrive at the Ziegfeld Theatre for the New York City premiere of *The Mirror Has Two Faces* (1996). There was no report of anybody shoving anybody.

Photo courtesy of Reuters
Fred Prouser/Archive Photos

professor falls in love with the Melinda version of his patient.

Review (Pro): "She [Streisand] is so fine that if I didn't know she was not terribly good at lip-sync, I would suspect someone else was reading her lines." — Vincent Canby (*New York Times*, June 18, 1970)

Reviews (Con): "Miss Streisand progresses pretty remarkably as an actress, while the movie around her keeps regressing, back through the Technicolored mists of time, to some of the dreariest, fustiest, mustiest habits of Hollywood's great musical-comedy era." — Joseph Morgenstern (*Newsweek*, June 29, 1970)

In her early scenes, she seems "like Jerry Lewis in drag." — (*Time*, January 29, 1970)

Of Note: Cecil Beaton designed the lavish period costumes for the film, while Arnold Scaasi did the costumes for the modern scenes—including a black chiffon pajama outfit rejected for this movie but which Barbra wore to the 1969 Academy Award ceremony. It was shockingly see-through to everyone who saw it, but Scaasi insisted it only *looked* that way.

Financial Statement: Rentals from *On a Clear Day You Can See Forever* were $5,350,000.

The Owl and the Pussycat (Columbia Pictures, 1970) 95 minutes, R-rated

Credits: Producer, Ray Stark; director, Herbert Ross; screenplay, Buck Henry; based on the play by Bill Manhoff; production design, John Robert Lloyd; art direction, Robert Wightman, Philip Rosenberg; costumes, Ann Roth; hairstyling, Robert Grimaldi; sound, Arthur Piantadosi, Dennis Maitland; cinematography, Harry Stradling, Andrew Laszlo; editor, John F. Burnett.

Cast: Barbra Streisand (*Doris*); George Segal (*Felix*); Robert Klein (*Barney*); Allen Garfield (*owner of dress shop*); Roz Kelly (*Eleanor*).

Music: composed and arranged by Richard Halligan; lyrics by Blood, Sweat and Tears; performed by Blood, Sweat and Tears.

The Story: A broad romantic comedy, set in New York City, about a street-smart hooker and an uptight would-be writer. They shed their facades to face life together.

Review (Pro): "The most amazing comic energy seen on the screen in a very long time." — Jack Kroll (*Newsweek*, November 16, 1970)

Review (Con): "She really ought to be called Barbra Strident. She comes on harsh and grating, seeking to win us by being unabashed about it. One reason she does, I think, is panic. *Funny Girl* fit her like a second skin, but then, bereft of Fanny Brice in the two musicals that followed, she grabbed a lot of other imitations to support her out there in the Brice-less cold. In her latest comedy, increasingly desperate, she leans on all the crassness she considers surefire, like a comic running out of material who can at least drop his pants." — Stanley Kauffmann (*The New Republic*, December 5, 1970)

Of Note: The original 1964 stage version starred Alan Alda and the African American actress Diana Sands, who had appeared onstage with Barbra back in 1961 in *Another Evening with Harry Stoones*.

Veteran cinematographer Harry Stradling (1901–1970) died during production. He had played a major part in the transformation of Streisand into a screen star by creatively finding the most flattering way to light and photograph her onscreen.

Financial Statement: Rentals from *The Owl and the Pussycat* were $11,645,000.

What's Up, Doc? (Warner Bros., 1972) 94 minutes, G-rated

Credits: Producer and director, Peter Bogdanovich; screenplay, Buck Henry, David Newman, Robert Benton; production design, Polly Platt; art direction, Herman A. Blumenthal; set decoration, John Austin; hairstyling, Lynda Gurasich; sound, Les Fresholtz; special effects, Robert MacDonald; cinematography, Laszlo Kovacs; editor, Verna Fields.

Cast: Barbra Streisand (*Judy Maxwell*); Ryan O'Neal (*Howard Bannister*); Kenneth Mars (*Hugh Simon*); Austin Pendleton (*Frederick Larrabee*); Sorrell Booke (*Harry*); Stefan Gierasch (*Fritz*); Mabel Albertson (*Mrs. Van Hoskins*); Michael Murphy (*Mr. Smith*); Graham Jarvis (*bailiff*); Madeline Kahn (*Eunice Burns*); Liam Dunn (*the judge*).

Songs: Barbra sings "You're the Top" behind the credits. She starts to sing "As Time Goes By" but it's just a tease. Music arranged and conducted by Artie Butler.

The Story: A largely successful attempt to make a modern 1930s screwball screen comedy. Free-soul Streisand takes the starch out of uptight O'Neal, with chase scenes all over San Francisco.

Review (Pro): "Although she never lets us forget the power that always seems to be held in uncertain check, she is surprisingly appealing, more truly comic than ever." — Vincent Canby (*New York Times*, March 10, 1972)

Review (Con): "Miss Streisand knows no subtleties in her comedy craft. She is an outrageous mugger. Nothing is done in low key. She could learn a great deal from Lucille Ball and Carol Burnett. — Bruce Bahrenburg (*Newark Evening News*, March 10, 1972)

Of Note: What's Up, Doc? began life as a 1970 Elliott Gould screen project called *A Glimpse of Tiger*, a black comedy about a man on drugs growing progressively mad; he has an affair with a prim young woman and murders her. Filming on *A Glimpse of Tiger* began in summer 1970, under the direction of Anthony Harvey. There were immediate problems. Elliott was deemed mentally fragile at the time, and filming halted. Later . . . Barbra and Ryan O'Neal were looking for a movie project to do together. Their mutual agent, Sue Mengers, suggested *A Glimpse of Tiger.* Director Peter Bogdanovich read the script and saw that it had its roots in thirties comedies. Hot, trendy writers Buck Henry, Robert Benton, and David Newman were hired, and *Tiger* became *Doc.*

Financial Statement: Rentals from *What's Up, Doc?* were $28,000,000.

Up the Sandbox (National General, 1972) 97 minutes, R-rated

Credits: A First Artists Presentation of a Barwood Film. Producers, Irwin Winkler and Robert Chartoff; associate producer, Marty Erlichman; director, Irvin Kershner; screenplay, Paul Zindel, from the novel by Anne Roiphe; production design, Harry Horner; set design, David M. Haber; set decoration, Robert De Vestal; hairstyling, Kaye Pownell; special effects, Richard F. Albain; cinematography, Gordon Willis; editor, Robert Lawrence.

Cast: Barbra Streisand (*Margaret*); David Selby (*Paul*); Ariane Heller (*Elizabeth*); Terry/Garry Smith (*the baby Peter*); Jane Hoffman (*Mrs. Yussim*); Jacobo Morales (*Fidel Castro*); Paul Benedict (*Dr. Beineke*); George Irving (*Dr. Keglin*); Cynthia Harris (*Stella*); and the Senegalese Dance Company.

The Story: A woman at the dawn of women's liberation is torn between love of family and home and wanting to fight for the cause. She finds escape in fantasy.

Reviews (Pro): "A superb display of acting. In this touching, funny, exhilarating and mature movie, Miss Streisand creates a remarkable portrait." — Donald J. Mayerson (*Cue*, December 23, 1972)

"A joy. Streisand's sixth film and her sixth hit." — Howard Thompson (*New York Times*, December 22, 1972)

Reviews (Con): "A confusing comedy. The screen adaptation jumps from reality to fantasy in the same unclear fashion as [the book]. The result is a jumbled story line." — Ann Guarino, (New York *Daily News*, December 22, 1972)

"Streisand . . . is still a monster. My image of her is of an egotistic animal gobbling the story, the audience, the very film stock on which her image is printed." — Stanley Kauffmann (*The New Republic*, November 10, 1972)

Of Note: Barbra said that the family portrayed in the movie was partly based on her family, that the scene at the door, telling her mother she doesn't want to see her, was played in real life with her own mother—and more than once. Then, also, don't forget the scene where she pushes her mother's face (actress Jane Hoffman) into a birthday cake.

Financial Statement: Rentals from *Up the Sandbox* were less than $4,000,000.

The Way We Were (Columbia Pictures, 1973) 118 minutes, PG-rated

Credits: A Rastar Production. Producer, Ray Stark; director, Sydney Pollack; screenplay, Arthur Laurents; production design, Stephen Grimes; set decoration, William Kiernan; costume design, Dorothy Jeakins, Moss Mabry; hairstyling, Kaye Pownell; sound, Jack Solomon; cinematography, Harry Stradling Jr.; supervising editor, Margaret Booth.

Cast: Barbra Streisand (*Katie*); Robert Redford (*Hubbell*); Bradford Dillman (*J. J.*); Lois Chiles (*Carol Ann*); Patrick O'Neal (*George Bissinger*); Viveca Lindfors (*Paula Reisner*); Allyn Ann McLerie (*Rhea Edwards*); Murray Hamilton (*Brooks Carpenter*); Herb Edelman (*Bill Verso*); Diana Ewing (*Vicki Bissinger*); Sally Kirkland (*Pony Dunbar*); Connie Forslund (*Jenny*).

Music: Marvin Hamlisch. "The Way We Were" composed by Marvin Hamlisch; lyrics by Marilyn and Alan Bergman; sung by Barbra Streisand.

The Story: Barbra is a political activist, Redford a college jock, in a New York-Hollywood love story set against the political issues (including Communism) of the late 1930s to the early 1950s.

Review (Pro): "Barbra Streisand does an acting job that consolidates her position as the foremost movie actress of her generation." — Joseph Gelmis (*Newsday*, October 26, 1973)

Review (Con): "Miss Streisand's furious determination is never very appealing but it is comprehensible, as is Redford's essential weakness. Miss Streisand is a formidable star. It's difficult enough to accept her as a wronged wife, and it's ludicrous when the movie presents her photographed in the sentimental manner once used on lovelorn movie heroines of forty years ago." — Vincent Canby (*New York Times*, October 26, 1973)

Of Note: Over the years, many of the principals have expressed interest in a sequel to the successful and popular *The Way We Were*. To date, no one has come up with a script everyone likes.

Financial Statement: Rentals from *The Way We Were* were $22,457,000.

For Pete's Sake (Columbia Pictures, 1974) 90 minutes, PG-rated

Credits: A Rastar Production. Producers, Martin Erlichman, Stanley Shapiro; executive producer, Phil Feldman; director, Peter Yates; screenplay, Stanley Shapiro, Maurice Richlin; production design, Gene Callahan; set decoration, Jim Berkey; costume design, Frank Thompson; Miss Streisand's hairstyles designed by Jon Peters; sound, Don Parker; cinematography, Laszlo Kovacs; film editor, Frank P. Keller.

Cast: Barbra Streisand (*Henry*); Michael Sarrazin (*Pete*); Estelle Parsons (*Helen*); William Redfield (*Fred*); Molly Picon (*Mrs. Cherry*); Louis Zorich (*Nick*); Vivian Bonnell (*Loretta*); Richard Ward (*Bernie*); Heywood Hale Broun (*Judge Hiller*).

Song: "For Pete's Sake (Don't Let Him Down)." Music, Artie Butler; lyrics, Mark Lindsay; performed by Barbra Streisand.

Story: A Brooklyn housewife tries to raise money for her cab driver husband and gets involved with the Mafia, a madam, and other comical characters.

Review (Pro): "An often boisterously funny old-time farce."—Vincent Canby (*New York Times*, June 27, 1974)

Review (Con): "Everyone involved . . . owes not only the audience but also his colleagues an apology for perpetrating this piece of schlock, certainly the worst Barbra Streisand package yet. Stale television frenzy does not a mad, mad comedy make." — (*New York*, July 15, 1974)

Of Note: Well aware of Barbra's social concerns, some Streisand fans were puzzled by the many politically incorrect aspects of this feature film: a lazy black maid who refers to herself as "the colored woman"; a lisping grocery store clerk who's told to keep his Fruit Loops; and Barbra's character, who is willing to become a prostitute for her husband. The movie also confirmed the criticisms of Barbra's megalomania in choosing weak male actors (such as Michael Sarrazin) who wouldn't dare try to steal scenes.

Financial Statement: Rentals from *For Pete's Sake* were $10,662,000.

Funny Lady (Columbia Pictures, 1975) 140 minutes, PG-rated

Credits: A Rastar Production of a Persky-Bright/Vista Feature. Producer, Ray Stark; director, Herbert Ross; screenplay, Jay Presson Allen, Arnold Schulman; story, Arnold Schulman; musical numbers directed by Herbert Ross; assistant to Mr. Ross, Nora Kaye; production design, George Jenkins; set decoration, Audrey Blasdel; costume design, Ray Aghayan, Bob Mackie; sound, Jack Solomon; special effects, Phil Cory; cinematography, James Wong Howe; special photographic effects, Albert Whitlock; editor, Marion Rothman.

Cast: Barbra Streisand (*Fanny Brice*); James Caan (*Billy Rose*); Omar Sharif (*Nick Arnstein*); Roddy McDowall (*Bobby*); Ben Vereen (*Bert Robbins*); Carole Wells (*Norma Butler*); Larry Gates (*Bernard Baruch*); Heidi O'Rourke (*Eleanor Holm*); Samantha Huffaker (*Fran*); Matt Emery (*Buck Bolton*); Gene Troobnick (*Ned*).

Music and Lyrics: John Kander and Fred Ebb; music arranged and conducted by Peter Matz.

Songs: "Blind Date," "More Than You Know," "I Like Him/Her" [with James Caan], "I Found a Million Dollar Baby in a Five and Ten Cent Store," "So Long Honey Lamb" [with Ben Vereen], "I Got a Code in My Doze," "Clap Hands, Here Comes Charley" [Ben Vereen], "Great Day," "How Lucky Can You Get?", "Isn't This Better?", "Me and My Shadow" [musical interlude for Aquacade], "If I Love Again," and "Let's Hear It for Me."

Story: Continuing the story of beloved entertainer Fanny Brice (1891–1951), who marries Broadway songwriter-producer Billy Rose (1899–1966), but can't forget her first love, gambler Nick Arnstein, who keeps sticking his handsome nose into her life.

Review (Pro): "What I find most impressive and likable about the performance is the softened, bittersweet maturity that Streisand lets us see in Fanny Brice. You sense that Streisand understands the star as well as she understood the impetuous young hopeful." — Charles Champlin (*Los Angeles Times*, March 14, 1975)

Review (Con): "*Funny Lady* continues [the Fanny Brice story] with all of the solemnity and attention to ritual that you might expect in the dramatization of a Norse legend." — Vincent Canby (*New York Times*, March 16, 1975)

Of Note: Herb Ross, the film's director, said: "[Barbra] was in love at the time [with hairdresser-producer Jon Peters], and she didn't seem to want to make the picture or play the part. It was a movie that was made virtually without her. She simply wasn't there in terms of commitment, and one of her greatest qualities is to make a thousand percent commitment."

Financial Statement: Rentals from *Funny Lady* were $19,313,000.

A Star Is Born (Warner Bros./First Artists, 1976) 140 minutes, R-rated

Credits: A Barwood/Jon Peters Production. Producer, Jon Peters; executive producer, Barbra Streisand; director, Frank Piereson; screenplay, John Gregory Dunne, Joan Didion, Frank Pierson; story, William Wellman, Robert Carson [who cowrote the original 1937 United Artists screenplay with Dorothy Parker and Alan Campbell]; production design, Polly Platt; art direction, William Hiney; set decoration, Ruby Levitt; sound mixer, Tom Overton; special effects, Chuck Gasper; cinematography, Robert Surtees; editor, Peter Zinner.

Cast: Barbra Streisand (*Esther Hoffman*); Kris Kristofferson (*John Norman Howard*); Gary Busey (*Bobby Ritchie*); Paul Mazursky (*Brian Wexler*); M. G. Kelly (*Bebe Jesus*); Joanne Linville (*Freddie Lowenstein*); Oliver Clark (*Gary Danziger*); Vanetta Fields and Clydie King (*The Oreos*); Marta Heflin (*Quentin*); Sally Kirkland (*Nikki*); Uncle Rudy (*Mo*).

Music: Musical concepts by Barbra Streisand; music supervised by Paul Williams; musical underscore by Roger Kellaway; musical conductor, Kenny Ascher; music and live recordings produced by Phil Ramone.

Songs: "Watch Closely Now" [Kris Kristofferson], "Queen Bee" [with the Oreos], "Everything," "Lost Inside of You," "Hellacious Acres," "Evergreen," "Woman in the Moon," "I Believe in Love," "Crippled Crow," "With One More Look at You," and "Watch Closely Now."

155

Story: The star-crossed love story of two rock music performers: Her career is on the rise, his is on the way down.

Review (Pro): "A superlative remake. Barbra Streisand's performance . . . is her finest screen work to date." — (*Daily Variety*, December 22, 1976)

Reviews (Con): "Truly the pits—it's the work of a madwoman. In *A Star Is Born*, Streisand becomes an honest-to-God monster—she's the real King Kong of our current movie season—and the more she hogs her scenes, the more she overacts, the more she shows off her personal wardrobe, the more she tries to fake being a rock-and-roll singer, the more monstrous she becomes." — Frank Rich (*New York Post*, January 15, 1977)

"Streisand's constant upstaging of Kristofferson often goes beyond the bounds of run-of-the-mill narcissism; the camera spends a great deal of time watching her watching him talk." — (*Newsweek*, January 10, 1977)

Of Note: Streisand reportedly confronted filmmaker Frank Pierson and asked that he share director's credit with her. He refused. She has credit as executive producer, star, contributing composer . . . and is credited onscreen with providing "musical concepts" and providing the clothes from her closet.

Financial Statement: Rentals from *A Star Is Born* were $37,100,000.

The Main Event (Warner Bros./First Artists, 1979) 112 minutes, PG-rated

Credits: A Barwood Film. Producers, Jon Peters, Barbra Streisand; executive producers, Howard Rosenman, Renee Missel; director, Howard Zieff; screenplay, Gail Parent, Andrew Smith; production design, Charles Rosen; sound, David Ronna; cinematography, Mario Tosi; editor, Edward Warschilka.

Cast: Barbra Streisand (*Hillary Kramer*); Ryan O'Neal (*Eddie "Kid Natural" Scanlon*); Paul Sand (*David*); Whitman Mayo (*Percy*); Patti D'Arbanville (*Donna*); Chu Chu Malave (*Luis*); Richard Lawson (*Hector Mantilla*); James Gregory (*Leo Gough*).

Music: Michael Melvoin; "The Main Event" written by Paul Jabara, Bruce Roberts; "Fight" written by Paul Jabara, Bob Esty; medley performed by Barbra Streisand.

The Story: Barbra plays a bankrupt Los Angeles perfume manufacturer who owns a not-so-terrific prize fighter. He had been a tax shelter, but now she sees him as a possible source of income. She becomes a fight manager. A comedy.

Review (Pro): "It's good to see Streisand reclaiming herself from the dramatic excesses of *A Star Is Born*, in which she presented a carved granite personality, its force reducing Kris Kristofferson to a helpless pulp. Here she can once again concentrate on the comic sense, with its finely tuned timing, that is so much a part of her talents. If only she didn't feel obligated to give so much of it, always to be on, twinkling and mugging and reacting." — (*New York Daily News*, June 22, 1979)

Review (Con): "The hegemony of Barbra Streisand over her films is less a matter of record than a plausible presumption, based on observation of her omnivorous Whitmanesque approach to character—her urge to appear dumb yet smart, funny-looking yet beautiful, tough yet cuddly, a good actress yet a famous singer. In view of her predilection for converting any handy vehicle into a one-woman show, the difficulties of designing a script for her and appointing a consort must be considerable. The strain is apparent in *The Main Event*." — Susan Lardner (*The New Yorker*, July 2, 1979)

Financial Statement: Rentals from *The Main Event* were $26,400,000.

With a Special Guest Appearance by Barbra's Amazing Butt!

No aspect of *The Main Event* received as much attention as Barbra Streisand's backside: The camera lingers on it for so long you wonder if the operator has gone on his coffee break. Despite the prominence given her derriere, and despite the critical acclaim, her butt was not given a screen credit: Barbra may not have wanted to pay its union dues. It's only fair then that it get proper recognition here.

"The most noticeable stylistic flourish [of director Howard Zieff] is his camera's peculiar fascination with the contours of Streisand's behind." — David Ansen (*Newsweek*, June 25, 1979)

"Were she not an unquestioned star, one would suspect *The Main Event* of being a vanity production—the sort of thing aging screen queens sometimes get their wealthy admirers to

---

buy for them so that the camera may once again be permitted to adore them. In particular, this star seems to labor under the delusion that it is not so much her face as her bottom that is her fortune—so many low angles of it upturned and bouncing about are featured. It's not a bad bottom, but you can't really make a movie of it. You can make a good movie that allows Streisand to employ fully her unquestioned gifts as singer and comedienne. But first, she's got to stop mooning around." — Richard Schickel (*Time*, July 9, 1979)

"Although her rear end seems reasonably decorative and probably is quite comfortable to sit on, it does little to advance the plot and may slow it down a bit." — (*Detroit Free Press*, June 22, 1979)

"Two years before Jane Fonda discovered a gold mine in workout tapes, Barbra would introduce aerobics to the national consciousness. Unfortunately, the manner in which the scenes were presented was patently offensive and inherently sexist. Howard Zieff's camera seems to have had some sort of magnetic attraction to Barbra's behind. But he alone can't be faulted. After all, she had final cut on the picture, and the appallingly gratuitous close-ups of her various body parts could have easily been excised." — Randall Riese (*Her Name Is Barbra*. New York: Birch Lane/Carol, 1993)

All Night Long (Universal Pictures, 1981) 99 minutes, R-rated
Credits: A Barwood Film. Producers, Leonard Goldbert, Jerry Weintraub; associate producers, Terrence A. Donnelly, Fran Roy; director, Jean-Claude Tramont; screenplay, W. D. Richter; production design, Peter Jamison; set decoration, Linda Spheeris; costume design, Albert Wolsky; sound, John K. Kean, Albert Morrona; cinematography, Philip Lathrop; editor, Marion Rothman.
Cast: Gene Hackman (*George Dupler*); Barbra Streisand (*Cheryl Gibbons*); Diane Ladd (*Helen Dupler*); Dennis Quaid (*Freddie Dupler*); Kevin Dobson (*Bobby Gibbons*); William Daniels (*Richard H. Copleston*); Terry Kiser (*day manager*); Vernee Watson (*Emily*); Chris Mulkey (*Russell Munk*).

158

Music: Ira Newborn, Richard Hazard; "Carelessly Tossed" composed by Alan Lindgren, lyrics by W. D. Richter. "Cheryl's Theme" composed by Dave Grusin.

Story: A wry California comedy of George Dupler's midlife crisis: He throws a chair through the boss's window and is demoted to running an all-night drugstore. He falls in love with his son's bleached blond, married girlfriend.

Reviews (Pro): "Barbra Streisand has never been so self-effacingly beautiful as in this film. But after the bombastic, emptily narcissistic performances in movies like *A Star Is Born* and *The Main Event*, this new, toned-down Streisand is a blessing. She makes us aware of how good she can be in the 'normal' range. Her Cheryl is both willful and evanescent—George's guardian-angel courtesan." — Peter Rainer (*Los Angeles Herald-Examiner*, March 6, 1981)

"Can one believe Barbra Streisand, the superstar, acting what is in fact a secondary role? The odd thing is one can. She does it with modesty, largely without mannerisms, and though her character isn't especially compelling, it's difficult to take one's eyes off her." — Vincent Canby (*New York Times*, March 6, 1981)

Reviews (Con): "The worst miscasting since John Wayne played Genghis Khan." — (*Boxoffice*, April 1981)

"Streisand looks and acts like a grotesque who ought to repel the Hackman who has been previously established. And to satisfy the star role, the script then goes through agonies of accommodation—trying to encompass some old-fashioned movie nonsense in a script that sets a tone of intelligence." — Stanley Kauffmann (*The New Republic*, March 21, 1981)

Of Note: All Night Long was chosen for inclusion in *The Hollywood Hall of Shame: The Most Expensive Flops in Movie History* by Harry and Michael Medved (New York: Perigree/Putnam, 1984). "What would have been a low-budget comedy except for the record-breaking $4 million fee paid to Streisand for her part."

Financial Statement: Rentals from *All Night Long* were below $4,000,000. [The negative cost was $14,000,000; domestic rentals were only $3,900,000.]

Yentl (MGM/United Artists, 1983) 134 minutes, PG-rated

Credits: A Barwood Film. Producer and director, Barbra Streisand;

co-producer, Rusty Lemorande; screenplay, Jack Rosenthal and Barbra Streisand; based on "Yentl, the Yeshiva Boy," by Isaac Bashevis Singer; production design, Leslie Tomkins, Roy Walker; costume design, Judy Moorcroft; wedding dance choreography, Gillian Lynne; sound, David Hildyard, Keith Grant; cinematography, David Watkin; editor, Terry Rawlings.

Cast: Barbra Streisand (*Yentl*); Mandy Patinkin (*Avigdor*); Amy Irving (*Hadass*); Nehemiah Persoff (*Papa*); Steven Hill (*Reb Alter Vishkower*); Allan Corduner (*Shimmele*); Ruth Goring (*Esther Rachel Vishkower*).

Music: Michel Legrand; lyrics by Alan and Marilyn Bergman; music orchestrated and conducted by Michel Legrand.

Songs: "Where Is It Written?", "Papa, Can You Hear Me?", "This Is One of Those Moments," "No Wonder," "The Way He Makes Me Feel," "Tomorrow Night," "Will Someone Ever Look at Me That Way?", "No Matter What Happens," and "A Piece of Sky."

Story: In nineteenth-century Poland, Jewish girls are denied an education. When her father dies, Yentl disguises herself as a boy, renames herself Anshel, and enters a yeshiva to study the Talmud. Eventually, she emigrates to America.

Review (Pro): "Streisand has gone for the emotional goods—to create a sweeping musical drama out of a tiny romantic triangle—and, miracle of miracles, she has delivered them." — Richard Corliss (*Time*, November 21, 1983)

Yentl is included in David Thomson's "20 Best Films Directed by a Woman" (*Movieline*, April 1998). Thomas calls it "a piece of magic."

Review (Con): It is the "vanity-picture aspects of *Yentl* that finally does it in. One can accept Streisand as a boy, but one can't accept so much of her; those insistent mannerisms and nonstop mugging will wear down all but the most stalwart." — Kenneth Turan (*California*, December 1983)

Of Note: The most outspoken critic of *Yentl* was Isaac Bashevis Singer, author of the original short story "Yentl the Yeshiva Boy." The *New York Times* (January 29, 1984) published Singer's self-interview about the new movie. He objects to the songs, saying that the passion for learning and the passion for singing are not related. He objects to Streisand hogging the movie: "The leading actress must make room for others to have their say and exhibit their talents. No matter how good you are, you don't take everything for yourself. Miss Streisand is always present, while poor *Yentl* is absent."

Singer's piece, worth reading in its entirety, is reprinted in *Diva: Barbra Streisand and the Making of a Superstar*, edited by Ethlie Ann Vare (New York: Berkley/Boulevard, 1996).

Singer's sister, Esther Streitman, is said to be the model for Yentl.

Also: Richard Gere was Barbra's first choice for the role of Avigdor. She then tried to interest Michael Douglas, singer Enrico Marcias, John Shea (who'd played Avigdor opposite Tovah Feldshuh in the 1975 Broadway play *Yentl*), and then signed singer Mandy Patinkin—known for his strong, clear voice—but who doesn't sing in the film.

Financial Statement: Rentals from *Yentl* were $19,680,127.

Nuts (Warner Bros., 1987) 116 minutes, R-rated

Credits: A Barwood Film. Producer, Barbra Streisand; director, Martin Ritt; screenplay, Tom Topor, Daryl Ponicsan, Alvin Sargent, from the play by Tom Topor; production design, Joel Schiller; art direction, Eric Orbom; costume design, Joe Tompkins; sound editors, Julia Evershade, Virginia Cook-McGowan; cinematography, Andrzej Bartkowiak; editors, Rick Spare, Jeff Werner.

Cast: Barbra Streisand (*Claudia Draper*); Richard Dreyfuss (*Aaron Levinsky*); Karl Malden (*Arthur Kirk*); Maureen Stapleton (*Rose Kirk*); James Whitmore (*Judge Murdoch*); Eli Wallach (*Dr. Herbert Morrison*), Leslie Nielsen (*client/victim*).

Music: Barbra Streisand; music arranged and conducted by Jeremy Lubbock.

Story: A high-priced Manhattan prostitute is charged with killing a client. She defiantly fights for the right to a trial—while the court, and her own parents, want to have her declared insane.

Review (Pro): "A damn sight better than it has any right to be, and that's largely because of Barbra Streisand's ferociously willed, all-out performance. Whether by edict or design, we get to see her in close-up more often than any actress since Falconetti played Joan of Arc" [referring to Carl Dryer's 1928 silent film *The Passion of Joan of Arc*] — Peter Rainer (*Los Angeles Herald-Examiner*, November 20, 1987)

Reviews (Con): "*Nuts* doesn't strive very hard for realism. From the first glimpse of one tawny, sun-streaked coiffure in the crowd at the Women's House of Detention, it's clear that the sanity issue is never even in question and that this is less a believable drama than a one-woman show. Miss Streisand, who produced *Nuts*, didn't direct it. And

Martin Ritt, who is the director of record, didn't either. The film is almost entirely adrift." — Janet Maslin (*New York Times*, November 20, 1987)

"As everyone but Streisand knows, she simply doesn't possess the physical attributes of a woman who turns men's heads whenever she passes by. Someone should have explained to Streisand that if women who looked like her actually could earn $300 for giving a handjob, prostitution would be the most overcrowded field in the country." — "Great Moments in Miscasting," by Virginia Campbell and Edward Margulies (*Movieline*, August 1994)

Of Note: Nuts is seen as Barbra's indictment of wicked stepfather Louis Kind, and an expression of the anger she feels toward her mother for not rescuing her from him.

This film is popularly referred to as "*Mentl*" (to rhyme with *Yentl*). More than one commentator has noted that of all the actors in Hollywood, Karl Malden is the only one with a nose more notable than Streisand's.

The New York stage production of *Nuts* starred Anne Twomey.

Editor's Note: James Spada and Anne Edwards each wrote a level-headed biography of Streisand (see **Appendix 1: An Annotated Bibliography**) but lost their perspectives (and their minds) when they came to the defense of *Nuts*. James Spada blames the film's failure on the advertising and marketing. Edwards said the critics couldn't see past their clichéd notions of prostitutes.

Yikes!

Financial Statement: Rentals from *Nuts* were $14,100,000.

The Prince of Tides (Columbia Pictures, 1991) 132 minutes, R-rated
Credits: Producers, Barbra Streisand, Andrew Karsh; director, Barbra Streisand; screenplay, Pat Conroy, Becky Johnston, from the novel by Pat Conroy; production design, Paul Sylbert, Richard Sylbert; art direction, W. Steven Graham; set decoration, Caryl Heller; costume design, Ruth Morley; sound, Dennis Maitland; special effects, Peter Knowlton; aerial photography, Michael Kelem; cinematography, Stephen Goldblatt; editor, Paul Zimmerman.
Cast: Nick Nolte (*Tom Wingo*); Barbra Streisand (*Dr. Susan Lowenstein*); Kate Nelligan (*Lila Wingo*); Blythe Danner (*Sallie Wingo*); Jason Gould (*Bernard Woodruff*); Jeroen Krabbe (*Herbert Woodruff*);

162

Melinda Dillon (*Savannah Wingo*); George Carlin (*Eddie Detreville*); Brad Sullivan (*Henry Wingo*).

Music: Music director, James Newton Howard.

Story: Long after the fact, members of a Southern family still suffer from a childhood brutalized by their father. A sister attempts suicide. A son drifts into affairs . . . and meets a glamorous New York psychiatrist who may help him.

Reviews (Pro): "Nothing about Barbra Streisand's previous acting or direction is preparation for her expert handling of *The Prince of Tides* . . . a film that is gratifyingly lean. Discretion and reserve . . . are very much in evidence this time. So is the frankly emotional style with which she is more often associated, a style perfectly attuned to this film's complex, stirring story." — Janet Maslin (*New York Times*, December 25, 1991)

"*The Prince of Tides* has a passion seldom found in contempo U.S. films and a quality not usually associated with Barbra Streisand—self-effacement." — Joseph McBride (*Variety*, December 9, 1991)

Reviews (Con): Rolling Stone (December 27, 1991) named this the second-worst film of the year, after the Bruce Willis debacle *Hudson Hawk*: "Director-star Barbra Streisand give Willis a run for the ego in this turgid dysfunctional-family saga whose plot is as nonsensical as its congratulatory reviews."

"If you want a piece of instant camp, see *The Prince of Tides*. It means with all its heart to be serious, and that's what makes it special." — Georgia Brown (*Village Voice*, December 24, 1991)

Of Note: Barbra Streisand said, "That's what *The Prince of Tides* is about in a way, learning to appreciate your mother." — (*Vanity Fair*, September 1991)

Two of Pat Conroy's autobiographical novels had been filmed earlier: *Conrack* (Twentieth Century-Fox, 1974) and *The Great Santini* (Warner Bros., 1979). *The Prince of Tides*, a bestseller, was published in 1986.

Financial Statement: Rentals from *The Prince of Tides* were $36,000,000.

The Mirror Has Two Faces (TriStar Pictures, 1996) 126 minutes, PG-13-rated

Credits: A Barbra Streisand/Barwood Films Production. Producers, Arnon Milchan, Ronald Schwary; executive producer, Cis Corman;

producer-director, Barbra Streisand; screen story and screenplay, Robert LaGravenese; production designer, Tom H. John; set design, John Alan Hicks; costumes, Theoni V. Aldredge; sound, Tom Nelson; cinematography, Andrzej Bartkowiak; film editor, Jeff Werner.

Cast: Barbra Streisand (*Rose Morgan*); Jeff Bridges (*Gregory Larkin*); Lauren Bacall (*Hannah Morgan*); George Segal (*Henry Fine*); Mimi Rogers (*Claire*); Pierce Brosnan (*Alex*); Brenda Vaccaro (*Doris*); Austin Pendleton (*Barry*); Elle Macpherson (*Candy*); Taina Elg (*female professor*).

Music: Love theme composed by Barbra Streisand; music composed and adapted by Marvin Hamlisch.

Story: This film is said to be based on the 1958 French movie drama *Le Miroir a Deux Faces*, an Andre Cayatte production starring Michele Morgan as a woman caught in a loveless marriage to an insensitive man. She has an accident, undergoes plastic surgery, emerges beautiful, and runs off with her brother-in-law. The husband shoots the plastic surgeon.

Streisand's rewrite is a romantic comedy of two Columbia University professors who enter into a strictly platonic marriage only to discover they are romantically, sexually attracted to each other.

So . . . how much money did Barbra pay for the rights to that French original? And should she ask for her money back?

Review (Pro): "For a romantic comedy, [this film] includes some surprisingly touching moments concerning the heroine's feeling about looking plain. [It] sometimes sharply examines the difficulties of being an outcast because of one's appearance." — Eric Monder (1997 *Motion Picture Guide*. New York: CineBooks, 1997)

Reviews (Con): "A really dumb idea." — Richard Schickel (*Time*, November 25, 1996)

"The unintentional self-revelation that leaks out of every scene in this jaw-dropping production is what makes *The Mirror Has Two Faces* such an astonishing full-Barbra experience—and a camp classic." — Lisa Schwarzbaum (*Entertainment Weekly*, November 22, 1996)

"Isn't Streisand a bit mature [fifty-four] to be playing a girl who shares a Manhattan apartment with a mom who keeps pushing marriage." — Peter Travers (*Rolling Stone*, October 11, 1996)

Of Note: The photo shown in the movie of Rose's parents is actually of Streisand's real father composited with actress Lauren Bacall.

Financial Statement: As of March 1998, the reported gross was $41,000,000, but the film's cost was more than this figure.

* * * * * *

(See also **Part II: 16. Barbra Streisand and Pauline Kael** for Pauline Kael's commentaries on these films.)

BARBRA ON VIDEOCASSETTE

All of Streisand's theatrical films are available on home video.

Funny Girl (Columbia TriStar Home Video)
Hello, Dolly! (Fox Video)
On a Clear Day You Can See Forever (Paramount)
The Owl and the Pussycat (Columbia TriStar Home Video)
What's Up, Doc? (Warner Home Video)
Up the Sandbox (Warner Home Video)
The Way We Were (Columbia TriStar Home Video)
For Pete's Sake (Columbia TriStar Home Video)
Funny Lady (Columbia TriStar Home Video)
A Star Is Born (Warner Home Video)
The Main Event (Warner Home Video)
All Night Long (Goodtimes Home Video)
Yentl (Fox Video)
Nuts (Warner Home Video)
The Prince of Tides (Columbia TriStar Home Video)
The Mirror Has Two Faces (Columbia TriStar Home Video)

**A Quick Look at the Movies that Barbra
Did Make . . . but What *Might* Have Been**

Funny Girl
If Fanny Brice's daughter (Mrs. Ray Stark) had had her way, Anne Bancroft would have starred in the original Broadway musical. Then, many viewers thought Shirley MacLaine was the best choice in Hollywood for the movie version.

Hello, Dolly!
Dolly was always the beloved Carol Channing—she did win the Tony Award as the Broadway Dolly, didn't she?—so the casting of Streisand in the movie was seen as slighting dear unbearable (to some) Carol.

On a Clear Day You Can See Forever

165

This musical was purchased for Audrey Hepburn, who said no, she just couldn't see starring in it.

The Owl and the Pussycat
Producer Ray Stark bought the rights to the play with Elizabeth Taylor and Richard Burton in mind. Remember them? They were the Demi Moore and Bruce Willis of their day.

What's Up, Doc?
One of the great amazing trivia nuggets: This began life as an Elliott Gould project!

Up the Sandbox
Barbra's first film for First Artists, so she had major input. The casting, for example. Here's a trivia question: What actor portrayed her husband? Don't bother to look in the Randall Riese biography or in the one by Anne Edwards—he's not even *mentioned*.

The Way We Were
Streisand read a fifty-page treatment and immediately agreed to do the movie. No other star was ever considered.

For Pete's Sake
Barbra was looking for sure-fire crass commercialism, so she chose this comedy by Stanley Shapiro and Maurice Richlin, who had co-authored several successful Doris Day projects: *Pillow Talk* (Universal, 1959) and *That Touch of Mink* (Universal, 1962) among them. Streisand should have let Doris Day have this one, too.

Funny Lady
They never considered anyone but you, Barbra.

A Star Is Born
This movie had been all but promised to Cher, when it was called *Rainbow Road*. Good loser that she is, Cher commented, "Barbra doesn't know *shit* about rock and roll!"

The Main Event
Diana Ross was the original choice. (She was also, trivially speaking, an ex-lover of costar Ryan O'Neal.)

All Night Long
A well-documented case of wretched excess. Shooting began

Upstaging a blind man: singing "Cryin' Time"
with living legend Ray Charles on her CBS-TV special
Barbra Streisand . . . and Other Musical Instruments (1973).
PHOTO COURTESY OF PHOTOFEST

on this movie with Lisa Eichhorn . . . but then Streisand was paid four million dollars to replace her, for box office insurance. *What* box office?

Yentl

Isaac Bashevis Singer, author of the original short story "Yentl the Yeshiva Boy," was unhappy with the movie version of his story. He felt that Tovah Feldshuh, who'd played Yentl on Broadway in 1975, was much better.

Nuts

Mark Rydell, the original director for this project, had Bette Midler in mind . . . or Debra Winger.

The Prince of Tides

This was Streisand's project, so naturally she would star. She wanted Robert Redford to costar but he balked at the idea of being directed by her. Lover Don Johnson didn't hang around long enough to snag the part. Warren Beatty was interested but was not willing to get as emotionally naked as Barbra demanded. So Nick Nolte was it.

The Mirror Has Two Faces

This also was Barbra's project from the beginning. Dudley Moore had been cast in the role of Henry, but the boss lady thought the comic too comedic and replaced him with George Segal.

CHAPTER 13

The Bare Barbra

For her fourth movie, after three all-singin,' all dancin' musicals, Barbra Streisand decided she was now ready for something completely different—she would portray a hooker-porno star and would be the first major star to say "Fuck off!" in a movie, and she would show her boobs on camera!

But then she got cold . . . uh, feet.

The movie is *The Owl and the Pussycat* (Columbia, 1970), which had been a 1964 Broadway comedy hit with Alan Alda and Diana Sands, the African American actress who had appeared with Barbra in *Another Evening with Harry Stoones*, the 1961 one-performance off-Broadway revue.

The owl of the title is an uptight, nervous type who works in a bookstore and tries to write novels at night. He's played by George Segal. The pussycat is Barbra's character, the hooker neighbor who makes so much noise the writer can't create. The two yell and fight until they realize they're in love.

For their big love scene, the script called for Barbra to be topless. Director Herb Ross had to coax her into doing it, assuring her she had a great body. "Pert" is the word James Spada uses to describe her breasts (*Streisand: Her Life*. New York: Crown, 1995); he also says George Segal was "completely alert" for the scene.

After the movie was finished, the leading lady changed her mind and asked that the topless scene be "fogged" so viewers couldn't clearly see what was happening.

However . . . certain frames escaped death by fogging and, nearly a decade later, Barbra in all her pert, topless splendor appeared in the November 1979 issue of *High Society* (a magazine for lowlifes), with "Barbra Streisand Nude!" boldly emblazoned on the cover.

Barbra sued, demanding that all copies of the magazine be recalled. The magazine's editor, the attractive Gloria Leonard, agreed but it was already too late. That issue now sells for over a hundred dollars on the collectors market.

When *The Owl and the Pussycat* came to video, Barbra's nudity, fogged or otherwise, was edited out.

* * *

Streisand had an earlier, apparently innocent, professional encounter with nudity.

For the 1969 Academy Awards, when she was in the running for Best Actress for *Funny Girl* (Columbia, 1968), she wore an outfit originally designed by Arnold Scaasi for her movie *On a Clear Day You Can See Forever* (Paramount, 1970) but not used. The outfit was a pajama-like pantsuit with greatly flared bell-bottom legs. It was made of glamorous black tulle with clear sequins and a white collar and sleeves. It seemed to display a generous amount of flesh. There's a publicity photo of it on page 100 of Allison J. Waldman's *The Barbra Streisand Scrapbook* (Secaucus, N.J.: Citadel/Carol, 1995).

When her name was announced as winner, in a tie with Katharine Hepburn for *The Lion in Winter* (Avco-Embassy, 1968), Barbra hurried down the aisle. Going up the stairs to the stage, she tripped on one of her bell-bottoms and stumbled. When the television lights hit the backside of her outfit, audiences in the auditorium got a clear and ample view of her near-naked, sequin-covered derriere.

Or didn't. Scaasi defended his creation, saying that it only seemed to be see-through, that the outfit was underlined with georgette crepe but the glaring lights and the flashbulbs washed out the black net covering. You only thought you were seeing skin.

* * *

In *A Star Is Born* (Warner Bros., 1976) Barbra is seen briefly wearing

Unlikely lovers in the popular *The Way We Were* (1973). Streisand agrees to Redford getting the higher salary, because he is so perfect for the film. However, he declines to work with her on *The Prince of Tides.*
PHOTO COURTESY OF PHOTOFEST

white short-shorts and a white T-shirt with the Superman logo. To keep the momentum going from the success of that film, she recorded an album of pop songs called *Streisand Superman* (1977). She posed in the white shorts for album photos.

Peter Reilly reviewed the album for *Stereo Review*: "Streisand's newest features . . . several rear-view photographs of her in an abbreviated track suit that permits an ample display of tushie. And a very pretty and appealing tushie it is, too. And also probably aimed directly, for bussing purposes, at the critics."

*   *   *

By the end of the 1970s, Barbra Streisand, age thirty-seven, had become quite enamored of her rear end. She put her buttocks on prominent display in *The Main Event* (Warner Bros., 1979). The reviews were mixed. Some critics appreciated the view, but many gave it a rump roast. (See **Part II: 12. A Hymn to Her: The Films of Barbra Streisand.**)

*   *   *

Then in 1991 Streisand went topless again . . . and changed her mind yet again. In an early version of a love scene with Nick Nolte for *The Prince of Tides* (Columbia), forty-nine-year-old Barbra filmed herself in such a way that audiences could see through her top. "I showed it in a preview. I got a feeling that it took people out of the scene," she explained. "It was like, all of a sudden, there's Barbra Streisand's breasts, instead of the emotion of the scene. So, I cut it differently. I made it into a two-shot in close-ups." — (*Drama-Logue*, December 19, 1991)

*   *   *

And that brings us to the porno film. It seems you really haven't made it to superstar firmament until it's revealed that you supposedly made a porno movie—and *of course* you did it only because you desperately needed the money. And the fact that a friend's father's cousin actually *saw* it is all the proof anyone needs.

In the October 1977 *Playboy*, Barbra discussed the porno film she's alleged to be in. She admits that the girl in the film has long hair just like she had in the sixties, but that she's chubby while Barbra was skinny. The giveaway is in a closeup of the girl's hands around the guy's you-know-what, and they're short, stubby fingers. Definitely not Streisand's!

CHAPTER 14

What Might Have Been: The Barbra Streisand Films Not Made

It's endlessly fascinating to speculate on What Might Have Been, espe-cially about someone with the range of talent, resources, and clout of Barbra Streisand. But how can you be sure of the reality of these unre-alized movie projects listed below? They could be what writer Norman Mailer calls "factoids": facts which have no existence before appearing in a magazine or newspaper. This is Hollywood: What's real? What's fan-tasy? What's press release? So one speculates. What if Streisand had made *Alice Doesn't Live Here Anymore* (Warner Bros., 1975) instead of *The Main Event* (Warner Bros., 1979)? Didn't the Triangle factory fire hold more promise of dramatic entertainment than *Nuts* (Warner Bros., 1987)? Wouldn't *anything* have been better than *Nuts*?

THE MUSICALS

Out of sixteen feature films to date, Streisand has made four tradi-tional musicals: *Funny Girl* (Columbia, 1968); *Hello, Dolly!* (Twentieth Century-Fox, 1969); *On a Clear Day You Can See Forever* (Paramount, 1970); *Funny Lady* (Columbia, 1975); the pop musical *A Star Is Born* (Warner Bros., 1976); and the fable-with-music *Yentl* (MGM/United Artists, 1983). She should/might have done more with the musical form, and may yet. God knows she's been offered just about every musical project out there, from Harold Arlen to Franz Lehar to Andrew Lloyd Webber. And one that she didn't make had "special" written all over it.

*   *   *

Hollywood super agent Ray Stark, who turned producer with the Broadway musical of *Funny Girl* (1964), signed Barbra Streisand to a four-picture deal, to begin with the movie adaptation of *Funny Girl*.

When Streisand announced that for her next star turn she would do *Hello, Dolly!*, Stark filed for an injunction to stop her from working for another movie company while under contract to him. He submitted two screen projects to her. The first was **Wait 'Til the Sun Shines, Nellie**, a musical inspired by the memorable Twentieth Century-Fox film (1952), a nostalgic evocation of small-town life starring Jean Peters and David Wayne. The second Stark proposal was **Seesaw**, the musical version of William Gibson's 1958 stage hit *Two for the Seesaw*, with a score by Cy Coleman and Dorothy Fields. This song-and-dance show had run for 296 performances on Broadway in 1973 with Ken Howard and Michele Lee. Lucie Arnaz and John Gavin had toured in the national company.

Streisand hated both suggested projects and threatened her own legal action to avoid making them for Stark. The stubborn star and the angry producer eventually settled their differences out of court. Neither of these two projects ever made it to the screen.

*   *   *

Streisand has had a long-time passion for all things French (French being her idea of classy) and particularly wants to portray on-screen the legendary actress **Sarah Bernhardt** (1844–1923), who was part Jewish and totally eccentric (she reportedly slept in a coffin). Barbra was offered the lead in a 1969 Broadway production of a play about the divine Sarah; it never materialized but even if it had, Barbra couldn't really face the thought of returning to the stage again.

She discussed Bernhardt with British film director Ken Russell, who'd filmed wonderfully flamboyant biographies of dancer Isadora Duncan, composers Peter Ilych Tchaikovsky and Gustav Mahler, and silent-screen legend Rudolph Valentino. They made a deal for a

Bernhardt movie biography, a spring 1972 start date was announced, and then Barbra began demanding changes to the script. When Russell refused, the project was killed.

This was maybe a Streisand goof. Here you had three over-the-top, in-your-face personalities—Bernhardt, Russell, and Streisand — made for each other. They mighta made it work.

A perfectly respectable Sarah Bernhardt film bio was made eventually, called *The Incredible Sarah* (British, 1976). It starred Glenda Jackson, was directed by Richard Fleischer, and was quickly forgotten. The Bernhardt name came up again in 1981 when Streisand asked United Artists to finance and distribute *Yentl*. The studio supposedly agreed because they wanted Barbra for a musical biography of Sarah Bernhardt (which has yet to materialize).

Another United Artists screen project discussed in the early 1980s was a musical based on the 1910 autobiographical novel *La Vagabonde* by Colette (1873–1954), one more of Barbra's French heroines. Sydney Pollack agreed to direct the screen adaptation if Arthur Laurents wrote the script and Stephen Sondheim composed the score. The project screeched to a halt when the studio couldn't get the rights to the novel.

Yet another unrealized United Artists project at that time was *House of Flowers*, based on the 1954 stage musical written by Harold Arlen and Truman Capote. This show features the song "A Sleepin' Bee," Streisand's favorite. (Actually, it was her audition song for her very first singing engagements; she considers it her lucky charm.)

But what role would Barbra have played in *House of Flowers*? The musical is set in Jamaica and has an all-native cast!

One Musical She Didn't Have a Chance to Reject

Following the smash success of *A Chorus Line* (1975) on Broadway, director-choreographer Michael Bennett was sought after by Hollywood. He wanted to make *Roadshow*, a musical about a touring production of *Two for the Seesaw*, with Bette Midler and Robert Redford in the leads. Universal insisted that Streisand should star, as Midler was too unattractive. Bennett packed his bags and escaped back to New York.

When critics (and fans) start totaling up Streisand's cinematic "mistakes" over the decades, turning down *Cabaret* (Allied Artists, 1972) is certainly near the top of the list. This story, of pre-World War II Berlin seen through the eyes of good-time American playgirl Sally Bowles, has been successful from the beginning: The original book *Berlin Stories* (1946) won acclaim for author Christopher Isherwood; the Broadway dramatization *I Am a Camera* (1952) and the movie version (DCA, 1955) won fame for actress Julie Harris; the hit Broadway musical adaptation (1966) did little for actress Jill Haworth; but Liza Minnelli won the Best Actress Oscar for the hugely popular movie version.

Would Streisand have been a sensational Sally Bowles? Imagine it! Why did she say no? Why? Why?

*   *   *

And, would you believe it, *Wait 'Til the Sun Shines, Nellie* also came around again, in 1974, when Streisand began thinking that, perhaps, it was a good idea after all. Lover-film producer Jon Peters called Jerry Schatzberg, then a currently hot director, to ask if he would be interested in directing the project. No, said Schatzberg, he was committed to directing *A Star Is Born*. What's that? asked Peters—it sounds interesting, send over the script. And that's how *that* 1976 Streisand movie began.

*   *   *

Born Yesterday has also had a long and varied history. The Garson Kanin comedy originated on Broadway in 1946, with Judy Holliday creating a sensation as not-so-dumb blonde Billie Dawn. She recreated the role in the film version (Columbia, 1950) and won the Best Actress Oscar. In 1954 songwriter Sammy Cahn envisioned a musical version of *Born Yesterday* with Marilyn Monroe as Billie and Frank Sinatra costarring as the loudmouth junk dealer who became a loudmouth millionaire. The project was scrapped when Marilyn ran off to marry baseball great Joe DiMaggio. When Barbra Streisand burst upon the scene in the late 1960s, Styne envisioned her and Sinatra being spectacular together. He made phone calls, author Garson Kanin made phone calls, but it never happened.

A nonmusical screen remake of *Born Yesterday* showed up in 1993

176

(Hollywood Pictures) starring Melanie Griffith and Barbra's ex-lover Don Johnson . . . who was Melanie's husband *and* her ex-husband. The film was dead on arrival.

*   *   *

In *People* magazine (April 26, 1976), Barbra recalled: "I was supposed to do **The Merry Widow** with Ingmar Bergman. He wrote the script. I read it and liked only the first half. I asked him to rewrite. He refused, so I refused to do the film." Instead, she made *Up the Sandbox* (National General, 1972).

With *The Merry Widow* she had the rare opportunity to work with one of the world cinema's undisputed masters. Yes, Swedish filmmaker Bergman is associated with the bleak vision of movies like *The Seventh Seal* (1957), *Winter Light* (1963), and *Persona* (1966). However, he also wrote and directed romantic dramas and sophisticated romantic comedies like *Smiles of a Summer Night* (1955) which became the classic musical *A Little Night Music* (1973). [In his first English-language film, *The Touch* (Swedish, 1971), Bergman had directed Barbra's ex-husband, Elliot Gould.]

Of greatest interest here, however, is Bergman's cinematic vision of *The Magic Flute* (1974), in which he turned Mozart's opera into a magical fairy tale. It's unaffected, unfussy, accessible. Imagine what Bergman could have done with *The Merry Widow*; that lush nineteenth-century romance of a European prince wooing a rich American widow to the sweeping waltzes of Franz Lehar. (The hit song is "Vilia.")

The Merry Widow had been filmed as a silent by Erich von Stroheim (MGM, 1925) starring Mae Murray and John Gilbert; as a sound feature by Ernst Lubitsch (MGM, 1934) with Jeanette MacDonald and Maurice Chevalier; and then again by Curtis Bernhardt (MGM, 1952) with Lana Turner and Fernando Lamas.

In addition to Mae Murray, Jeanette MacDonald, and Trudy Erwin (the singing voice of Lana Turner), *The Merry Widow* has been performed in far-flung stage productions and record albums by many of this century's greatest singers: Rise Stevens, Kitty Carlisle, Dorothy Kirsten, Anna Moffo, Lisa Della Casa, Patrice Munsel, Roberta Peters, Hilde Gueden, Joan Sutherland, Beverly Sills, Elisabeth Schwarzkopf, and Cheryl Studer. Streisand has the voice—she would have fit right in . . . wonderfully.

*　　*　　*

In 1978, Streisand and Neil Diamond each recorded the song "**You Don't Bring Me Flowers.**" A disc jockey in Louisville recognized that they were both singing in the same key, so (you must remember this) he cleverly created a duet by splicing together the two versions and created a hit. Columbia put the two singers together in a studio and created a real duet *and* a real big hit. At the 1980 Grammy ceremony, Streisand and Diamond were a sensation when they appeared on opposite ends of the stage singing their hit. "You Don't Bring Me Flowers" won the Grammy Song of the Year.

The next big idea was to develop a movie of the same name to star these two top-name performers. Various screenplays were written but never to Barbra's satisfaction. *Barbra* magazine (vol. 2, no. 1, 1981) reported that Diamond was moving ahead on his own, with actress Mary Steenburgen set to costar in *You Don't Bring Me Flowers*. Diamond did move ahead, but, instead, chose to star in *The Jazz Singer* (Associated Film Dist., 1981), a stink bomb which effectively ended his screen acting career.

*　　*　　*

In spring 1979, after *The Main Event*, Barbra acquired the screen rights to the rousing Irving Berlin musical **Annie Get Your Gun.** The original 1946 Broadway production had showcased Ethel Merman. Judy Garland was to star in the 1950 MGM movie but dropped out for health reasons, and was replaced by Betty Hutton. Jon Peters was to produce the Streisand movie version. Could the brash Brooklynite have brought it off? Listen, if Ethel Merman could do it. . . .

*　　*　　*

In the mid-1980s there was talk of filming **They're Playing Our Song**, a 1978 Broadway musical based on the lives of composer Marvin Hamlisch and songwriter Carole Bayer Singer . . . who wrote the music and lyrics for the stage show. Streisand was slated for the lead in the movie musical with ex-husband Elliott Gould, who swore, "It's definite." Marvin Hamlisch said, "I have heard about it, but I swear to God no one has spoken to me yet." And, apparently, no one did . . . ever.

*　　*　　*

178

In early 1989 Barbra was said to be considering the role of Mama Rose in a big-screen remake of *Gypsy* . . . with Madonna as daughter Gypsy Rose Lee. (Say, *that* would have been interesting!)

Mama Rose is another role, like Annie Oakley, created by the one-woman brass band named Ethel Merman, who headlined the original 1959 Broadway hit production, with Sandra Church as Gypsy Rose Lee. The 1962 Warner Bros. film featured Rosalind Russell as Mama Rose (with Lisa Kirk singing the harder parts) and Natalie Wood as her stripper daughter (with Marni Nixon supplying the high notes). There have been two successful Broadway revivals: with Angela Lansbury in 1974 and Tyne Daly in 1989.

The Streisand project eventually evolved into a network TV special, televised in December 1993, with Bette Midler as Mama and Cynthia Gibb as Gypsy Rose Lee.

*   *   *

And then there is . . . ***Evita!***

Andrew Lloyd Webber and Tim Rice, creators of the phenomenally successful musical *Evita* (1978), the story of Argentina's charismatic strong woman Eva Peron (1919–1952), publicly stated in the early 1990s that Barbra Streisand was their choice for the movie—their only choice.

Barbra's no-bull response was recorded by *Drama-Logue* (December 19, 1992): "Let's get this straight," she said, suddenly transforming into that pugnacious, outspoken Brooklyn girl who endeared herself to a legion of fans. "I went to see *Evita*, they [the producers] wanted me to see it, to do Evita. I hate the show! Print that if you want to. I hated it! The producers kept putting out, 'Barbra Streisand wants to play the part.' I would call them, write them letters saying 'Please stop using me to promote your project.' I don't want the thing. I don't even like the song, 'Don't Cry for Me, Argentina'!"

*   *   *

Streisand recently came close to making another musical . . . maybe.

Miramax Films tycoon Harvey Weinstein made Barbra Streisand a 'very firm' offer to star in the screen version of the Bob Fosse musical ***Chicago***, the tale of publicity-hungry showgirl Roxie Hart, who shoots her lover. It debuted on Broadway in 1975 with Gwen Verdon

179

and Chita Rivera. Successful revivals of *Chicago* are currently playing in New York and Los Angeles.

There was speculation that if Streisand were interested in this film venture she'd also produce and direct it. But there's "many a slip 'twixt the cup and the lip" (Palladas, A.D. 400), and Goldie Hawn and Madonna were signed instead for Roxie's big-screen outing. Did Barbra miss another golden opportunity? We'll never know, will we?

TORN FROM THE HEADLINES!

Barbra Streisand has discussed a number of media projects that reflect her concerns with the world's social and political problems.

* * *

In the late 1970s, Barbra made it known she wanted to do "something important" on television. She was sent the script of ***Playing for Time***, written by super-important playwright Arthur Miller. This is the true story of Fania Fenelon, a half-Jewish nightclub singer who was sent to the Auschwitz concentration camp during World War II, where she became part of an all-female orchestra that entertained the Nazis. Streisand rejected this project because of salary problems: Art or not, she demanded the salary of a *star*. In this case the figure she had in mind was double the entire budget of the TV movie. The producers had to "settle" for Vanessa Redgrave, who is just an actress . . . but she won the Emmy for Best Actress.

The movie aired on NBC in 1980.

* * *

"Barbra will be costarring with Jane Fonda in ***The Triangle Fire***, script by Naomi Foner, from a novel by Leon Stein. The Triangle factory fire was a shocking tragedy in turn-of-the-century New York City, with dozens of lives lost among the mostly female workers. The public outrage over the lack of safety precautions resulted in more humane working conditions for factory workers. The film will be produced by longtime Streisand associate Cis Corman" (*Barbra* magazine, vol. 2, no. 1; Summer 1981).

However, this publicity hype was for naught. This movie would have been a must-see for the casting alone, as Streisand has never yet shared the screen with an actress of equal stature. Too bad for us. Too bad for Barbra.

*   *   *

One of Barbra's unrealized screen projects has created more attention and caused more controversy than some of her efforts that did make it—Larry Kramer's AIDS play *The Normal Heart*.

This emotional call-to-arms, first presented in New York City in 1985, tells of the gradual discovery of the virus, the growing alarm in the gay community, and of the government's indifference or reluctance in seeking a cure.

Streisand optioned the drama in spring 1986. From the beginning, playwright Larry Kramer worried that Barbra saw his play as a starring vehicle for herself, portraying Dr. Emma Brookner—who is an important but minor character in the story.

When it came time to sign the final contract, Barbra insisted that she, not Kramer, would write the final screenplay. Kramer refused to give up control of his story, so the deal was dead. Instead, Barbra made *Nuts*.

Time passed. In the spring of 1990, Streisand and Kramer compromised: He would write the script but she would have the final word. Kramer had been HIV positive for two years; he was desperate to get *The Normal Heart* on the screen before he was dead, so he agreed to her terms.

In spring 1994 Streisand was *still* working with Larry Kramer on rewrites . . . *and* working with writer Richard LaGravenese on *The Mirror Has Two Faces* (TriStar, 1996). When she announced that *Mirror* would be her next film, Kramer was justifiably furious.

In January 1996 Barbra's ten-year option on *The Normal Heart* expired. On April 8 of that year, Kramer was quoted in *Variety*: "She was all set to make *The Normal Heart* about a worldwide plague, and at the last minute she switches to a film about a woman who gets a facelift. I didn't think that was decent of her to do to me, her gay fans, and the people with AIDS she talks so movingly about."

Biographer Anne Edwards (*Streisand: A Biography*. Boston: Little, Brown, 1997) was interviewed in the July 1997 issue of *Icon* magazine. Her criticism: "Barbra did something unconscionable—she held onto that play for too long. She held it to the point where the play was no

181

longer 'the hot property'—it's not relevant politically anymore."

In thinking back, Kramer concludes that he may have made a mistake in presenting Streisand with a book with graphic photos of gays making love—to help her understand the subject of her movie. "She really freaked out," he says. "She said, 'This is what you do?' I began to see that maybe she was more prudish than I'd been led to believe, considering she's the mother of a gay son" (*The Advocate*, June 11, 1996).

STORY INTO FILM

The filmography of Streisand's movies-that-never-were include projects plucked from the bestseller lists.

* * *

At the time she was preparing *A Star Is Born*, in 1975, Robert Benton and David Newman were writing **The Gift Shop** for Barbra, adapted from the 1966 suspense novel by bestselling author Charlotte Armstrong.

Benton and Newman earlier had written *What's Up, Doc?* (Warner Bros., 1972), one of Streisand's most successful movies. But a Hitchcock-type woman in distress? Do they make that kind of movie anymore? Certainly Barbra Streisand don't!

* * *

In 1985 Streisand and Robert De Niro jointly purchased the rights for **To a Violent Grave: An Oral Biography of Jackson Pollock** by Jeff Potter. The story details the tumultuous relationship between Pollock, the famous abstract artist, and his wife-manager, artist Lee Krasner. This project is particularly meaningful to De Niro, as his father (also known as Robert De Niro) was an artist of note.

* * *

"Dynamic young producer (and former real estate tycoon) Keith Barish has acquired movie rights to the D. M. Thomas bestseller **The White Hotel** (New York: Viking, 1981) which features the kind of juicy role actresses fight for—Lisa Erdman, an opera singer in turn-of-the-century Vienna, who undergoes psychiatric analysis by Sigmund Freud himself for hysterical symptoms. Vivid sexual

182

fantasy sequences contribute to the uniqueness of the role" (*Barbra*, vol. 2, no. 2; 1981).

ILL-ADVISED REMAKES AND SEQUELS

In April 1985, Robert Redford told a reporter that there was a definite possibility of a sequel to the mega-hit *The Way We Were* (Columbia, 1973), and it would costar Barbra. The new project would incorporate unused footage from the original film, and would be called *The Way We've Changed*.

Director Sydney Pollack scoffed at reports of a pending big-screen sequel: "We'd have to do it from wheelchairs. Everybody's getting too old," he says. But seriously, "We've tried to make a sequel work. I've done two scripts myself. [Producer] Ray Stark has two scripts. But we couldn't find anything that didn't sound like it was being done just to capitalize on the first film" (columnists Marilyn Beck and Stacy Jenel Smith, Los Angeles *Daily News*, February 24, 1997).

*　　*　　*

At the time she was prepping *The Prince of Tides* (Columbia, 1991), Streisand was also planning a big-budget screen remake of Claude Lelouch's *And Now My Love* (French, 1974), a multigenerational love story, which had starred Marthe Keller and André Dussollier.

In light of the care Barbra took with the Jewish story *Yentl* (MGM/United Artists, 1983), this project is of interest in that it also involves the lives of European Jews and the Holocaust.

*　　*　　*

There was talk in the mid-1980s of a remake of *The Captain's Paradise* (British, 1953), the classic comedy with Alec Guinness as a ship's captain who has wives in opposite ports. In the proposed new rendition, Streisand would be a ship's cruise director with a husband in every port. As with the other projects detailed here, *The Captain* never arrived.

*　　*　　*

For a long time, a remake of *The Women* kept showing up on lists as an upcoming Streisand screen idea. At one point, Faye Dunaway and Raquel Welch were even listed as costars.

183

A bitch fest, Clare Boothe Luce's *The Women* was first produced on Broadway in 1936. MGM's 1939 movie version starred Joan Crawford, Norma Shearer, and Rosalind Russell. There was a musical remake, *The Opposite Sex* (MGM, 1956) with June Allyson, Joan Collins, and Dolores Gray. (This rendition gave the women onscreen husbands and boyfriends.)

The idea of a Streisand celluloid variation was foolish from the beginning—the very idea of her sharing the screen with a dozen other women!

THE OFFERS SHE REJECTED
(and Maybe Lived to Regret)

After Streisand's first singing appearance in Los Angeles, in August 1963, at the legendary Cocoanut Grove, she received numerous movie offers. Producer/director Samuel Goldwyn, Jr. offered her the lead in *The Young Lovers* (MGM, 1964). She wanted to accept but couldn't: After her club tour ended in December, she would immediately start rehearsals for *Funny Girl* (1964) on Broadway. *The Young Lovers* (1964) was made with Peter Fonda, Sharon Hugueny, Nick Adams, and Deborah Walley. And surely Barbra was lucky to have lost this love.

* * *

Before production began on *A Star Is Born* (1976), Jon Peters formed his own company and signed a three-movie deal with Columbia Pictures. He optioned the thriller *Eyes* (to become *The Eyes of Laura Mars*, 1978). Columbia hoped that Streisand would star as the photographer who has premonitions of murder. Streisand said it was not a role she wished to play. (Faye Dunaway wasn't as choosy. However, she should have been.) Barbra did consent to sing "Prisoner" over the opening credits (one of the few Streisand endeavors never available on CD).

* * *

Many of Barbra's thumbs-down movie-making decisions have caused loyal fans to question her instinct for doing what's "right for me." She turned down *They Shoot Horses, Don't They?* (National General,

1969) because she didn't want to do all that dancing. Jane Fonda took the challenge and, as a result, was rewarded with an Oscar nomination for Best Actress. Streisand turned down *Klute* (Warner Bros., 1971), and, once again, Jane Fonda stepped into the part and, this time, won the Best Actress Oscar. Barbra turned down *The Devils* (Warner Bros., 1971), which became a critical success for Vanessa Redgrave, and turned down *Cabaret*, with which Liza Minnelli went home with an Academy Award.

In turn, Streisand rejected two projects that made actress Ellen Burstyn's day: first, as the anguished mother in *The Exorcist* (Warner Bros., 1973), which won Burstyn a Best Acress nomination for her work in that horror classic. Then, Streisand declined to work with Martin Scorsese on *Alice Doesn't Live Here Anymore*, reasoning that, at the age of thirty-one, she was much too young to play the mother of a twelve-year-old. Ellen Burstyn, forty-one years old, won an Oscar for her performance as Alice the waitress.

And yet throughout the 1970s quixotic Streisand frequently expressed dissatisfaction with her acting career. With the exception of *Up the Sandbox* and most of *The Way We Were*, she felt she had not yet fulfilled her potential as a dramatic actress.

This is not to say that Barbra would have taken the Academy Awards that Jane Fonda and Liza Minnelli and Ellen Burstyn did. However, there would certainly have been the possibility of "fulfilling her potential"—a possibility that's sorely missing from the clinkers she has made instead. Barbra, phone home!

*   *   *

After the success of *A Star is Born* in 1976, First Artists proposed a project originally meant for **Steve McQueen** and **Ali MacGraw**: that of a midwest farm girl and the city man who sweeps her off her feet. Barbra refused.

*   *   *

As early as 1977 Streisand was considering *Third Time Lucky*. This psychological love drama concerns a mentally unstable ex-actress living in a squalid London flat with her small son. A man enters her life and a bittersweet love story blossoms. It's from a novel by screenwriter Stanley Mann.

185

A Come-as-a-Marx-Brother costume party, in a scene from *The Way We Were* (1973). The real Groucho drops by to buss Barbra as Harpo. The Groucho on the right is Bradford Dillman.
PHOTO COURTESY OF J. C. ARCHIVES

In 1981 *Variety* reported that after years of discussion, the movie had been reinstated as a property for Barbra, to be produced by Jon Peters and Peter Guber through Polygram Pictures.

Fortunately, I think, *Third Time Lucky* didn't happen. Unfortunately, *Nuts* did.

*   *   *

In 1995 *The New Yorker* published writer-editor Michael Korda's profile on the late **Jacqueline Susann** (1921–1974), the wonderfully flamboyant author of the trash classic *The Valley of the Dolls* (New York: Bernard Geis, 1966). TriStar paid Korda $750,000 for the movie rights and hired Paul Rudnick to write the screenplay for producers Andy Bergman and Mike Lovell.

Bette Midler expressed interest, as did Streisand. Bette won, Barbra lost.

*   *   *

After *What's Up, Doc?* Barbra considered **Bent Jane** as her next movie project. The screenplay by W. D. Richter (who wrote *All Night Long*; Universal, 1981) is about a woman with a compulsion to kill. It was to be directed by Lee Katzin. It didn't happen. Barbra as a murderess? Her fans would have killed her!

*   *   *

A start date of spring 1975 was given for **Suppose They Met**, a romantic comedy developed by Streisand and Jon Peters, from a screenplay by Joane A. Gil. The story is about a feminist leader who falls in love with a sexist millionaire playboy (was Peters planning to costar?).

*   *   *

Barbra continues to develop her own projects. One that keeps coming up in conversation is the film biography of the famous *Life* magazine photographer **Margaret Bourke-White** (1904–1971). Streisand talks of Richard Gere for the part of Southern writer Erskine Caldwell (*Tobacco Road*, 1932), Bourke-White's husband of five years.

THE DIRECTORS SHE REJECTED

"The only American directors who've asked me to be in their movies are Peter Bogdanovich [with whom she'd made *What's Up, Doc?*] and Irvin Kershner [with whom she'd made *Up the Sandbox*]. And then foreign directors. John Schlesinger asked me a long time ago to be in a movie. Bertolucci asked me once, and Ingmar Bergman. And then Percy Adlon, the German director, asked me to be in *Bagdad Cafe* (West German, 1988). I was almost going to be in it just because he wanted me! It was so sweet, to be wanted by a director" (*Vanity Fair*, November 1994).

*   *   *

Biographer Randall Riese (*Her Name Is Barbra*. New York: Birch Lane, 1993) reports that Italian director Bernardo Bertolucci had been scheduled to direct *The Mirror Has Two Faces*. Many saw this as a good sign, as Streisand has worked with so few strong directors in her Hollywood endeavors.

But come on! The idea of Bernardo Bertolucci (*The Conformist*, 1970; *Last Tango in Paris*, 1972; *1900*, 1976; *The Last Emperor*, 1987) directing fluff like *The Mirror Has Two Faces*—well, it strains credulity!

THE DIRECTING JOB SHE REJECTED

Streisand says she was asked to direct the movie *Shadowlands* (Savoy Pictures, 1993), the story of the love of British writer C. S. Lewis (1898–1963) for dying American poet Joey Gresham.

She turned it down, but Richard Attenborough bravely accepted the assignment. The movie starred Anthony Hopkins and Debra Winger. The *TV Guide* ad called it "the most unusual love story of all time." What was really unusual was how fast it was in and out of movie theatres.

THE OFFERS SHE DIDN'T GET

Barbra Streisand desperately wanted to play the title role in ***Sophie's Choice*** (Universal, 1982), a film based on William Styron's 1979 bestseller. Styron himself wanted Swiss-Italian actress Ursula Andress (a very curious casting choice); director Alan J. Pakula hoped for Norwegian-Swedish actress Liv Ullmann; German actress Marthe Keller was also a top contender.

As the contest for the coveted pivotal role heated up, Meryl Streep is said to have actually begged Pakula for the screen assignment. Streisand went her one better and offered to play Sophie without salary in exchange for a percentage of the profits. However, the British mogul Sir Lew Grade, who was involved in financing the picture, didn't care for Streisand's looks. Thus, Meryl Streep won the part *and* the Oscar.

*   *   *

After Barbra and Don Johnson split in 1988, she threw herself into her work. She had wanted to star on camera in the vicious comedy *The War of the Roses* (Twentieth Century-Fox, 1989), but director Danny

DeVito instead chose Kathleen Turner. Streisand also sought the female lead in *Frankie & Johnny* (Paramount, 1991), but director Garry Marshall preferred Michelle Pfeiffer to play opposite Robert De Niro.

COCKAMAMY IDEAS

After *A Star Is Born*, in the mid-1970s, Streisand and Peters began working on a **clown project** because Streisand is wild about clowns. They did not actually have a story, so they flew in Arthur Laurents (who wrote *The Way We Were*, both novel and screenplay) to see if he could offer help. Laurents couldn't think of any clown ideas either.

*   *   *

"Cindy Adams reports that TriStar is trying to influence Barbra to star in *Lady in a Cage*. The film story parallels the Princess Diana tragedy, in that the screenplay is about a Hollywood star dealing with "stalkerazzi" photographers and ends with tragic consequences. The project is described as an update of Paramount's 1964 Olivia de Havilland film of the same title. If Barbra doesn't do the film, TriStar hopes to move on the project with either Bette Midler or Madonna" (*Just Like Buttah*, no. 12, 1997).

For those lucky enough to have missed the 1964 Olivia de Havilland thriller: This is the story of a rich but lonely widow trapped in a private elevator in her home during a power failure who is then terrorized by James Caan and other screen thugs. At the stand-up-and-cheer finale, the brave little widow pokes out James Caan's eyes; he staggers away, and, because a freeway runs right in front of the house, a car runs over his head.

The parallels to the Princess Diana tragedy should be obvious.

*   *   *

Barbra (vol. 1, no. 3; 1979) reports that screen veteran **Shelley Winters** is writing her autobiography and announced that Barbra Streisand wants first dibs on the screen rights so she can play the title role.

Two-time Oscar winner Shelley Winters published the first installment of her autobiography, *Shelley: Also Known as Shirley* (New York: William Morrow), in 1980. Thus far, it has not been filmed. Part two

A scene from the comedy *For Pete's Sake* (1974) with Michael
Sarrazin as husband Pete, because no major star would play the part.
PHOTO COURTESY OF J. C. ARCHIVES

was *Shelley II: The Middle of My Century* (New York: Simon and
Schuster, 1989). This one, also and alas, hasn't been filmed, yet. In this
second volume, Winters tells of spending a 1960 weekend at the beach
with writer Arthur Laurents. She says she told him stories of things
that had happened to her . . . that wound up happening to Barbra
Streisand in Laurents' screenplay for *The Way We Were*.

CHAPTER 15

Barbra Streisand as Movie Producer

THEATRICAL MOVIES

First Artists was introduced as a new production company on June 11, 1969—a joint venture of Barbra Streisand, Paul Newman, and Sidney Poitier. (Steve McQueen joined the moviemaking firm in 1971, Dustin Hoffman a year later.) The stated aim was to start a new business in developing and producing theatrical motion pictures, as well as give the stars complete creative control over these feature films.

Each partner would develop three movies in which they believed. They would have final cut; they would take no up-front money but would receive a percentage of a picture's gross.

Barbra weighed various projects in the early 1970s: *Bent Jane*, about a woman with a compulsion to kill; a biography of Sarah Bernhardt to be directed by Ken Russell; and a remake of *The Merry Widow* to be helmed by Ingmar Bergman. (See **Part II: 13. What Might Have Been.**) She decided instead on the feminist *Up the Sandbox* because she "wanted to do something about something" (Joseph Gelmis, "On Being Barbra," *Newsday*, January 21, 1973). The film was a critical and box office failure.

In April 1974 when Streisand became interested in remaking *A Star*

191

Barbra quells the crowd of 50,000 rock fans who show up for the outdoor concert scene in *A Star Is Born* (1976). Trying to speak their lingo, she tells them, "All you motherfuckers have a great time!"
PHOTO COURTESY OF J. C. ARCHIVES

Is Born (Warner Bros., 1976), one of her demands was that First Artists take over the project, with Warner Bros. acting only as distributor. Warners acquiesced. *A Star Is Born* is still the top-grossing movie of Barbra's career.

In October 1978 Barbra began filming *The Main Event* (Warner Bros., 1979) to fulfill her contract with First Artists, seeing this as a frivolous, commercial venture after the grueling experience of *A Star Is Born*. *The Main Event* was a hit.

First Artists was sold to an Australian firm in early January 1979. This move was denounced by Ed Holly, vice president of First Artists, as "a strong indication of how little First Artists meant to the stars themselves. . . ." (quoted in Anne Edwards. *Streisand: A Biography*. Boston: Little, Brown, 1997).

Streisand calls her company Barwood Productions (Barbra plus Hollywood). Longtime loyal agent Marty Erlichman is an executive with the company. Cis Corman, Barbra's oldest friend, is president. To date, Barwood has been associated with seven of Barbra's sixteen movies (see **Part II: 12. A Hymn to Her: The Films of Barbra Streisand** for full credits):

- *Up the Sandbox* (National General, 1972)
  A First Artists Presentation of a Barwood Film.
- *A Star Is Born* (Warner Bros./First Artists, 1976)
  A Barwood/Jon Peters Production.
- *The Main Event* (Warner Bros./First Artists, 1979)
  A Barwood Film.
- *All Night Long* (Universal, 1981)
  A Barwood Film.
- *Yentl* (United Artists, 1983)
  A Barwood Film.
- *Nuts* (Warner Bros., 1987)
  A Barwood Film.
- *The Mirror Has Two Faces* (TriStar Pictures, 1996)
  An Arnon Milchan-Barwood Films Production.

MOVIES PRODUCED FOR TV

Serving In Silence: The Margarethe Cammermeyer Story
(NBC, February 6, 1995) 100 minutes

Storyline: The true story of a much-decorated U.S. Army nurse who was discharged in 1992, after twenty-six years in the military, for revealing that she was a lesbian. A colonel, she was the highest-ranking official ever discharged for being a lesbian. She became a leader in the fight to overturn the military's ban on homosexuals.

Cast: Glenn Close, Judy Davis, Jan Rubes, Wendy Makkena, Susan Barnes, William Converse-Roberts.

Credits: Producer, Richard Heus; executive producers, Barbra Streisand, Glenn Close, Craig Zadan, Neil Meron, Cis Corman; director, Jeff Bleckner; screenplay, Alison Cross.

Rescuers: Stories of Courage—Two Women
(Showtime, October 5, 1997) 100 minutes

Storyline: True stories of non-Jews who risk their lives to help save victims of the Holocaust during World War II.

Cast: Elizabeth Perkins, Sela Ward, Fritz Weaver, Anne Jackson.

Credits: Producer, Jeff Freilich; executive producers, Barbra Streisand, Cis Corman; director, Peter Bogdanovich; screenplay, Susan Nanus, Ernest Kinoy, based on the book *Rescuers: Portraits of Moral Courage in the Holocaust* by Gay Block and Malka Drucker (New York: Holmes & Meier, 1992).

Of Note: Barbra Streisand introduces the made-for-cable-TV movie.

The Long Island Incident
(NBC, May 3, 1998) 120 minutes

Storyline: Based on the ordeal of Long Island housewife Carolyn McCarthy, whose husband was killed and son severely wounded when a crazed gunman opened fire on the passengers inside a Long Island Railroad commuter train. McCarthy later ran for Congress on an antigun platform and was elected.

Cast: Laurie Metcalf, Mackenzie Astin, Tyron Benskin.

Credits: Producers, Rick Rosenberg, Bob Christiansen; executive producers, Cis Corman, Barbra Streisand; co-executive producer, Jordan Davis; director, Joseph Sargent; screenplay, Maria Nation.

Rescuers: Stories of Courage—Two Couples
(Showtime, May 10, 1998) 120 minutes

Storyline: Two true stories of non-Jews who bravely save Jews from the Nazis.

Cast: Dana Delany, Linda Hamilton, Martin Donovan, Alfred Molina.

Credits: Producer, Jeff Freilich; executive producers, Barbra Streisand,

Executive producer Barbra Streisand and producer Jon Peters watch
a playback from *A Star Is Born* (1976).
It's their movie, and probably their story that's on the screen.
It remains Barbra's most successful movie.
PHOTO COURTESY OF J. C. ARCHIVES

Cis Corman; directors, Tim Hunter, Lynne Litman; screenplay, Paul
Monash, Cy Chermak, Francine Carroll.

Of Note: Barbra Streisand introduces this made-for-cable-TV movie.

Projects announced by Barwood:

Rescuers: Stories of Courage—Two Families
Scheduled to air in the winter of 1998.

Cast: Daryl Hannah, Tim Matheson.

195

Two Hands That Shook the World

The story of Yitzhak Rabin, Yasser Arafat, and their attempts to bring peace to the Middle East.

Barbra spoke to journalists about her intent to make this project, in 1995. When Israeli Prime Minister Rabin was assassinated in 1997, Barbra announced plans to proceed with the production.

What Makes a Family

A projected TV movie for CBS, first announced in February 1996. The true story of a lesbian who fights a legal battle to gain custody of her dead lover's daughter.

The project is to be a coproduction of Barwood (Streisand and Cis Corman) and Storyline Entertainment (Craig Zadan and Neil Meron), the producers of *Serving In Silence: The Margarethe Cammermeyer Story*, in association with Touchstone Television.

Varian's War

A TV movie project first announced in April 1997: the story of a Harvard graduate who rescued 4,000 artists, scientists, and politicians from Nazi persecution during World War II.

A Showtime production, in association with Barwood Films and London-based Griffin Productions. Streisand and Cis Corman of Barwood and Michael Deakin of Griffin are executive producers. Lionel Chetewynd is the scriptwriter. The telefeature is to be filmed in Marseilles, France.

CHAPTER 16

Barbra Streisand and Pauline Kael: Pauline Tries Not to Rain on Barbra's Parade

Pauline Kael is frequently referred to as "the doyenne of American film critics," which means oldest (which she's not), or best by reason of long experience (which she is). However, that doesn't begin to fill in the picture. No other American movie critic has Pauline's fierce love for movies and movie stars, her raucous humor, her built-in bullshit detector—passions that often provoke and intimidate both fellow critics and loyal readers.

David Ansen of *Newsweek* said, "She's the only critic who can make you feel like an asshole for disagreeing with her" (*People*, April 18, 1983). Her reviews of thirty years have been collected in fourteen published books.

Pauline Kael grew up in Northern California, the daughter of a Polish-born Jewish farmer. She hasn't written of her Jewishness that I can remember, but it must have given her some insight into Barbra Streisand, the most proudly Jewish of today's show biz celebrities. Roy Blount wrote about Pauline in *The Atlantic Monthly* (December 1994), in which he says, "As a child, she was regarded as such an inspired comedian that her parents thought she might be the next Fanny Brice."

Kael was an early champion of Streisand, which meant a lot to the singer. Barbra was quoted in the *New York Post* (September 28, 1968)

197

Hiding from the bad guys in fizz-free comedy *For Pete's Sake* (1974).
Did Barbra also pick out the fabrics?
PHOTO COURTESY OF PHOTOFEST

as saying she particularly liked Pauline's comment that "the message of Barbra Streisand in *Funny Girl* is that talent is beauty."

A *New York Times* story (December 2, 1991) says that "besides her mother, Streisand looks for approval from people like Marlon Brando, the film critic Pauline Kael (who praised *Yentl* [MGM/United Artists, 1983]) and 'whatever man is in my life.' "

The critic described her side of the relationship in *Modern Maturity* (March/April, 1998):

Question: Do you avoid making friends in the movie business because it would be hard to review them?

Kael: I only spoke with actors or directors if they contacted me after a movie was out. Barbra Streisand called me after I panned *Funny Lady* [Columbia, 1975] to tell me she agreed with me.

Question: Rumor has it Streisand solicited your opinion on *The Prince of Tides* [Columbia, 1991] before its release.

Kael: She phoned me afterwards to ask what I thought. I was very rough.

Question: You didn't want to let her down easy?

Kael: Barbra Streisand doesn't need to be let down easy.

*   *   *

Pauline Kael was movie critic for *The New Yorker* for six months of each year from 1968 to 1980, then mainly year-round until 1991. During that period she wrote at length on a number of Streisand's movies.

Funny Girl (Columbia, 1968)

"Let's dispose at once of the ugly-duckling myth. It has been commonly said that the musical *Funny Girl* was a comfort to people because it carried the message that you do not need to be pretty to succeed. That is nonsense; the "message" of Barbra Streisand in *Funny Girl* is that talent is beauty."

"The end of the movie, in a long single take, is a bravura stroke, a gorgeous piece of showing off, that makes one intensely, brilliantly aware of the star as performer and of the star's pride in herself as performer. The pride is justified."— *The New Yorker*, September 28, 1968

Hello, Dolly! (Twentieth Century-Fox, 1969)

"Barbra Streisand has a protean, volatile talent that calls for a new era in movie musicals. . . . Streisand totally dominates the screen whenever she's on. . . . She energizes and transforms the prancing rubbish."
— *The New Yorker*, January 30, 1970

On a Clear Day You Can See Forever (Paramount, 1970)

[This movie opened when Pauline Kael was off duty, but she included this comment in her later review of *The Owl and the Pussycat*.]

"Streisand is an intuitive actress who needs someone to play against. In her last picture, with Yves Montand, there was no contact; their scenes together looked as if the two had been photographed separately and matched in the editing room, and she was stranded on the screen.

"It's good to see Streisand get out from under the archaic produc-

199

tion values of large-scale movies—especially after *Hello, Dolly!* and the thudding dialogue of *On a Clear Day You Can See Forever*, that huge picture with only one redeeming sequence, when Streisand, gowned by Cecil Beaton, toyed with a glass of champagne. . . . She may never again look as smashing as she did in that high-style champagne bit, but if the price of that glamour is the paralysis of talent, it isn't worth it."   — *The New Yorker*, November 14, 1970

The Owl and the Pussycat (Columbia, 1970)
"A cheering, satisfying romantic comedy. Like some of the thin and totally concocted screwball comedies of the thirties, it draws its life from the performers. Streisand, self-conscious and self-mocking, combative but wistful, is an intuitive actress who needs someone to play against. . . . She and Segal have the temperamental affinity to make a romantic comedy take off. Their rapport has a beautiful, worked-out professionalism. Were [Katharine] Hepburn and [Spencer] Tracy this good together, even at their best, as in *Pat and Mike* [MGM, 1952]? Maybe, but they weren't better."
      — *The New Yorker*, November 14, 1970

What's Up, Doc? (Warner Bros., 1972)
"Streisand comes off much better than Ryan O'Neal . . . she does her own shtick—the rapid, tricky New Yorkese line readings. She is tanned and elegant, and she works at making brashness adorable, but she doesn't do anything she hasn't already done. She's playing herself—and it's awfully soon for that.
"Streisand sings a sizzling version of 'You're the Top' behind the titles, and there's a moment in the movie when the audience cheers as she starts to sing 'As Time Goes By,' but it's just a teaser, and it has to last for the whole movie. Why? Nothing that happens in the movie—none of the chases or comic confusions—has the excitement of her singing."
      — *The New Yorker*, March 25, 1972

Up the Sandbox (First Artists/National General, 1972)
"Barbra Streisand has never seemed so mysteriously, sensually fresh, so multi-radiant. . . . She's a complete reason for going to a movie, as Garbo was.

200

For the new version of *A Star Is Born* (1976) Streisand looks for onscreen chemistry with Kris Kristofferson as they'd had a brief affair a few years earlier. But new lover Jon Peters watches like a hawk.
PHOTO COURTESY OF J. C. ARCHIVES

"In *Up the Sandbox*, she shows a much deeper and warmer presence and a freely yielding quality. . . . She is a great undeveloped actress—undeveloped in the sense that you can feel the natural richness in her but can see that she's idiosyncratic and that she hasn't the training to play the classical roles that still define how an actress's greatness is expressed. But in movies new ways may be found."

— *The New Yorker*, December 30, 1972

The Way We Were (Columbia, 1973)

"*The Way We Were* is a fluke—a torpedoed ship full of gaping holes which comes snugly into port. . . . Yet the damned thing is enjoyable. It stays afloat because of the chemistry of Barbra Streisand and Robert Redford."

— *The New Yorker*, October 15, 1973

For Pete's Sake (Columbia, 1974)

"An abomination."

— *The New Yorker*, January 10, 1977

"Her instinct played her false when she decided to do *For Pete's Sake*, a slapstick sitcom with exhausted jokes and no characterization. Her intuitive timing didn't work on the lines that were programmed to be pounded out, and she was a cartoon of her worst mannerisms. She was, in fact, what people who didn't like her had always said she was—shrill."

— *The New Yorker*, March 17, 1975 (reviewing *Funny Lady*)

Funny Lady (Columbia, 1975)

"Streisand is in beautiful voice, and her singing is terrific—too terrific. It's no longer singing, it's something else—that strident over-dramatization that turns a song into a big number. The audience's attention is directed away from the music and onto the star's feat in charging it with false energy. . . . The dialogue throughout is sharp and bitchy, and Streisand's inflections are beyond criticism—she doesn't deliver a wisecrack, she detonates it—but the cracks, too, are high-powered, designed to blitz us rather than to reveal character. This Fanny Brice isn't human. Streisand's performance is like the most spectacular, hard-edged female impersonator's imitation of Barbra Streisand."

— *The New Yorker*, March 17, 1975

A Star Is Born (Warner Bros., 1976)

"[Streisand] seems at half-mast, out of it, and you don't get engrossed in reading her face, because she's reading it for you. She wants to make sure we get what's going on all the time. That kills any illusion—that and the camera, which is always on her a second too soon, and seconds too long, emphasizing how admirable she is, how strong yet loving.

"Streisand has more talent than she knows what to do with, and the heart of a lion. But she's made a movie about the unassuming, unaffected person she wants us to think she is, and the image is so truthless she can't play it."   — *The New Yorker*, January 10, 1977

All Night Long (Universal, 1981)

"The tone . . . is slapstick irony. The film is an idiosyncratic, fairy-tale comedy about people giving up the phony obligations they have accumulated and trying to find a way to do what they enjoy.

"We don't know who Streisand is. She doesn't use her rapid-fire New York vocal rhythms in this movie, and a subdued Streisand doesn't seem quite Streisand. . . . It's a Marilyn Monroe flower-child, crazy-lady role, and there was a certain amount of discomfort in it for us when Monroe did it, too—but a different kind of discomfort. The character came out of Monroe; with Streisand it isn't clear what it comes out of. She's a thin-faced, waiflike question mark walking through the movie, and you can't quite grasp why [the Gene Hackman character] would respond to Cheryl's bleached-blonde tackiness."

— *The New Yorker*, March 9, 1981

Yentl (MGM/United Artists, 1983)

"When she starts a song, her hushed intensity makes you want to hear her every breath, and there's high drama in her transitions from verse to chorus. Her phrasing and inflections are so completely her own that the songs make the movie seem very personal. Her singing has an ardent, beseeching quality—an intimacy. And her vocal fervor lifts the movie to the level of fantasy.

"The movie loses its sureness of touch now and then, but it's unassuming. It's a homey, brightly lighted fantasy.

"Where Streisand's instinct as an artist fails her is in her not recognizing that Yentl exists on a magical plane, and that the attempt to make her a relevant, contemporary heroine yanks her off it."

— *The New Yorker*, November 28, 1983

203

*　　　*　　　*

Because she was at *The New Yorker* for just six months of some years, Pauline Kael didn't write on all the new Streisand movies; her early retirement precluded her reviewing other titles. Thus, she did not review **The Main Event** (Warner Bros., 1979), **Nuts** (Warner Bros., 1987), **The Prince of Tides** (Columbia, 1991), or **The Mirror Has Two Faces** (TriStar, 1996).

*　　　*　　　*

A James Brolin Bonus!

In her wealth of movie judging, Pauline Kael provides a very interesting take on James Brolin, who became the passionate love of Barbra Streisand's life since July of 1996.

Pauline reviewed the extremely unsatisfying biographical entry *Gable and Lombard* (Universal, 1976), in which James Brolin portrays movie legend Clark Gable (1901–1960) to Jill Clayburgh's Carole Lombard (1908–1942) [Gable's real-life movie star wife].

"By conventional standards of symmetry, James Brolin, who appears as Clark Gable in the new film *Gable and Lombard*, is much more handsome than Gable, though he manages to look quite a bit like him and does a pretty fair imitation of Gable's voice besides. But Brolin's manner is keyed to moderate involvement; he's primarily a TV actor—you can watch him with only half an eye and ear and not miss a thing. As Gable, Brolin doesn't totally disappear; he has his own TV actor's engaging, lightweight presence. But he doesn't have a dominant personality, and the more he tries to fill the big screen the more callow he seems. He lacks what was the essence of Gable's appeal: his cocksure masculinity. (Gable was one of the few actors never thought to be, even a little bit, homosexual.) There was also something tough and slightly shady about Gable that redeemed his virility act. There was the gleam of a bad boy in him; he looked as if he'd been around. When Brolin uses Gable's vocal rhythms, the faintly derisive, unrespectable overtones are missing; the character has a hollow ring. He's wooden—unmagical."

—*The New Yorker*, February 23, 1976

204

CHAPTER 17

And the Winner Is...
The Award-Winning
Barbra Streisand

Barbra Streisand has won Oscar, Tony, Emmy, Grammy, and Golden Globe awards . . . and so has Liza Minnelli. However, no one else has also won a Georgie, a CableACE, a Peabody, a People's Choice Award, and awards from *Cue*, *Playboy*, *Billboard*, *US*, and *People*. If she were the boasting type, Barbra could also claim to be the first performer to have acquired all of the major show business awards.

Here then are Barbra's major awards and other prizes of interest, to demonstrate her incredible popularity over the decades. Dates listed are the years in which the award was actually presented.

Oscar (The Academy Award)
given by The Academy of Motion Picture Arts and Sciences
1969 — Best Actress, *Funny Girl* (Columbia, 1968)
1977 — Best Song, "Love Theme from *A Star Is Born* (Evergreen)" (Warner Bros., 1976). Shared with Paul Williams.

Grammy
given by The National Academy of Recording Arts and Sciences
1964 — Album of the Year, *The Barbra Streisand Album*
Best Vocal Performance, Female, *The Barbra Streisand Album*

And after the tumult and the shouting comes the party for
A Star Is Born (1976) at Manhattan's Tavern-on-the-Green, where
the Association for a Better New York honors Streisand, flanked here
by Peters and Kristofferson.

PHOTO COURTESY OF J. C. ARCHIVES

1965 — Best Vocal Performance, Female, *"People"*

1966 — Best Vocal Performance, Female, *My Name Is Barbra*

1978 — Best Pop Female Vocal, "Evergreen," the love theme from
A Star Is Born

    — Song of the Year, "Evergreen"

1981— Best Pop Performance by a Duo or Group with Vocal,
"Guilty" (with Barry Gibb)

1987 — Best Pop Female Vocal, *The Broadway Album*

1992— The Living Legend Award, bestowed to "individuals or
groups for ongoing contributions and influence in the recording field"

1995 — Lifetime Achievement Award, for "creative contributions of outstanding artistic significance to the field of recordings"
Note: Barbra Streisand is the youngest artist to win the top album prize (in 1964, she was twenty-two).

Emmy

given by The National Academy of Television Arts and Sciences
1965 — Outstanding Individual Achievement, *My Name Is Barbra*
— Outstanding Program Achievement, *My Name Is Barbra*
1995 — Best Variety or Music Special, *Barbra: The Concert*
— Best Individual Performance, *Barbra: The Concert*

Tony (The Antoinette Perry Award)

given by the National Academy of the Living Theater Foundation
1970 — The first "On-Stage Hall of Fame Award" as Star of the Decade

London Drama Critics Award

1967 — Barbra Streisand, Best Foreign Actress, *Funny Girl*

Golden Globe

given by The Hollywood Foreign Press Association
1969 — Best Motion Picture Actress, Comedy or Musical, *Funny Girl*
1970 — World Film Favorite, Female
1971 — World Film Favorite, Female
1975 — World Film Favorite, Female
1977 — Best Motion Picture, Comedy or Musical, *A Star Is Born*
— Best Motion Picture Actress, Comedy or Musical, *A Star Is Born*
— Best Original Song, "Evergreen," love theme from *A Star Is Born*
1978 — World Film Favorite, Female
1984 — Best Motion Picture Director, *Yentl* (MGM/UA, 1983)
— Best Motion Picture, Comedy or Musical, *Yentl*
Note: Barbra's ten Golden Globe awards are the most won by any star to date.

People's Choice

given by the People's Choice Awards
1975 — Favorite Motion Picture Actress
1975 — Favorite Female Singer

1977 — Favorite Motion Picture Actress
1978 — Favorite Motion Picture Actress
1985 — Favorite All-Around Female Entertainer
1988 — Favorite All-Time Musical Performer

Georgie Award

given by The American Guild of Variety Artists (AGVA)
1970 — Entertainer of the Year
1972 — Singing Star of the Year
1977 — Singing Star of the Year
1980 — Singing Star of the Year

CableAce

given by the cable TV industry
1995 — Performance in a Music Special or Series, *Barbra: The Concert*
— Best Direction of a Music Special or Series, *Barbra: The Concert*

Peabody Award

given by the George Foster Peabody Broadcasting Pioneers for
Distinguished Achievement in Television
1966 — *My Name Is Barbra*
1995 — *Barbra: The Concert*

New York Drama Critics Poll

1962 — Best Supporting Actress in a Musical, *I Can Get It for You Wholesale*
Note: This was Barbra Streisand's first award of any kind.

Top Ten Box Office Stars

A poll conducted by Quigley Publications (publisher of the International Motion Picture Almanac) of circuit and independent movie exhibitors.
1969 — Barbra Streisand, Number Ten
1970 — Barbra Streisand, Number Nine – Top Female Star
1972 — Barbra Streisand, Number Five – Top Female Star
1973 — Barbra Streisand, Number Six – Top Female Star
1974 — Barbra Streisand, Number Four – Top Female Star
1975 — Barbra Streisand, Number Two – Top Female Star
1977 — Barbra Streisand, Number Two – Top Female Star
1978 — Barbra Streisand, Number Ten
1979 — Barbra Streisand, Number Five

1980 — Barbra Streisand, Number Nine

Fanny Brice Award
given by The National Association of Gagwriters

1962 — Barbra Streisand, Best Comedienne

Entertainer of the Year Award
given by Cue *magazine*

1963 —Barbra Streisand

1969 —Barbra Streisand

NARM
given by the National Association of Record Merchandisers

1963 — Best Selling Female Vocalist

1964 — Best Selling Female Vocalist

1965 — Best Selling Female Vocalist

1966 — Best Selling Female Vocalist

1976 — Best Selling Female Vocalist

1977 — Best Selling Soundtrack, *A Star Is Born*

1978 — Best Selling LP by a Female Vocalist, *Barbra Streisand's Greatest Hits, Volume 2*

1981 — Best Selling LP by a Female Vocalist, *Guilty*

1988 — President's Award

Billboard's No. 1 in the Nation
given by Billboard *magazine*

1964 — Female Vocalist

1974 — Top Pop Single, "The Way We Were"

1977 — Top Pop Single, "Evergreen," love theme from *A Star Is Born*

— Top Female Pop Singles Artist

— Top Easy Listening Artist

— Top Soundtrack, *A Star Is Born*

ASCAP Awards
given by The American Society of Composers and Publishers

1969 — Pied Piper Award

1985 — Songwriter's Award: for composing one of the most performed pop standards of the previous decade, "Evergreen," the love theme from *A Star Is Born*

1994 — Harry Chapin Humanitarian Award

The 1977 Academy Awards: presenter Neil Diamond smiles as Barbra
Streisand and Paul Williams show off their Oscars for writing
"Evergreen," the theme song from *A Star Is Born* (1976)
PHOTO COURTESY OF PHOTO ARCHIVES/FOTOS INTERNATIONAL

National Association of Theater Owners (NATO)

1968 — Star of the Year
1980 — Star of the Decade

Crystal Award
given by Women in Film

1984 — Barbra Streisand
1992 — Dorothy Arzner Special Recognition Award to Barbra Streisand

People Magazine Readers Poll

1979 — Favorite Motion Picture Actress
1981 — Favorite Female Vocalist
1982 — Favorite Female Vocalist
1983 — Favorite Female Vocalist
1986 — Favorite Female Vocalist

210

1989 — Favorite Female Vocalist
1990 — Favorite Female Vocalist

Playboy Music Poll

1965 — Leading Female Vocalist
1979 — Leading Female Vocalist, Jazz

US Magazine Readers Poll

1980 — Top Female Vocalist of the Seventies (with Donna Summer)
1982 — Favorite Pop Singer

CUE Magazine Entertainer of the Year

1963 — Barbra Streisand
1970 — Barbra Streisand

Liberty Award

*given by The Western Regional Office of
Lambda Legal Defense and Education Fund*

1995 — Barbra Streisand, as executive producer (with Glenn Close, Craig Zadan, Neil Meron, and Cis Corman) for *Serving in Silence: The Margarethe Cammermeyer Story* (NBC)

211

CHAPTER 18

The Ultimate Barbra Trivia Quiz, Part Two: The Songs

31. In which song did Barbra substitute a harmonica for a trumpet solo? Who's that on the harmonica?
32. One of Streisand's soundtrack albums is only thirteen minutes long. Which is it?
33. What's the popular duet from a Broadway musical that Barbra sang as a solo?
34. What is the first-ever Streisand album to debut on the *Billboard* chart at number one?
35. In which film does Barbra sing a duet with herself?
36. *Classical Barbra* (1976) won Streisand a Grammy nomination for Best Classical Vocalist, Solo Performance. Ironically, the award went to an opera singer going the other way—singing popular songs! Name the highbrow performer.
37. What is the unique album on which all the music was written just for Barbra Streisand?
38. Who wrote the liner notes for her debut offering *The Barbra Streisand Album* (1963)?
39. Music-wise, what makes October 31, 1964, significant?
40. Which song in the Broadway production of *Funny Girl* (1964) did both director Garson Kanin and producer Ray Stark think was not right for the show?

41. The original soundtrack recording of *Funny Girl* (Columbia, 1968) was released a month in advance of the film . . . but there was already a *Funny Girl* album on the market, made by another superstar. Who?

42. At the time Streisand began shooting the screen version of *Hello, Dolly!* (Twentieth Century-Fox, 1969), the musical was still playing on Broadway, and three stars had already recorded cast albums. There was the Carol Channing version, of course, but who were the other two?

43. In October 1967 Barbra signed a new Columbia Records contract with a royalty rate higher than that received by the Beatles—at Barbra's demand. Just how much higher was her royalty rate?

44. The lyrics of which Streisand song hint at oral sex?

45. When Barbra sings "Look at That Face" in the *Color Me Barbra* special (CBS, 1966), to whose profile is she referring?

46. What is the song Barbra has long considered her good-luck charm?

47. How many Streisand albums can you name that have one-word titles?

48. The first album collaboration between Barbra and lover-coproducer Jon Peters was called *ButterFly* (1974) because _____.

49. At the 1969 Academy Awards, Streisand tied with Katharine Hepburn for Best Actress—the only award *Funny Girl* received. The title tune, nominated for Best Song, was sung at the Oscars by _____.

50. One of Barbra's million-selling hits was first heard in a Broadway musical by . . . husband Elliott Gould. Can you name it?

Streisand as blonde Cheryl Gibbons, a characterization evoking
Marilyn Monroe, in *All Night Long* (1981), reputed to be one of the
most expensive flops of all.
PHOTO COURTESY OF PHOTOFEST

215

ANSWERS TO TRIVIA QUIZ, Part 2

31. "Can't Help Lovin' Dat Man" from *Show Boat* (1927), on *The Broadway Album* (1985). Stevie Wonder provides the harmonica solo.
32. *Nuts* (Warner Bros., 1987), released as a mini-CD. It contains the five main themes, composed by Streisand.
33. "All I Ask of You" from *Phantom of the Opera* (1987).
34. *The Broadway Album* (1985).
35. *On a Clear Day You Can See Forever* (Paramount, 1970), the song, "Go to Sleep."
36. Beverly Sills, singing Victor Herbert.
37. *Guilty* (1980).
38. Composer-friend Harold Arlen.
39. On this date, five of her albums were on the *Billboard* Top 100 chart: *The Barbra Streisand Album* (1963), *The Second Barbra Streisand Album* (1963), *Barbra Streisand/The Third Album* (1964), the Broadway cast album of *Funny Girl* (1964), and *People* (1964).
40. "People," of course.
41. Diana Ross. The album is *Diana Ross and the Supremes Sing and Perform* Funny Girl (1968).
42. Mary Martin, Pearl Bailey.
43. A penny an album.
44. "Love in the Afternoon," on the *ButterFly* album (1974).
45. Sadie the poodle.
46. "A Sleepin' Bee," from the Broadway musical *House of Flowers* (1954).
47. There are nine so far: *People* (1964), *ButterFly* (1974), *Songbird* (1978), *Wet* (1979), *Guilty* (1980), *Memories* (1981), *Yentl* (1983), *Emotion* (1984), and *Nuts* (1987).
48. Because Jon Peters said Barbra reminded him of a butterfly.
49. Aretha Franklin.
50. "He Touched Me" from the short-lived Broadway musical *Drat! The Cat!* (1965). Elliott sang it as "She Touched Me."

PART ③
HER
WORLD

CHAPTER 19

The Barbra Streisand Dictionary of Yiddish

"She is perhaps the only Hollywood star in its history who has been so publicly proud of being a Jew," wrote biographer Anne Edwards in *Streisand: A Biography* (Boston: Little, Brown, 1997).

From the beginning, Barbra has emphasized her ethnic style. In 1961, for example, she was doing Smothers Brothers-type comedy patter between song numbers in her club act—heavy Jewish material that some thought too heavy, detracting from the subtle songs that followed. She included Yiddish songs in her performances at The Town & Country Club in Winnipeg, Manitoba, Canada, which had an older Jewish audience.

When Streisand was fighting for the starring role in the Broadway musical *Funny Girl* (1964–1967), based on the life of singer-comic Fanny Brice (1891–1951), director Garson Kanin and his actress wife Ruth Gordon took Barbra's side, arguing that she had the quirkiness and the Jewish shtik that once had made Brice so popular with the public.

Movie reviewer Gene Siskel (one thumb of "Two Thumbs Up!") was in the audience at Barbra's 1993 New Year's Eve concert at the MGM Grand Hotel in Las Vegas. He delighted in the "speedball Yiddishisms" between Barbra and comic Mike Myers, spurring Siskel to reflect on "the importance of Streisand as a stand-up Jew."

Said Siskel: "As the film world properly celebrates Steven Spielberg's brilliant Jewish coming-of-age with *Schindler's List* (Universal, 1993), consider Streisand's career: It was built on a nose that would not be altered and was suffused with an ethnicity that was as fresh in its time as JFK's youth. Her pride and Sandy Koufax's refusal to pitch in the 1965 World Series on Yom Kippur—the same year she was starring in *Funny Girl* on Broadway—were towers of strength to young Jews everywhere" (*Entertainment Weekly*, January 14, 1994).

Yiddish is . . .

Jewish people do not speak Jewish: They speak Hebrew, the holy language of prayer, and Yiddish, the lingua franca of the general populace—the common language of the synagogue, the street, and the home. Yiddish is descended from the German language adopted by Jewish immigrants from France a thousand years ago. Along the way it has incorporated words and dialects from many European languages, plus borrowings from English in English-speaking countries.

In his "relaxed lexicon" *The Joys of Yiddish* (New York: McGraw-Hill, 1968), Leo Rosten says, "Yiddish [is] a language of exceptional charm. [It] lends itself to an extraordinary range of observational nuances and psychological subtleties." For example, what other language would have such a glorious symphony of hissing disdain as this Yiddish line-up of losers: *shlemiel* (a simpleton), *shlepper* (a drag, a jerk), *shlimazel* (a born loser), *shlub* (a bumpkin), *shlump* [or *shloomp*] (a wet blanket), *shmegegge* (a petty person), *shmendrik* (a pipsqueak), *shmo* (a boob), *shmuck* (a prick), *shnook* (a sad sack), *shnorrer* (a moocher), *shtunk* (a fool, a dope)—all very similar sounding yet with subtle differences.

For the benefit of those goys *furtumphed* about the difference between *fahrklempt* and *feckuckteh*, here is my *Barbra Streisand Dictionary of Yiddish*.

Most of these classic Yiddish words and phrases have been used by Barbra in interviews or in performance; others are from media writers discussing her. Spellings have been standardized.

baleboosteh /bol-eh-BOOSS-teh/ A good homemaker.

In 1961 Barbra shared a one-bedroom walk-up in New York City with Elaine Sobel, a friend from acting school. Said Elaine: "She was just not a *baleboosteh*—she wasn't neat around the house" (James Spada, *Streisand, Her Life*. New York: Crown, 1995).

bar mitzva or ***bar mitzvah*** /bar-MITZ-vah/ The ceremony in which a thirteen-year-old boy reaches the age and duties of a man. On January 5, 1980, Jason Gould's bar mitzvah is held at the Pacific Jewish Center, a traditional synagogue in Venice, California. Standing with Jason are his father, actor Elliott Gould, and Gould's father Bernard, following custom. Proud mother Barbra watches from the front row of the women's section.

bubeleh /BUB-eh-leh/ A term of endearment for babies, sweethearts, husbands, and wives.
Barbra apparently was never her mother's favorite little *bubeleh*, and it has drastically colored her whole life.

bubkes or ***bobkes*** /BOP-kess/ Triflings, nothing (literally, goat droppings). A great Yiddish word of indignation, scorn, contempt. *The Prince of Tides* (Columbia, 1991) gets seven Oscar nominations, including Best Picture and Best Actor, but wins nothing—*bubkes!*

choleria /kha-LEH-ree-a/ A curse in the shape of a woman; a hellcat; a ball-breaker.
Before filming begins on *Hello, Dolly!* (Twentieth Century-Fox, 1969), director Gene Kelly meets with Streisand to discuss her reputation for being difficult. "Me?" she replies. "I'm a nervous *choleria* maybe, but I'm not difficult" (Anne Edwards, *Streisand: A Biography.* Boston, Little, Brown, 1997).

chozzerai /khoz-zair-EYE/ Junk.
All those *tsatskes* in Barbra's house: Are they valuable, or just *chozzerai?*

chutzpa /KHOOTS-pah/ Audacity; incredible nerve; effrontery.
Cis Corman, Barbra's oldest and dearest friend, phones and says she's found the first person in a long time who reminds her of Streisand—Madonna. Corman and Streisand take Madonna out to a Chinese meal—and the young singer orders a whole fish! Says Barbra, "When I go out with people, I don't order lobster or steak. I think maybe they can't afford it or something. I would never do that. I mean, that takes *chutzpa* to order a whole fish. I was knocked out by her *chutzpa*" (*Vanity Fair*, September 1991).

cockamamy /COCK-a-may-me/ Ridiculous; pointlessly complicated; stupidly messed up.
In 1963 Barbra's club act doesn't go over well with audiences at the Cafe Pompeii at the Eden Roc Hotel in Miami Beach, because

221

her material is too *cockamamy* for the older Jewish clientele, "the rocks and lox crowd," as she calls them.

fahrklempt /far-KLEMPT/ Emotional, upset, a nervous wreck.

In 1994 Barbra performs in New York City for the first time in years, in Madison Square Garden: "The audience went berserk and there was just such an outpouring of love that she was *fahrklempt* at one point herself. You could see she was very close to crying. It was that overwhelming" (Spada, *Streisand: Her Life*).

farbissener (male), *farbisseneh* (female) /far-BIS-sen-er-eh/ A sourpuss, an unpleasant or unlikable person.

When she was young, the insistent buzzing in Barbra's ears was a constant source of distraction. It made her walk around like a *farbisseneh*.

fekukteh /fuh-COCK-teh/ Crappy, useless, screwed up.

Barbra jokes with her audience at the International Hotel in Las Vegas in 1969: "This is an absolutely *fekukteh* place, you know? There are no clocks here. They want everybody out in the casino, so the television sets in your rooms don't work, right?"

Diet guru Richard Simmons has been an obsessive Streisand fan since the eighth grade. He keeps offering to cook for her. "It's not like I'm a stalker," he says. "I'm an equal now. I'm worth just about as much as she is. I just don't have all those *fekukteh* Tiffany lamps" (*Entertainment Weekly*, April 15, 1994).

furtumph or *furtummelt* /fur-TUMPH/ Flustered.

On the day Barbra auditions for the 1962 Broadway musical *I Can Get It For You Wholesale* she has, that morning, moved into her first apartment and is all excited and *furtumphed*.

geshrey /gesh-RYE/ A holler, a yell.

gita geshrey / Someone hollering.

"Sometimes when I hear that first record of mine (*The Barbra Streisand Album*, 1963), where I'm *geshreying*, and getting so emotional, I think, Oh, my God, how did they ever like me?" (*Playboy*, October 1977).

goy (singular), *goyim* /GOY-im (plural)/ Anyone not a Jew.

goyish (adjective), *goyisher* (masculine), *goyisheh* (feminine)

Barbra is partial to handsome *goyisher* guys, both on screen (like Robert Redford) and off screen (like Don Johnson).

to put the kibosh on /KY-bosh/ To put an end to something; to squelch.

222

The *New York Post* reports (January 1993) that Barbra is thinking of running for Congress. Barbra puts the *kibosh* on the story quickly.

kishkas /KISH-kehs/ The intestines, the guts, innards.

From the beginning of her movie career, Barbra dreams of one day producing and directing her own film, one that has a theme that she wants to present, something so good she can feel that it comes from her *kishkas*.

kvetch (rhymes with fetch) / Complain, bitch, nag, delay, fuss.

In New York for her 1994 concert tour, Barbra makes a surprise visit to TV's *The Late Show with David Letterman*. The scarcity of Streisand tickets had been a running gag on Dave's CBS network talk program. She hands Letterman two tickets and tells him to "stop *kvetching*, already."

Peter Bogdanovich, director of *What's Up, Doc?* (Warner Bros., 1972), says, "She's a real *kvetch*—she's always moaning about something or other. When she's *kvetching* I simply say: 'Shut up and give me a little kiss, will ya, huh?' or 'Stick out your boobs, they're beautiful.' And after that she's fine for the next ten minutes" (David Shipman, *Movie Talk: Who Said What About Whom in the Movies.* New York: St. Martin's, 1988).

marinkele / A little nothing.

"I was always trying to prove [to my mother] that I was worthwhile, that I wasn't just a skinny little *marinkele*" (*Playboy*, October 1977).

mensh or **mench** (rhymes with bench) / A human (not an animal); a person of great moral character or upbringing (man or woman); someone to inspire you.

Barbra looked at lover Jon Peters (the hairdresser who became a movie titan) and she was proud. He had made it into the big time, the *very* big time. "Look at you," her expression said, "You're a *mensh*, a real *mensh*!" (Anne Edwards, *Streisand: A Biography*).

meshugge /m'SHU-geh/ Crazy, offbeat.

A common early dismissal of Barbra Streisand, especially when she was appearing on the Mike Wallace *P.M. East* TV talk show in the early 1960s.

mieskeit /MEES-kite/ An ugly person.

"[Barbra's mother] Diana thinks her teenage daughter too much of a *mieskeit* to be successful. Barbra would look in the mirror and call herself *mieskeit* — 'Who the hell wants me?' " (James Spada,

Streisand: Her Life).

Super-agent Sue Mengers remembers seeing Barbra off-Broadway in *Another Evening with Harry Stoones* (1961): "When I saw her walk out on the stage I thought, it sure takes a lot of balls for a *mieskeit* like that to get up in front of people and perform" (*Vanity Fair*, September 1991).

mishegass /mish-eh-GASS/ Crazy antics, madness, insanity.

While filming *Funny Girl* (Columbia, 1968), Streisand's *mishegass* — her compulsive behavior, lateness on the set, her need to be involved in every aspect of the film—barely fazes veteran movie director William Wyler.

mitzva, mitzvah /MITZ-veh/ A good deed, a meritorious act.

Talking about her relationship with actor James Brolin, Barbra says, "It's a *mitzvah*. It's a blessing. It's a joy" (*New York Times*, November 11, 1997).

nudnik /NUD-nik/ A nuisance, a nagger.

Barbra treats autograph collectors as *nudniks*.

plotze (rhymes with watts) / Blow up, explode, fall on your face.

On her 1973 TV special *Barbra Streisand . . . and Other Musical Instruments* she has 150 musicians from around the world, playing all sorts of instruments, but this is seen as little more than a gimmick. Said Jim Farber of the New York *Daily News*, June 20, 1994: "Barbra makes a big stretch—playing music from around the world—and *plotzes* bad."

potchkee /POTCH-kee/ Putter; to act aimlessly or idly.

Barbra relishes her private time when not performing in public. She *potchkees* around, remodeling and redecorating her homes.

shlep /SHLEP/ To drag or pull yourself; walk laboriously; lag behind.

In 1963 Barbra worked almost nonstop, *shlepping* around the country from one club engagement to another.

shlump /SHLUMP/ A careless or untidy person; a foolish person.

In her career, Barbra has played several variations on the persona of Fanny Brice—that of the *schlumpy* nobody who finds success.

shmaltz (rhymes with dolltz) / Ambience; with heart and soul.

Barbra wanted Joan Didion and John Gregory Dunne to rewrite their script for *A Star Is Born* (Warner Bros., 1976). She wanted less rock and roll and more love story, more *shmaltz*.

shmatte /SHMOT-ta/ Rags, cheap clothes.

224

Elliott Gould (boyfriend, later husband) remembers living with Barbra in 1962 in a tiny Manhattan apartment above a fish store on Third Avenue, *shmattes* hanging everywhere!

shmeikel /SHMEK-el/ To fast-talk, to con, to kiss ass (vulgarly, ***toches lecker*** /TOOK-us LECK-er/)

Barbra's a little sharp with director Frank Pierson (*A Star Is Born*) and apologizes: "I have a problem with tact. I'm sorry, I don't know how to *shmeikel* you" (*Playboy*, October 1977).

shmooze (rhymes with ooze) / Chat, talk, gossip.

The chorus girls in the original Broadway stage production of *Funny Girl* (1964–1967) dislike Barbra because she never *shmoozes* with them.

shnorrer /SHNOR-rer/ A beggar, a cheapskate, a moocher.

Choreographer Jerome Robbins, who helps to guide Barbra through the stage musical *Funny Girl*, marvels at how she can study script changes at the same time as she is *shnorring* part of his sandwich and someone else's coke.

shnoz, shnozzle /SHNAZ, SHNAZ-al/ Nose; large or unattractive nose.

In 1961 Abel Greene, publisher of the show biz bible *Variety*, writes that Streisand should consider "a *shnoz* bob."

shpilkes /SHPIL-kas/ Pins and needles (usually sitting on *shpilkes*—nervous)

February 3, 1995: Barbra appears at Harvard University, at the John F. Kennedy School of Government, to deliver a speech on "The Artist as Citizen." She's more nervous than anyone has seen before—"You've heard of *shpilkes*?" (James Spada, *Streisand: Her Life*).

shtik /sh-TICK/ A characteristic bit of acting; a show biz gimmick, a bit of "business."

While appearing in Las Vegas in 1971, Barbra does this *shtik* of passing around a joint to the band members

tsatske or tsatskeleh /TSAHTS-keh/ Originally: worthless trinkets, doodads, whatnots, gewgaws. In English, it's come to mean collectible or favorite trinkets, doodads, etc. Also used to describe a person of not so perfect character.

Many of Barbra's treasured *tsatskes* are broken or destroyed in the 1994 Los Angeles earthquake, which prompts her to sell off much of her remaining collection.

trayf (rhymes with safe) / Any food that is not kosher (that is, not prepared according to dietary rules).

On Saturday afternoons in Brooklyn, young Barbara is able to escape into the opulent Loew's Kings Theatre on Flatbush Avenue. The refreshment stand tempts her with its smell of buttered popcorn and spicy frankfurters, which she is forbidden to eat—they are *trayf.*

tsuris, tsouris /TSOO-riss/ Troubles, problems, misery.

You think you got *tsuris*—in 1992 Barbra can't sell her twenty-two-acre Malibu, California, ranch, and has to give it away!

yenta /YEN-ta/ A woman who stands around gossiping and spreading rumors. (A man who does this is also called a *yenta*.) Also, a vulgar woman of little breeding.

Says acidic film critic John Simon: "Her speaking voice seems to have graduated with top honors from the Brooklyn Conservatory of Yentaism. . . ." (Shipman, *Movie Talk*, New York: St. Martin's Press, 1988).

While performing at the International Hotel in Las Vegas in 1963, Barbra calls out to her audience, "And now for your *yenta*tainment pleasure . . . ."

yeshiva /yeh-SHEE-va/ Originally, a house of religious study only. In America it's a school (can be from elementary to graduate) teaching both secular and religious subjects, or only religious.

Barbra's first three years in grade school (1947–49) are spent at the *yeshiva* on Willoughby Street in Brooklyn, where her father Emanuel had taught. Defiant at an early age, Barbra would call out "Christmas! Christmas!" when the rabbi left the room, shocking the other kids with her "profanity."

zaftig /ZOFF-tig/ Pleasingly plump, well rounded.

In all honesty, Roslyn Kind, Barbra's stepsister, was more than *zaftig*. At thirteen, she weighed twice as much as Barbra.

CHAPTER 20

The Son Also Rises: The Acting Career of Jason Gould

Jason Gould was five years old when he made his first screen appearance. This was in one of his mother's less successful screen ventures, *Up the Sandbox* (National General, 1972), where he's briefly glimpsed riding a merry-go-round. (Streisand and his father, actor Elliott Gould, had been divorced the year before.)

Jason started making home movies at age six. At nine he was making eight-millimeter monster movies with his friend Christopher Peters, son of his mother's lover, Jon Peters and Peters' ex-wife, actress Lesley Ann Warren.

As a high school graduation gift in 1984, his mother financed a home movie that Jason would write, produce, direct, and edit. Called *It's Up to You*, it starred his father, Elliott Gould, his grandmother Diana Kind, and aunt Roslyn Kind. Barbra assisted him during production and in the editing room.

* * *

Jason studied filmmaking at the University of California at Berkeley before pursuing an acting career in 1988. He worked as a production assistant for Steven Spielberg (did mom put in a word for him?) and made brief appearances in three films released in 1989:

The Big Picture (Columbia), directed by Christopher Guest. Jason

227

Publicity photo for *Yentl* (1983): Streisand in costume as superstar,
director, producer, co-writer, and star.
PHOTO COURTESY OF PHOTOFEST

Gould appears as Carl Manknik in this comedy about a naive student
filmmaker who tries to get inside the movie industry but gets swal-
lowed instead. The movie stars Kevin Bacon, Emily Longstreth, J. T.
Walsh, Jennifer Jason Leigh, and Teri Hatcher.

Say Anything . . . (Twentieth Century-Fox), written and directed by Cameron Crowe. A teenage comedy-drama about loner John Cusack, who pursues honor student Ione Skye and finds that love has its dark secrets. Also starring are John Mahoney, Lili Taylor, Amy Brooks, Pamela Segall, Bebe Neuwirth, Eric Stoltz, and Chynna Phillips. Jason is Mike Cameron, a zonked-out partygoer with a bad haircut who can't remember where he lives.

Listen To Me (Columbia), directed by Douglas Day Stewart. The story of a college debating team on one of those wholesome, gung-ho college campuses you see only in movies like this. It stars Kirk Cameron, Jami Gertz, Roy Scheider, Amanda Peterson, Tim Quill, and Christopher Atkins. Jason is Hinkelstein.

When Barbra began work on *The Prince of Tides* (Columbia, 1991), Jason asked for the role of rebellious Bernard, the teenage son of the psychiatrist Barbra was portraying. The director-mother said no, he wasn't right for it. But then Pat Conroy, author of the original novel, saw a photo of Jason—not knowing who it was—and insisted that this was the actor to play Bernard. His mother finally agreed.

*   *   *

In May of 1990, the *Star* tabloid claimed that twenty-five-year-old Jason was gay. In July of 1991 another tabloid, the *Globe*, alleged that Jason had "married" underwear model David Knight. In the Randall Riese biography (*Her Name Is Barbra*. New York: Birch Lane, 1993), Knight is quoted as saying he'd never met Jason. In the James Spada version (*Streisand: Her Life*. New York: Crown, 1995), the two might not have been married but were certainly involved.

The fanzine *All About Barbra* (no. 46, 1997) has this news note: Jason's film *Inside Out* (1997) was shown at the Sundance Film Festival (the haven/hangout for independently made movies). Originally written as a feature, Jason cut it down to a twenty-seven-minute short. Semi-autobiographical, it tells the story of a gay celebrity scion confronted by a supermarket tabloid story of his marriage to a male model.

The film is described as being very personal and a study of a person's right to privacy. Jason is quoted as saying, "I wasn't sure if my father was going to be in it. I love his sense of humor, but I didn't know if that was crossing the line."

229

Barbra spoke about Jason's debut at Sundance to British TV host Des O'Connor, saying she is "very proud of Jason."

*   *   *

The fanzine *Just Like Buttah* (no. 12, 1997) reports that Jason Gould appeared for six weeks in Jonathan Tolins' play *The Twilight of the Golds* at the Arts Theatre in London, to generally positive reviews.

The Twilight of the Golds concerns Mr. and Mrs. Gold, their gay son David, and married daughter Suzanne. When the daughter learns that she's pregnant, she submits to genetic testing, which shows that her unborn son will likely be gay. Should she have an abortion? David learns that if his parents had had such an option, they would have chosen abortion rather than have a gay child—*him*. David then begins to fight for the life of the unborn baby.

The theater critic for *Just Like Buttah* had this to say: "The play is very touching and moving. Jason Gould portrayed David with a strong, positive, masculine approach. There was plenty of humor too, in this serious treatment of a controversial subject, as Jason's character was also very funny. He proved that he has excellent comic timing and delivery."

The Twilight of the Golds was filmed by Hallmark Entertainment and presented on Showtime in 1997. In this cable TV version the gay son is portrayed by Brendan Fraser, costarring with Faye Dunaway, Garry Marshall, Jennifer Beals, Jon Tenney, and Rosie O'Donnell.

*   *   *

Jason's latest screen project is as the star of the movie *Subterfuge*, a 1998 release. It's a production of The Subterfuge Company and Storm Entertainment. David Frost is producer; Herb Freed is co-executive producer, and director.

CHAPTER 21

Somewhere There's a Place for Them: Barbra Streisand as a Gay Icon

She was asked why gay men respond to her.

"Because I can be imitated?" she says, sounding stumped. "Because I seem bigger than life?" She shrugs. "I guess because I was so odd" (*Vanity Fair*, September 1991).

Get your act together, Babs—you owe your career to gay men!

*   *   *

Barry Dennen and Barbra Streisand met in early 1960 when they were portraying insects in an off-Broadway play. Dennen's usually identified as Barbra's first lover, although, reportedly, he was also sleeping with guys at the same time. Through his huge record collection, Dennen introduced Barbra to the great song stylists: Edith Piaf, Ruth Etting, Billie Holiday, Mabel Mercer, Helen Morgan, Libby Holman—singers whose style could be described as *acting* the songs. Dennen helped create Barbra's performance style.

Dennen's friend Bob Schulenberg designed a new face for her, artfully using makeup to give her the look of a fashion model. Terry Leong, another pal, went scavenging in thrift shops to piece together her unusual one-of-a-kind outfits.

Thus psyched up, made up, dressed up, Streisand stood up in front of the all-gay audience at The Lion bar and knocked 'em dead. From that club she went to the classier Bon Soir, which wasn't known as a gay club, but those well-dressed guys at the bar weren't fooling anyone. The Blue Angel was a snootier uptown joint, but audience response let Barbra know her friends were there also.

James Gavin writes that Streisand was frightened to move from the loose, informal Bon Soir to the stiffer Blue Angel. The Village club felt like home to her because of the enthusiastic gay clientele. Bob Schulenberg is quoted as saying, "I have a feeling that Barbra, like Bette Midler later on, felt like a social outlaw, and that's why she identified with them. And Barbra had almost exclusively gay friends in those days" (*Intimate Nights: The Golden Age of New York Cabaret*. New York: Grove Weidenfeld, 1991).

(Bette Midler, you'll remember, was first noticed singing in a gay *bathhouse*.)

Streisand was "a misfit among misfits," says Randall Riese in his biography *Her Name Is Barbra* (New York: Birch Lane, 1993). "When she sang about the pain of being unloved, she really felt the lyrics. Gay men related to that pain, that rejection.

"She related, too, to their humor, their 'camp' sensibility. This eighteen-year-old ragamuffin kid not only refused to suppress her differences, she was flaunting them in the face of a straitlaced society—and she was being accepted. She was breaking all the rules—she was *winning*. To some gay men, she provided a vicarious thrill. To many others, she was downright liberating.

"It can also be said that there probably would never have been a Madonna if there hadn't first been a Streisand."

However, you can't give nine-hundred performances of *Funny Girl* to gay-only audiences. And you can't sell them three million CDs, even if they are show tunes. Barbra Streisand's specialness touches people of every shape and color and sexual persuasion. Nevertheless, gays were in the forefront of those touched first. Then, as happens with many trends and tastes, she was absorbed into mainstream America.

*　　　*　　　*

Jump ahead in time to the Age of AIDS in the 1980s and 1990s, and Streisand is under fire for not doing more.

A touching (and touchy) moment from *Yentl* (1983): gentle Hadass (Amy Irving) wants to be a good wife but is confused because her husband (forty-year-old Streisand as the boy Yentl) runs away from her.
PHOTO COURTESY OF PHOTOFEST

"Of all the celebrities who should have done more for gay men during the AIDS crisis it's Barbra," says an industry bigwig who's active in AIDS charities in Los Angeles. "Whenever you call Madonna or Bette Midler or Liz Taylor, they're there, no questions asked. But what has Barbra done? She hides behind this stage-fright crap, but she got up and raised millions for a bunch of politicians. We are the people who discovered her, who have loved her. Where is she? It's shameful."

Streisand is unapologetic. "That's their opinion. I give loads of money. I've given a lot to pediatric AIDS through my foundation, and all the proceeds from the single 'Somewhere' from my Broadway album went to The American Foundation for AIDS Research. I don't give public appearances; Madonna and Bette like to perform and I don't. Elizabeth has this as her one cause. She gives speeches. I did have a passion to film *The Normal Heart* (Larry Kramer's play concerning the genesis of the AIDS epidemic). I wanted to give back something through my work, which is the best way I know how" (*Vanity Fair*, September 1991).

* * *

It does seem that Streisand came out as a fighter for gay rights only after the tabloid account of her son Jason's "marriage" to a fellow usually described as an underwear model.

1. She appeared at a benefit concert for an AIDS Project L.A. in November 1992 and attacked Colorado's recent passage of an amendment that would deny certain rights to gays. She called for a boycott of the state, saying "the moral climate there is no longer acceptable." She urged her fellow performers to boycott the Aspen ski resort, a popular celebrity getaway.

She also spoke out against the homophobia of that year's Republican convention, at which Pat Buchanan railed against gay couples having the legal rights of heterosexual couples.

The benefit concert ended with Barbra in duet with Johnny Mathis singing "One Hand, One Heart" and "I Have a Love." She closed the show by herself, singing "Somewhere (There's a Place for Us)," which many consider the gay national anthem.

2. In 1995 Barbra produced the TV movie *Serving in Silence: The Margarethe Cammermeyer Story*, about the highest-ranking military official ever kicked out of the service for being a lesbian.

3. In 1996 she announced the TV movie *What Makes a Family*, based on the true story of a lesbian who fought for custody of her dead lover's child.

4. However, Streisand's "passion" to film *The Normal Heart* petered out after she'd held on to the rights for ten long years.

* * *

Nonetheless, Streisand as a gay icon continues to glow:
1. "Hello Gorgeous!" opened on Castro Street in San Francisco in

234

1996 as the world's first boutique/museum/shrine devoted to Barbra Streisand. Ken Joachim mortgaged his home to open the memorabilia store.

"Mr. Joachim agreed that Ms. Streisand's appeal seems to go beyond the world-class talent as a singer, actress, and director. "Particularly among gay people and Jews," he said, "it seems to hinge partly on the adversity and prejudice she had faced down from all the people who said she was not pretty enough or white-bread enough or able enough to succeed.

" 'With my own background, being a gay man, being oppressed, I feel my life is very parallel,' he said" (*New York Times*, May 21, 1996).

2. *In & Out* (Paramount, 1997), an "Is he or isn't he?" comedy, highlights Barbra's status as a gay entertainment icon. Kevin Kline plays a married high school teacher whose sexuality is questioned. The fact that he's a big Streisand fan is seen as proof that he's gay.

3. Andy Medhurst's review of *The Mirror Has Two Faces* (TriStar, 1996) in the February 1997 *Sight and Sound* has this summation: "Straight women and gay men will love it, which is perhaps just as it should be with any text bearing the Streisand imprimatur."

Barbra as the unwed, unloved heroine of *The Mirror Has Two Faces* (1996), a film seen by many as unintentional self-revelation.
PHOTO COURTESY OF PHOTOFEST

235

CHAPTER 22

'Cause They Cried a River Over Her!

In June 1960 at the suggestion of friend and struggling actor Barry Dennen, Barbra Streisand agrees to sing in an amateur contest at The Lion, a gay bar in New York City's Greenwich Village.

As Barbra had never performed in public before, she asks her then-roommate, fellow would-be actress Marilyn Fried, to listen to her sing a song and tell her if she was any good. However, Barbra insists that Marilyn not *watch* her, that she face the wall instead. Marilyn agrees.

Barbra screws up her courage and sings something familiar from a Broadway musical. She finishes and Marilyn doesn't budge.

"What's the matter?" Barbra asks. "You're not laughing, are you? Tell me if it was terrible."

Marilyn turns around slowly, tears trickling down her face (Barry Dennen. *My Life with Barbra, A Love Story*. New York: Prometheus, 1997).

(In another version, it's Cis Corman, Barbra's oldest friend, who is asked to listen and is overwhelmed and can't stop crying.)

What is this with the tears?!

*　　　*　　　*

Bob Schulenberg, another New York friend from the pivotal summer of 1960, remembers Barbra performing at The Bon Soir club, her second public appearance:

"I knew that she sang, but I'd never heard her, because she didn't appear anywhere for a couple of months after The Lion [the club where she'd made her debut]. Peter Daniels was the pianist, and they'd never ever seen each other. But she came out and Peter took the music, and it was just incredible. I mean, I started crying. I don't think she's ever, ever been recorded like she used to sound there. Afterwards, I was like melted butter on the floor. She said, 'How was it?' and I couldn't talk" (James Spada: *Streisand: The Woman and the Legend*. New York: Doubleday, 1981).

*   *   *

Moving right along:
On September 9 of that same year, 1960, Barbra begins a two-week engagement at the uptown The Bon Soir . . . which stretches into ten weeks of work.

Songwriters Marilyn and Alan Bergman—future friends and collaborators of Barbra—are in the audience. Marilyn reports: "I was tired and distracted, but when she began singing, I started crying. I cried through the whole show" (Bob Thomas, Los Angeles *Daily News*, December 24, 1993).

*   *   *

Richard Simmons, the zaftig diet and exercise guru, is co-publisher of *BARBRA bilia*, an unofficial enthusiast magazine. He recalls vividly sitting in the Winter Garden Theatre on Broadway watching a live performance of *Funny Girl* (which would have been 1964–1965). "I remember the sound of 'the voice with a heart and soul,' and how it brought tears to my eyes."

*   *   *

Kathie Lee Gifford frequently discusses Streisand on the TV morning show *Live with Regis & Kathie Lee* (ABC). "I first heard it [The Voice] when I was twelve years old," she says. "I heard 'People' come on the radio, and it stopped me dead in my tracks. I had tears sobbing down my face. And I wasn't even in puberty at this point, so don't think it was hormonal" (*Entertainment Weekly*, April 15, 1994).

238

A high-priced prostitute kills a client in *Nuts* (1987), then fights to prove her sanity so she can receive a fair trail. Sometimes referred to as Mentl (to rhyme with *Yentl*).
PHOTO COURTESY OF PHOTOFEST

* * *

Streisand was the top client of powerful ICM talent agent Sue Mengers. Their professional relationship ended because Mengers felt strongly that 'Barbra shouldn't make *Yentl* (MGM/United Artists, 1983). Confessed Mengers after the fact, "To my chagrin, I was wrong. I remember going to see it . . . and crying and saying 'Thank God she didn't listen to me.' " (Allison J. Waldman. *The Barbra Streisand Scrapbook*. Secaucus, N.J.: Citadel/Carol, 1995)

CHAPTER 23

Hello Gorgeous!
A History

When Ken Joachim, a vintage clothing dealer in San Francisco, mortgaged his house in 1996 to open a Barbra Streisand store/museum in the Golden Gate city, he names the establishment Hello Gorgeous!

Like, what else would he have called it?

* * *

The greeting is the first words of *Funny Girl*, on both stage and screen. In the original 1964 Broadway production, Barbra, as comedian-singer Fanny Brice, enters and wanders across the bare stage into her dressing room. She pulls her hat down over her forehead and sarcastically addresses herself in the mirror—"Hello, Gorgeous."

The 1968 Columbia movie makes a bigger deal of it. The camera follows Fanny Brice from behind as she crosses Broadway, walks down an alley beside the theatre, and enters the stage door. She walks toward the stage, then stops before a large mirror. Cut to her reflection in a mirror and we see the striking face of Barbra Streisand for the first time on the movie screen. "Hello, Gorgeous," she says, with a touch of sarcasm, a tear glistening in the corner of her eye.

A year later, on April 14, when Academy Award presenter Ingrid Bergman announces the Best Actress of 1968—a tie between

Streisand and Katharine Hepburn—Barbra rushes up to the stage, nearly tripping over the hem of her sequined black-net pajama outfit. Publicist Jack Brodsky had suggested she use the opening line of the film, if she won. Following his advice, she coos to Oscar, "Hello, Gorgeous!"

*   *   *

The *New York Times* (May 21, 1996) described Ken Joachim's Hello Gorgeous! memorabilia store/museum as "a reverently glitzy little shrine" situated in the largely gay Castro section of San Francisco, dealing in all things Barbra."

But what did the real Barbra think of this tribute? *Entertainment Weekly* (October 4, 1996) reported: "Five months later, Barbra still had not acknowledged the store. A spokesman maintains that she has no reason to feel guilty about not dropping in: 'We have cult followings everywhere,' " he said.

Hello Gorgeous! was at 549-A Castro Street, San Francisco, California.

Barbra takes a break during the filming of *The Prince of Tides* (1991), the second movie she officially directed.

PHOTO COURTESY OF J. C. ARCHIVES

Ken Joachim says he had to beg for it, but he eventually received a letter from the diva: "For Ken Joachim. A Jewish shrine? Thanks and best wishes, Barbra Streisand."

Sadly, there just hasn't been enough foot traffic to keep the store open. Hello Gorgeous! closed its doors on Castro Street on May 24, 1998. The contents of the museum were auctioned. However, Joachim continues to sell Streisand memorabilia through the mail and on the Internet.

> Hello Gorgeous!
> P.O. Box 1255
> Kenwood, CA 95452–1255
> (707) 833-6998
> http://www.grin.net/~hellogorgeous
> E-mail: hellogorgeous@grin.net

Ken Joachim issued a press release at the time of the closing: "I can no longer stand by and be a part of the hype, the manipulation of the public and press, and sadly even her fans, by Streisand and her people. It makes it difficult for me to respectfully own and operate a dedicated public monument to someone who, I have learned, is not very truthful or nice."

CHAPTER 24

The Ultimate Barbra Trivia Quiz, Part Three

51. Barwood is the name of Streisand's production company: *Bar* from Barbra and *wood* from Hollywood—that one's easy. What's Ellbar?

52. *July Pork Bellies* was the original title of which Streisand feature film?

53. Which Streisand lover had been an extra in Cecil B. DeMille's big-screen epic *The Ten Commandments* (Paramount, 1956) and rode a donkey into the Red Sea?

54. What silent screen lovers are the original inspiration for *A Star Is Born* (Warner Bros., 1976)?

55. Can you name the three earlier screen versions of *A Star Is Born*?

56. One of Streisand's lovers was said to jog in the nude on the beach at Malibu, California —"He wasn't easy to ignore," said high-profile neighbor Diana Ross.

57. This one is classic Streisand: What is the message Barbra's father sent her, via the medium's table pounding on the floor?

58. If you look real close, you might spot stepsister Roslyn Kind in which of Barbra's films?

59. Name another entertainer who, like Streisand, produced, directed, and starred in his own films—and also scored the music.

60. Who did Barbra originally want to play the son of Dr. Lowenstein

(the part Jason Gould performed) in *The Prince of Tides* (Columbia, 1991)?

61. Barbra supposedly rejected an offer to play the mother in *The Exorcist* (Warner Bros., 1973), a monster hit for director William Friedkin. She did work with Friedkin on another project—which one?

62. The Friars theatrical club in New York City paid tribute to Barbra in 1969 as Entertainer of the Year—only the second woman so honored up to that time. Who was the first?

63. In January 1994 Barbra got a bichon frise. What would you do with a brichon frise: pet it, eat it, convert it to Judaism, or see a doctor?

64. Which name does not belong in this list:
Harold Arlen, Ray Charles, Barry Gibb, Don Johnson, Johnny Mathis, Jon Peters

65. Fill in the blanks below (the same word goes for both):
" _____ is having a baked potato come out of the oven just right. Not raw and not overdone. _____ is having ten honeydew melons and eating only the top half of each one."

66. How was Angelina Scarangella related to Barbra?

67. Said Barbra of her business associates: "All the others love money, but _____ loves me."

68. Producer Ray Stark bought out the Broadway stage contract of *Funny Girl* (1964) costar Sydney Chaplin because he was causing problems behind the footlights. Chaplin's understudy, George Reeder, stood in until a Barbra-approved replacement arrived. Name of . . . ?

69. *Rainbow Road* was the first title for which Streisand screen project?

70. Elvis Presley supposedly said he wouldn't appear opposite Barbra in *A Star Is Born* (Warner Bros., 1976) because he'd played opposite a formidable female once before and lived to regret it. Who was that *femme terrible*?

71. Talk to the animals, ask them who they are:
* Cupid * Gonzola * Leo * Sadie * Shot
A. _____, a lively horse, a present from Jon Peters.
B. _____, a large rat that Barbra shared an apartment with in New York City.
C. _____, a stallion that roamed around Streisand's Malibu ranch in California.

D. _____, a fluffy white poodle.

E. _____, a mountain lion, sometimes in a cage.

72. Name two who costarred onscreen with Marilyn Monroe and with Barbra Streisand.

73. Name the year in which Barbara became Barbra.

74. In what movie did Barbra push her screen mother's face into a birthday cake?

75. Barbra sang for President John F. Kennedy and called him "a doll." She sang for President Bill Clinton and spent the night in the White House. Did she sing for any other presidents?

76. Who is the top glamour photographer seriously bitten by one of Barbra's doberman guard dogs?

77. When Barbra accepts your invitation to come for dinner, how will you prepare the baked potatoes? And the rice pudding: Will that be with or without raisins?

78. One of Barbra's screen lovers also lusted after screen sexpot Raquel Welch. Who's the actor, and what are the respective movies?

79. When a certain cinematographer was hired for one of Barbra's movies, he felt he already knew her because his father often spoke about working with her. Who are the father and son cinematographers?

80. Before *Funny Girl* (Columbia, 1968) and *Funny Lady* (Columbia, 1975) Alice Faye portrayed Fanny Brice, thinly disguised, in what Hollywood movie?

A much publicized (and ridiculed) romance: Barbra and actor Don Johnson. Here they're attending the premiere of his 1988 romantic comedy *Sweet Hearts Dance*.

PHOTO COURTESY OF ARCHIVE PHOTOS/DARLENE HAMMOND

ANSWERS TO TRIVIA QUIZ, Part 3

51. *Ell* from Elliott Gould, and *bar* from Barbra. This was the name of their production company which produced her first three TV specials.
52. *For Pete's Sake* (Columbia, 1974).
53. Jon Peters.
54. John Bowers and Marguerite De la Motte.
55. (a) *What Price Hollywood?* (RKO, 1932) with Lowell Sherman and Constance Bennett. (b) *A Star Is Born* (United Artists, 1937) with Fredric March and Janet Gaynor. (c) *A Star Is Born* (Warner Bros., 1954) with James Mason and Judy Garland.
56. Ryan O'Neal.
57. "S-I-N-G P-R-O-U-D."
58. Roslyn appears as a nonspeaking extra in 1976's *A Star Is Born*, where she sits at Streisand's table during the Grammy Awards scene; in *The Main Event*, (Warner Bros., 1979) she's one of the women working out in the aerobics class at the beginning of the film.
59. Charles Chaplin.
60. Chris O'Donnell.
61. William Friedkin directed her music video *Somewhere* (1985).
62. Sophie Tucker (1884–1966).
63. Whatever turns you on: It's a fluffy white dog with dark button eyes and an affectionate nature.
64. Jon Peters. All the others recorded duets with Barbra.
65. Success.
66. That's a name Barbra assumed when she enrolled in two different acting schools when she first moved to Manhattan from Brooklyn in the late 1950s. She also hid behind this name at the hospital when she gave birth to Jason.
67. Marty Erlichman, Barbra's manager, who worked for her without a contract.
68. Johnny Desmond.
69. *A Star Is Born.*
70. Ann-Margret in *Viva Las Vegas* (MGM, 1964). Elvis thought she stole the picture and vowed never again to have such a dynamic costar onscreen.
71. (a) Cupid (b) Gonzola (c) Shot (d) Sadie (e) Leo

72. Yves Montand: *Let's Make Love* (Twentieth Century-Fox, 1960), with Marilyn; *On a Clear Day You Can See Forever* (Paramount, 1970) with Barbra. Lauren Bacall: *How to Marry a Millionaire* (Twentieth Century-Fox, 1953) with Marilyn; *The Mirror Has Two Faces* (TriStar, 1996) with Barbra.
73. 1960.
74. *Up the Sandbox* (National General, 1972).
75. January 15, 1965, she sang for President Lyndon B. Johnson's Inaugural Eve Gala at the National Armory in Washington, D.C. She sang at a benefit for the Special Olympics, held at the Kennedy Center, March 9, 1975, with President Gerald Ford in the audience.
76. Francesco Scavullo.
77. Bake the potatoes two days ahead, and then reheat them so they're "hard on the outside and mooshy on the inside" (instructions to *Time*, April 10, 1964). As for the rice pudding, skip the raisins.
78. John Richardson, who plays Robert Tentrees, the dashing, handsome nineteenth-century English aristocrat in *On a Clear Day You Can See Forever*. Barbra silently seduces him across the banquet table, singing "Love with All the Trimmings." Richardson had grunted seductively at Raquel Welch in *One Million Years B.C.* (Twentieth Century-Fox, 1966).
79. Harry Stradling: *Funny Girl, Hello, Dolly!* (Twentieth Century-Fox, 1969), *On a Clear Day You Can See Forever*, *The Owl and the Pussycat* (Columbia, 1970), and Harry Stradling, Jr.: *The Way We Were* (Columbia, 1973).
80. *Rose of Washington Square* (Twentieth Century-Fox, 1939). Fanny Brice sued, saying she'd been slandered. The case was settled out of court and the movie was withdrawn from theatrical distribution.

APPENDIX 1:

An Annotated Bibliography:

Books and Significant Magazine Pieces

Abitan, Guy. *Barbra Streisand: Une Femme Libre*. Paris: Editions-orban, 1979.

"A landmark biography—a landmark in misinformation," says Michel Parenteau in *Barbra* magazine no. 8, 1982. The only thing to be said in defense of the book is a fourteen-page interview with composer Michel Legrand. He makes reference to an aborted 1974 album project with Barbra called *The Life and Death of a Young Woman*.

Alexander, Shana. "A born loser's success and precarious love." *Life*, May 22, 1964, cover story.

This is the source of many familiar stories about Barbra and Elliott Gould at the time of *I Can Get It For You Wholesale* (1962).

Black, Jonathan. *Streisand*. New York: Leisure Books, 1975.

A superficial paperback biography of Barbra as living legend. A few photos.

Bly, Nelly. *Barbra Streisand: The Untold Story*. New York: Windsor Pub. Corp., 1994.

Reviewed in *Just Like Buttah*, no. 5, 1995. "The book consists of a series of paragraphs and short chapters taken from newspaper and magazine articles, television interviews, and previous biographies."

Brady, Frank. *Barbra Streisand: An Illustrated Biography*. New York: Grosset & Dunlap, 1979.
Barbra magazine no. 3, 1979, calls it "a rehash of material previously published . . . a positive portrait . . . (but) with no new insights." Many pictures, mainly publicity photos.

Bronson, Fred. *The Billboard Book of Number One Hits* (revised and expanded edition). New York: Watson-Guptill, 1997. A breezy, invaluable chronological history of the popular music singles that reached the number one position in sales/popularity, according to the trade paper *Billboard* (the definitive industry chart). The history begins with "Rock Around the Clock" in the week of July 9, 1955—which is identified as the beginning of the "rock era." Streisand has had six number one hit singles. (See **Part II: 10. The Complete Streisand Discography.**)

Carrick, Patrick. *Barbra Streisand: A Biography*. London: Robert Hale, 1991.

Considine, Shaun. *Barbra Streisand: The Woman, the Myth, the Music*. New York: Delacorte, 1985.
Considine says his book is "a story of what contributed to her legend the most—her music; and it is told by the people . . . who were there, including this writer." He says "Evergreen" was written by another songwriter who was never credited—a claim which prompts Streisand fans to totally reject this important book. It is "so frank it rises above the genre, presenting Barbra as a kind of Beloved Medusa, a creature of Mythic Narcissism" (*Kirkus Reviews*). There is no index, which the author acknowledges as a mistake.

Dennen, Barry. *My Life With Barbra, A Love Story*. New York: Prometheus, 1997.
With never-published photos and sketches. A valuable first-person account of Barbra Streisand's rise to fame by a friend/lover who says he played a major role in her early success. Hopelessly overwritten, Dennen's 279-page story of his long-ago relationship with Barbra is concisely told in several pages of James Spada's biography.

Edwards, Anne. *Streisand: A Biography*. Boston: Little, Brown, 1997.
Basically an affectionate biography, though Edwards is critical of her subject's excessive egomania. Edwards states that over a hundred people discussed their involvement with Streisand, with many of them requesting anonymity because of Streisand's "climate of fear."

Edwards concentrates on her subject's personal and emotional life, and her career on the stage and in films. While praising the singer's voice, she has little to say about Streisand's many albums. Anne Edwards notes that she worked on and cowrote the screenplay of *Funny Girl* (Columbia, 1968) with Sidney Buchman. They were taken off the project when production started, to be replaced with Ben Hecht and John Patrick, and then later by Isobel Lennart, who received final screenplay credit.

Gavin, James. *Intimate Nights: The Golden Age of New York Cabaret.* New York: Grove Weidenfeld, 1991.

A fascinating, readable history. Gavin says Streisand came to nightclubs through the encouragement of Barry Dennen . . . then later claimed she did it all by herself: "Streisand became notorious for burning those early bridges" (p. 251).

Griffin, Nancy, and Kim Masters. *Hit & Run: How Jon Peters and Peter Guber Took Sony for a Ride in Hollywood.* New York: Simon & Schuster, 1996.

The story of how a Beverly Hills hairstylist (Peters) became one of the most important and controversial producers in the industry—a climb to the top that began when he met Barbra Streisand.

Grobel, Lawrence, interviewer. "Playboy Interview: Barbra Streisand." *Playboy*, October 1977 (pp. 79–107, 193–200).

A lengthy interview covering much of her life and career, meant to be her "definitive statement." Many of her answers to interview questions since then have essentially drawn upon this interview— even to using the identical words and phrases. *Barbra* magazine, Spring 1979, interviews Grobel about his Barbra interview. He says that the more "gossipy" parts left out of *Playboy* were later printed in the newspaper *Newsday*.

Haber, Joyce. "Barbra's Directing Her First Movie." *New York*, April 15, 1968 (pp. 50–51).

An unfriendly witness writes about the making of *Funny Girl*. First appearance of the quip, "Willie [*Funny Girl* director William Wyler] shouldn't be so hard on her. After all, this is the first picture she's ever directed."

Hamill, Pete. "Barbra the Great: Talented Girl on a Triumphal March." *Cosmopolitan*, February 1968.

Harvey, Diana Karanikas and Jackson Harvey. *Streisand: The Pictorial*

Biography. Philadelphia: Courage Books/Running Press, 1997. Brief text with a hundred photos, most in color.

Hirsch, Foster. "The Way She Is," *After Dark* magazine, April 1975. An excellent analysis of Streisand and her first eight movies. "In most of her films, she plays characters who educate stuffy writers and professors and who teach her men how to loosen up and live right. She's the creature of instinct and heart who rescues controlled men from a life of sober reason. Blatantly anti-intellectual, her characters are American-Jewish versions of Zorba the Greek."

Jordan, René. *The Greatest Star*. New York: Putnam's, 1975. *Barbra* magazine no. 3, 1979: "Early (though suspect) biography." *Barbra* magazine no. 8, 1982: "Mean-spirited."

Kael, Pauline. *For Keeps: 30 Years at the Movies*. New York: Dutton, 1994. A 1,250-page selection of Kael's movie reviews from *The New Yorker*. This collection includes much of what Kael has written about Barbra Streisand.

Kimbrell, James. *Barbra—An Actress Who Sings*. Boston: Branden, 1989. _____. *Barbra—An Actress Who Sings, volume II*. Boston: Branden, 1992. Although it sometimes has the feel of a vanity publication, this is a straightforward, fact-filled, double-volume work. It defends its subject without making a mushy fool of itself. However, there is no obvious reason for this work to be in two parts. The author died of AIDS before publication; his sister finished his work.

King, Larry. *The Best of Larry King Live: The Greatest Interviews*. Atlanta: Turner Publishing, 1995. Includes King's CNN cable interview with Streisand from February 6, 1992, in which she discusses her political and social positions, and pushes *The Prince of Tides* (Columbia, 1991).

Lewis, Richard Warren, interviewer. "Playboy Interview: Elliott Gould." *Playboy*, November 1970 (pp. 77–94, 262–264).

Lurie, Diana. "It's scary—it could suddenly all fall apart." *Life*, March 18, 1966, cover story on Barbra after the great success of her Broadway hit *Funny Girl* (1964–1965). This story features the memorable photo, taken at a Chanel fashion show, of Barbra flanked by four elegant women, including Marlene Dietrich, all dressed in classic Chanel outfits. Barbra sits stiffly, staring ahead, wearing an absurd jaguar-print suit and hat she designed herself.

Madsen, Axel. *William Wyler, The Authorized Biography*. New York: Crowell, 1973.

Wyler directed Streisand in her first film, Funny Girl. He could envision himself in the Streisand-Gould relationship—a husband in the shadow of his movie-star wife—because he'd been there: He'd been married to incandescent blonde star Margaret Sullavan for two troubled years. Wyler felt Elliott Gould handled the situation far better than he had.

Newfield, Jack. "Diva Democracy." *George*, November 1996 (pp. 144–47, 160–62). "Her political journey—from a close encounter with her late father to her intimate bond with the first family." "As Streisand declared in her Harvard speech, 'I have opinions. No one has to agree.' Nonetheless, her political judgments have stood the test of time remarkably well. When all the wise men from Harvard assured the nation that the Vietnam War was winnable, Streisand, who never went to college, knew better. When Richard Nixon and Pat Buchanan were trashing Martin Luther King, Jr., she was singing for King at a benefit. When the issue of legal abortion was hanging by a thread in the United States courts, Streisand belted out the songs that raised the money that elected the senators that stopped Robert Bork's appointment to the Supreme Court. When measured against all other celebrity icons, history will judge that Barbra Streisand used her gigantic fame, wealth, and power to fight for justice. She not only sings proud, she thinks and acts proud."

Parish, James Robert and Michael R. Pitts. *Hollywood Songsters*. New York/London: Garland, 1991.

Profiles of 104 performers who have had success both as singers and as film stars. Photos, filmographies, discographies.

Pierson, Frank. "My Battles with Barbra and Jon." *New York*, November 15, 1976. The same piece appeared in *New West* at the same time. Pierson, nominal director of *A Star Is Born* (Warner Bros., 1976), writes that Streisand was impossible to work with for a variety of unflattering reasons: She was a megalomaniac, abusive, disruptive, rude to everyone, monstrously self-absorbed. Jon Peters was described as jumping up and down threatening violence, full of "mad schemes" and "incompetent." Said Barbra: "No other article has ever touched off this deep sense of injustice in me. I felt totally helpless and impotent knowing so many people would probably believe what they were reading" (*Playboy*, October 1977).

Quart, Barbara Koenig. *Women Directors: The Emergence of a New Cinema*. New York: Praeger, 1988.

A survey of the unprecedented number of movies by women beginning in the late 1970s, and the impact on the industry of women as directors and producers. *Yentl* (MGM/United Artists, 1983) is seen as proving that a feminist director can work within the Hollywood system and make accessible ideas previously found only in serious writing.

Queenan, Joe. *If You're Talking To Me, Your Career Must Be in Trouble: Movies, Mayhem, and Malice*. New York: Hyperion, 1994. A collection of celebrity profiles, "informed viciousness," mostly reprinted from *Movieline* magazine. Queenan says that Streisand's is one of the truly weird careers . . . that she could have been a terrific comedienne had she not succumbed to her own self-delusions. According to Queenan, by the time she made *Nuts* (Warner Bros., 1987) she had lost touch with reality. Also: "In the history of idiotic movies . . . there are very few scenes more shamefacedly self-adulatory than the moment [in *A Star Is Born*] when Streisand . . . captivates a roomful of hard rock fans with her schlocky ballads." And: "Streisand embodies everything that is tacky and cheap and hopelessly corny and unsophisticated about Middle America."

Reed, Rex. *Do You Sleep in the Nude?* New York: New American Library, 1968.

A collection of celebrity interviews, mainly from the *New York Times*. Reed's Streisand question-and-answer session was "the first high-profile piece to paint her as an unreasonable perfectionist who was demanding, paranoiac, rude, driven, arrogant, and contemptuous of her fans" (Spada: *Streisand, Her Life*, p. 173).

Riese, Randall. *Her Name Is Barbra*. New York: Birch Lane, 1993.

The best-written of the major Streisand biographies, succinct and straightforward. Riese says he interviewed two hundred people for his book, many of them requesting anonymity.

Rivers, Joan, with Richard Meryman. *Enter Talking*. New York: Delacorte, 1986.

Her first autobiography, covering her early days. In 1958, Rivers worked with Streisand in an off-Broadway play called *Driftwood*, a vanity production staged in the home of the playwright, Maurice Tei Dunn. Rivers played a lesbian in love with Barbra's stage character. There's a photo of them in this book not seen elsewhere. Rivers' first impression of Streisand: "A tough little hustler, paying her way by working part time as a cashier at a Chinese restaurant" (p. 90).

Rosen, Craig. *The Billboard Book of Number One Albums; The Inside Story Behind Pop Music's Blockbuster Records*. New York: Billboard Books, 1996.

The definitive industry chart. To date, Streisand has had seven number one albums. (See **Part 2: 10. The Complete Streisand Discography.**)

Ruhlmann, William. *Barbra Streisand*. London: Maagna Books; Stamford, CT: Longmeadow Press.

A sale/bargain book, with mainly photos. A brief bio with emphasis on her recording career.

Scharf, Walter, "accompanied by Michael Freedland." *Composed and Conducted by Walter Scharf*. London: Vallentine, Mitchell & Co., 1988. Remembers Scharf: "She sang songs that I had orchestrated, and demanded that musicians of sometimes thirty and forty years experience bow to wishes that were pointless and made no musical sense." However, he grew to like Streisand. Scharf thinks he coined the word 'superstar.'

Sessums, Kevin. "Queen of Tides." *Vanity Fair*, September 1991 (pp. 174–79, 228–35).

Barbra seen as a forty-nine-year-old show-biz grande dame. She's currently a fervent follower of New Age pop psychologist John Bradshaw and claims she can now look at her mother with love.

Sharif, Omar, with Marie-Therese Guinchard. *The Eternal Male*. New York: Doubleday, 1977.

A casual overview of his life and loves, with a few comments on Barbra, his movie costar in *Funny Girl* and *Funny Lady* (Columbia, 1975) and off-screen lover.

Spada, James. *Barbra: The First Decade — The Films and Career of Barbra Streisand*. Secaucus, N.J.: Citadel, 1974.

A complete account of her career through *The Way We Were* (Columbia, 1973): Broadway, recordings, television, movies, with more detailed information than available in any other source. Many rare and unfamiliar photos. (The second decade book was written by Karen Swenson in 1986.)

_____. *Streisand: Her Life*. New York: Crown, 1995.

After his two earlier versions, Spada achieves the best, the most comprehensive biography. "A portrait that fans and critics can agree on: Streisand is her own best friend and worst enemy" (John Clark, *Premiere*, December 1995).

_____, with Christopher Nickens. *Streisand: The Woman and the Legend*. New York: Doubleday, 1981. An affectionate and admiring pictorial biography.

_____. same, revised and updated paperback. New York: Pocket Books, 1983.

Streisand, Barbra. "Who Am I, Anyway?" *Life*, January 9, 1970 (pp. 90–96).

An interview with the questions edited out, resulting in an important autobiographical sketch. (She acknowledges no one.)

Swenson, Karen. *Barbra: The Second Decade*. Secaucus, N.J.: Citadel, 1986.

This picks up where James Spada left off in *Barbra: The First Decade*, with a detailed account of her life and work since 1974. (Swenson is said to have worked for Barbra's agent Marty Erlichman.)

Teti, Frank, photo editor. Text by Karen Moline. *Streisand Through the Lens*. New York: Delilah/Putnam, 1982.

Oversize quality paperback. A collection of 116 photos of Barbra over a twenty-year period, plus interviews with the photographers represented in the book: Cecil Beaton, Yani Begakis, Bob Deutsch, Ron Galella, Tony Rizzo, Santiago Rodriguez, Frank Teti. Many unflattering papparazzi photos but also great glamour shots by Beaton and others. The interviews are on the trivial side.

Vare, Ethlie Ann, editor. *Diva: Barbra Streisand and the Making of a Superstar*. New York: Berkley/Boulevard Books, 1996.

A "biography-in-the-raw," a compilation of magazine and newspaper stories from the early 1960s to 1995, covering all aspects of the superstar's life and career. Includes a 1962 interview from *The New Yorker*; Rex Reed's bitch profile; Isaac Beshevis Singer on what has she done to my Yentl; Glenn Gould comparing Barbra to opera legend Elisabeth Schwarzkopf; profiles and think pieces by feminist writers Camille Paglia, Nora Ephron, Gloria Steinem; and other important material not easily available.

Waldman, Allison J. *The Barbra Streisand Scrapbook.* Secaucus, N.J.: Citadel/Carol, 1995.

A fan's tribute book with wonderful color photos, much valuable information. There's a collection of fifty quotes in praise of Barbra and three (!) against; one of the three is filmmaker Robert Altman defending her against vitriolic critic John Simon. Of most interest is a lengthy itemization of scenes cut out of Barbra's movies and of songs unreleased. There's a photo from *Up the Sandbox* (National General, 1972) of Barbra shoving the mother's face into a birthday cake (p.11), and two surprisingly unflattering shots (pp. 106 and 232) of a flabby Barbra (as a Cycle Slut in *The Owl and the Pussycat* (Columbia, 1970).

Whitburn, Joel. *The Billboard Book of Top 40 Hits*, sixth edition. New York: Billboard, 1996.

Winnert, Derek. *Barbra Streisand: Quote Unquote.* Avenel, N.J.: Crescent/Random House, 1996. One in a series on celebrities, an eighty-page collection of photos and quotes by Barbra Streisand on life, love, and career.

Zec, Donald, and Anthony Fowles. *Barbra.* New York: St. Martin's, 1981.

Lucy Gardner, in *Barbra* magazine no. 8, 1982, calls this British biography "a rehash," with the exception of an Elliott Gould interview and new data on Barbra's various trips to England.

APPENDIX 2:

Her fans Reach Out to Touch Barbra

Fan Magazines

All About Barbra. Lynne Pounder, publisher and editor-in-chief. AB Publications, 17 Adrian Place, Peterlee, Co. Durham SR8 5SR, England. Allison J. Waldman is listed as U.S. Executive Editor. Published from 1985. The current issue, from 1997, is no. 46.

BARBRA bilia. Anthony Andrich, Richard Simmons, publishers. Anthony Andrich, editor-in-chief.
The fall/holiday 1995 issue is no. 6/7.

The Barbra File. Allison J. Waldman, editor. P. O. Box 822232, South Florida, FL 33082–2232.
A monthly newsletter, published from 1994.

Barbra magazine–fan newsletter. *No longer published* (Note that the numbering is erratic.)
Chris Nickens, Robert Scott, James Spada, Karen Swenson, editors: vol.1, no. 1 (1979); no. 2 (1979); no. 3 (1979).
Chris Nickens, Robert Scott, Karen Swenson, editors:
vol. 1, no. 4 (1980).
James Spada, publisher and editor-in-chief; Chris Nickens, editor:
vol. 2, no. 1 (1981); vol. 2, no. 2 (1981) and no. 7 (1982).

261

Barbra became *Barbra Quarterly* in 1982:
  no. 8 (1982), no. 9 (1982), and no. 10 (1983).

Just Like Buttah, *A Barbra Streisand Fan Magazine*. Thomas, Galyean,
  Publisher-editor. JLB Publishing, P.O. Box 6152, Arlington, TX
  76005–6152 .
  Quarterly, published since 1993.

Fan Clubs

Barbra International Network
c/o Donald Farrell
P.O. Box 24221
San Jose, CA 95154–4221

Barbra Streisand Association
c/o Chris Every
36 Toppham Drive
Low Edges, Sheffield S8 7NT
United Kingdom

Barbra Streisand Fan Club
Postbus 103
2250 AC Voorschoten
Holland

"How Lucky Can You Get"
c/o Vincent Ricci Jr.
304 North Park Avenue
Buffalo, NY 14216–1938

Simply Streisand
c/o Mary Grifin
629 37th Street
Richmond, CA 94805–1757

The Internet
Please Note: URLs for Internet Web sites frequently change.

Australian Barbra Streisand Association (ABSA):
  http://www.geocities.com/Hollywood/Set/4824/

BABS Club (Beloved Appreciators of Barbra Streisand):
http://www.geocities.com/WestHollywood/5931/babsclub.htm

The Barbra File:
http://members.aol.com/barbfile/barbpage/TBF2.html

Barbra Joan Streisand:
http://www.haydennet.com/barbra.htm

Barbra on the Internet:
http://acs2.bu.edu:8001/~pimentel/tidbits.htm

Barbra Pictures:
http://members.aol.com/cbrown1269/index.htm

Barbra Streisand:
http://www.barbra-streisand.com/

Barbra Streisand:
http://www.geocities.com/~chris_hardin/Barbra/

Barbra Streisand Fan Magazine:
http://www.tnef.com/cgi-bin/buttah.cgi

The Barbra Streisand FAQ (frequently asked questions):
http://members.aol.com/markjayeye/bjsfaq/

The Barbra Streisand Memorabilia Museum:
http://mgfx.com/barbra

Barbra Streisand Music Guide (or Directory):
http://members.aol.com/barbramusc/index.html

The Barbra Streisand Songbook:
http://kac.net/yankec/bsongbk.htm

Barbra Streisand Web Page:
http://acs2.bu.edu:8001/~pimental/bjsweb.html

Barbra Streisand's Generous Donation:
http://ns2.con2.com/~erashum/Streisand.html

Biteside — The Mirror Has Two Faces:
http://www.bitesite.com/new/mirror.html

263

The Broadway Singer:
http://www.geocities.com/Broadway/5607

Classic Movies:
http://www.geocities.com/Hollywood/9766/streisand

DIVA Collectables:
http://www.kac.net/diva/index.htm

Flicks Interview:
http://whyy.org/flicks/Streisand interview.html

The I Love Barbra Catalog:
http://members.aol.com/iluvbarbra

Just Like Buttah:
http://members.aol.com/JLBPub/index.htm

The Keller Collection (memorabilia):
http://mgfx.com/barbra/

The Mirror Has Two Faces:
http://movieweb.com/movie/mirror

The Mirror Has Two Faces:
http://www.music.sony.com/Music/ArtistInfo/TheMirror

My Life with Barbra by Barry Dennen:
http://members.aol.com/bazdennen/index.htm

Neil Stoter — A Barbra Streisand Page:
http://home.clara.net/rmns/barbra1.htm

Never the Hollywood dumpling, Streisand still:
http://detnews.com/1996/menu/stories/74992.htm

A Streisand Homage!:
http://www.kac.net/yankee/barbra.htm

The Ultimate Barbra Streisand Experience:
http://www.fortunecity.com/lavender/scaremoucho/22/index.internet

Where Is It Written?:
http://acs2bu.edu.8001/~pimentel/sources.htm

*   *   *

At present there is no e-mail address for fans to reach Barbra. Mail for her may be sent to:
Barbra Streisand
521 Fifth Avenue
New York, NY 10175–0003

Barbra Fan Reunions

Information on upcoming reunions may be had from:
Barbra: The Reunion
P.O. Box 54402
Tulsa, OK 74155–0402

The Barbra Store

Hello Gorgeous!
P.O. Box 1255
Kenwood, CA 95452–1255
(707) 833-6998

http://www.grin.net/~hellogorgeous
E-mail: hellogorgeous@grin.net

Index

About the Author

Ernest Cunningham is the author of *The Ultimate Marilyn* (1998), the first in a pop culture series from Renaissance Books.

His background is in entertainment advertising, notably as a copywriter for the New York City agency Diener-Hauser-Bates, as well as for two major TV networks.

He is now a dealer in movie memorabilia. He also does freelance copywriting, editing, proofreading, and researching.

He is intrigued by the phenomenon of Barbra Streisand, but is more fascinated by the star's legions of fans—both those who love her and those who love to "hate" her.